General Editor's Introduction

Nicola Lacey's writings have been at the forefront of scholarship on legal theory for some years now. This towering monograph not only develops some of the major themes of her work on criminal law theory but also argues for a particular methodology for general jurisprudence. In relation to criminal responsibility, the book traces the emergence of capacity theory, character theory, outcome-responsibility and paradigms of risk and prevention, in their historical and institutional settings. Examples of different phases in ideas of responsibility are discussed, without suggesting a historical progression in which one set of ideas replaced another but rather suggesting a layered accumulation in which elements of various ideas remain influential. Another of the book's major themes is the institutional context of the criminal law and its effect on conceptions of criminal responsibility. The influence of economic and social changes, the media and broader political trends is charted, and special attention is paid to the interaction between the written criminal law and the practices of the police, prosecutors, and regulatory agencies.

The upshot of this historical and inter-disciplinary analysis is a strong and well-documented argument that criminal responsibility is an idea embedded in the social practices of criminalization, which are themselves located within an institutional context that is changing over time. The emphasis is on reflexivity between the raw phenomena of legal rules and doctrines and ideas and institutional influences, as a methodology for explicating what might be termed the second level of interpretive analysis – the concept of responsibility being the prime example in this work. But Nicola Lacey then takes the argument to a third level, questioning the relationship between the concept of law itself and the changing social and institutional facts that constitute the context to which the concept of law must be applied. The monograph therefore ends by challenging the notion of a single unchanging concept of law, arguing that legal theorists must preserve an openness to revising the concept of law by adopting a reflexive methodology. Thus, in both its advances in the analysis of criminal responsibility and its arguments on general jurisprudence, this monograph will rank as a major scholarly work of our time.

Andrew Ashworth

OXFORD MONOGRAPHS ON CRIMINAL LAW AND JUSTICE

In Search of Criminal Responsibility

OXFORD MONOGRAPHS ON CRIMINAL LAW AND JUSTICE

Series Editor: Professor Andrew Ashworth, Emeritus Vinerian Professor of Law at All Souls' College, Oxford

This series aims to cover all aspects of criminal law and procedure including criminal evidence. The scope of this series is wide, encompassing both practical and theoretical works.

OTHER TITLES IN THIS SERIES

Character in the Criminal Trial
Mike Redmayne

Preventive Justice
Andrew Ashworth and Lucia Zedner

Homicide and the Politics of Law Reform
Jeremy Horder

The Insecurity State
Vulnerable Autonomy and the Right to Security in the Criminal Law
Peter Ramsay

Manifest Madness
Mental Incapacity in the Criminal Law
Arlie Loughnan

The Ethics of Plea Bargaining
Richard L. Lippke

Punishment and Freedom
Alan Brudner

Prosecuting Domestic Violence
A Philosophical Analysis
Michelle Madden Dempsey

Abuse of Process and Judicial Stays of Criminal Proceedings
Andrew L.-T. Choo

A Philosophy of Evidence Law
Justice in the Search for Truth
Ho Hock La

The Criminal Justice System and Health Care
Edited by Charles A. Erin and Suzanne Ost

Rethinking Imprisonment
Richard L. Lippke

Killing in Self-Defence
Fiona Leverick

Delayed Prosecution for Childhood Sexual Abuse
Penney Lewis

Lying, Cheating, and Stealing
A Moral Theory of White Collar Crime
Stuart P. Green

Defining Crimes
The Special Part of Criminal Law
Edited by Anthony Duff and Stuart P. Green

Criminal Responsibility
Victor Tadros

Proportionate Sentencing
Exploring the Principles
Andrew von Hirsch and Andrew Ashworth

Appraising Strict Liability
Edited by Andrew Simester

In Search of Criminal Responsibility

Ideas, Interests, and Institutions

Nicola Lacey

OXFORD
UNIVERSITY PRESS

OXFORD
UNIVERSITY PRESS

Great Clarendon Street, Oxford, OX2 6DP,
United Kingdom

Oxford University Press is a department of the University of Oxford. It furthers the University's objective of excellence in research, scholarship, and education by publishing worldwide. Oxford is a registered trade mark of Oxford University Press in the UK and in certain other countries

First Edition published in 2016

Impression: 1

Published in the United States of America by Oxford University Press
198 Madison Avenue, New York, NY 10016, United States of America

British Library Cataloguing in Publication Data
Data available

Library of Congress Control Number: 2015958967

ISBN 978–0–19–924820–9 (hbk.)
ISBN 978–0–19–924821–6 (pbk.)

Printed and bound by
CPI Group (UK) Ltd, Croydon, CR0 4YY

Preface

The book has grown out of a long-term project with two substantive purposes: first, to understand the ways in which English criminal law's conception of responsibility—its very conception of what it is to be a subject of criminal law—has changed since the eighteenth century; and second, to explore the relationship between these changes in legal framework and broader social, political, cultural, and economic developments. The project is premised on the assumption that criminal law may usefully be examined not only as an institution in its own right but also as an index of broad social changes; it is therefore a project in social theory as much as in legal history.

Building on my previous analysis in *Women, Crime and Character* (2008), I aim in this book to do two things. First, using the concept of responsibility as my prime example, I make a case for bringing together philosophical, historical, and socio-legal methods in legal theory and, indeed, in legal scholarship more generally. I understand criminal responsibility as a practice of attribution which is specific to criminal law yet which is connected with prevailing intellectual ideas, including—though, obviously, not restricted to—philosophical theories about the nature of human beings. This specificity and practical orientation of responsibility in criminal law, I shall argue, entails a relationship between philosophical and legal conceptions of responsibility that is more oblique than is generally assumed in criminal law theory. Moreover, it makes it possible—though it does not prove it to be the case—that multiple and philosophically inconsistent conceptions of responsibility are operating within legal practices of attribution without any necessary illogicality or incoherence in these distinctive practices. My intellectual starting point is, therefore, sceptical about the propriety of an a priori unitary approach to theorizing criminal responsibility. My approach accordingly moves away from a conception of criminal law theory as founded primarily in analytic philosophy and the systematic analysis of legal doctrine. Rather, my aim is to historicize the structure as well as the content of criminal law within a broad socio-theoretic framework, drawing links between: the conceptual structure or form of criminal law doctrine; the institutions through which it is produced, interpreted, and executed; the interests which have shaped both doctrine and institutions; and the substantive social functions which criminal law and punishment have been expected to perform at different points in history. Hence I attempt to construct a dialogue between criminal law theory of a doctrinal and philosophical temper and socio-historical studies of criminal justice.

Second, deploying this pluralist methodology, I provide an analysis of the idea of responsibility, of its development over time in English criminal law, and of what drives that development. In a nutshell, I argue that while multiple patterns of responsibility-attribution can be discerned throughout the period under consideration, we can nonetheless discern some broad trends in the alignment of these different patterns—trends which are themselves produced by shifts not only in prevailing ideas but also in the structure of institutions and the play of powerful interests. We have moved, I argue, from a criminal law dominated by character and outcome responsibility in the eighteenth century through a period in which the idea of responsibility as founded in capacity was gradually established at the core of criminal law, with outcome responsibility practically significant but ideologically marginal. Our current phase is one in which character responsibility, combined in interesting ways with a new discourse of responsibility as founded in risk, is enjoying a renaissance. In offering this interpretation of responsibility—and of method in legal scholarship—I also aim to unravel some of the oppositions which have structured scholarly debate about responsibility in recent years.

I present this analysis of responsibility as a case study of methodology in legal scholarship more generally. In developing this approach, I aspire to tread a middle path between an internal, doctrinally focused legal analysis and an external, social analysis: a middle path which explores the distinctive institutional organization, techniques, and assumptions of the legal order while investigating their implications for social systems beyond the law. I therefore attempt to escape the narrowness of doctrinal scholarship by aligning myself with a long line of traditions that resist the idea of legal scholarship as autonomous and that insist on the importance of studying law and legal practices in a social, historical, and institutional context: the Process School in the United States; Law and Society and socio-legal scholarship; and critical legal scholarship. Equally, however, I aim to avoid several unhelpful oppositions that have sometimes characterized critical or socio-legal, cross-disciplinary studies of law by acknowledging a concern with both agency and structure. My approach focuses on both cultural and material forces as important factors in the explanation of how law evolves and works, explores law's autonomy while also attending to its heteronomy, and recognizes the importance of both intellectual and material history for explaining the evolution of law. Of key importance to the socio-theoretic dimension of jurisprudence and to the evolving shape of its subject matter, I argue, is the changing modality of law's own normative system—a changing modality which can best be discerned by examining law's role in shaping and realizing ideas such as criminal responsibility over a significant period of time.

My work on this book has taken place over such an extended period, and under the aegis of such a number of institutions in which I have had the good fortune to work or to spend time as a visitor, that it is impossible to reconstruct the list of all my debts of gratitude. The initial research was conducted at the Wissenschaftzkolleg in Berlin: I am truly grateful for the Kolleg's hospitality, and in particular for access to its marvellous library services. A further tranche of the research was conducted during a Leverhulme Senior Research Fellowship, and I remain indebted to the Leverhulme Trust for this precious time. I would like to thank the many colleagues and friends who have commented over the last fifteen years on the papers, published and unpublished, which feed into this monograph; as well as the students whom it has been my privilege to teach and supervise over this period. In particular, my graduate students have been a constant source of intellectual stimulation, and I would especially like to acknowledge the various contributions that Arlie Loughnan, Ely Aaronson, Manuel Iturralde, Zelia Gallo, and Geoffrey Shaw have made to the development of the ideas expressed in this book. I have hugely benefited from the intellectual environment at LSE, and in particular from its lively and collegial criminal law group, convened and animated by Emmanuel Melissaris and Federico Picinali. In addition, I have been fortunate to be working in the field of criminal law theory during a period in which cross-disciplinary scholarship has burgeoned. My intellectual friendships with Andrew Ashworth, Peter Cane, Markus Dubber, Antony Duff, Lindsay Farmer, John Gardner, Bernard Harcourt, Jeremy Horder, Arlie Loughnan, Sandra Marshall, Alan Norrie, Peter Ramsay, Carol Steiker, Victor Tadros, Celia Wells, James Whitman, and Lucia Zedner have been of huge importance: echoes of my joint work with Celia on *Reconstructing Criminal Law* and with Lucia on comparative criminal justice sound throughout this book.

As the book finally neared completion, I benefited from the patience and continuing interest of Alex Flach at OUP; and it has been a pleasure to work with Natasha Flemming and Nicole Leyland in the final stages of preparing it for publication. I am also grateful to Nicholas Bromley for meticulous copy editing. Anne Phillips read and gave me exceptionally helpful comments on an early version of the book. Jacob Bronsther did fantastic editorial work and commented extensively and incisively on the penultimate draft of the manuscript. Ely Aaronson, Andrew Ashworth, Lindsay Farmer, and Arlie Loughnan gave incisive and generous comments on the final draft. My warmest thanks go to each of them. I would also like to acknowledge the precious support, advice, and encouragement of Neil Duxbury, Moira Gatens, David Garland, Emily Jackson, Martin Loughlin, Tori McGeer, Linda Mulcahy, Jill Peay, Philip Pettit, Hanna Pickard, Peter Ramsay, Jeremy Waldron, and—last but not least, and always my most valuable, and treasured, interlocutor—David Soskice. My discussions with David over the last thirty years, as well as our more recent collaboration on the comparative political economy of crime and punishment, have fundamentally shaped my approach, and are directly reflected in Chapter 5's aspiration to produce a political economy of criminal responsibility.

For much of the last decade, my work on character responsibility has been made much more enjoyable, and considerably less intellectually lonely, by regular exchanges with my friend and colleague Mike Redmayne, whose fine book on character evidence, *Character in the Criminal Trial*, appeared in the spring of 2015, just two months before his tragically early death. This book is dedicated to his memory, with gratitude.

Nicola Lacey

London
January 2016

Acknowledgements

The text of this book draws in part on the following previously published papers: 'In Search of the Responsible Subject: History, Philosophy and Criminal Law Theory' 64 *Modern Law Review* (2001) 350–71; 'Responsibility and Modernity in Criminal Law' 9 *Journal of Political Philosophy* (2001) 249–77; 'Criminalization as Regulation: The Role of Criminal Law', in Christine Parker, Colin Scott, Nicola Lacey, and John Braithwaite (eds), *Regulating Law* (Oxford University Press 2004) pp. 144–67; 'Character, Capacity, Outcome: Towards a Framework for Assessing the Shifting Pattern of Criminal Responsibility in Modern English Law', in Markus D. Dubber and Lindsay Farmer (eds), *Modern Histories of Crime and Punishment* (Stanford: Stanford University Press 2007); 'Space, Time and Function: Intersecting Principles of Responsibility Across the Terrain of Criminal Justice' 1 *Criminal Law and Philosophy* (2007) 233–50; 'Historicising Criminalisation: Conceptual and Empirical Issues' 72 *Modern Law Review* (2009) 936–61; 'Psychologising Jekyll, Demonising Hyde: The Strange Case of Criminal Responsibility' 4 *Criminal Law and Philosophy* (2010) 109–33; 'The Resurgence of Character: Responsibility in the Context of Criminalization', in Anthony Duff and Stuart Green (eds), *Philosophical Foundations of Criminal Law* (Oxford: Oxford University Press 2011); 'What Constitutes Criminal Law?', in R. A. Duff, Lindsay Farmer, S. E. Marshall, Massimo Renzo, and Victor Tadros (eds), *The Constitution of the Criminal Law* (Oxford: Oxford University

Press 2012); 'Institutionalising Responsibility: Implications for Jurisprudence' 4(1) *Jurisprudence* (2013) 1–19; 'Comparative Criminal Justice: An Institutional Approach', 24 *Duke Journal of Comparative and International Law* (2014) 501–27; 'Jurisprudence, History, and the Institutional Quality of Law' 101 *Virginia Law Review* (2015) 919–45.

Table of Contents

Table of Cases

HISTORICAL CASES

UNITED KINGDOM CASE LAW

EUROPEAN COURT OF HUMAN RIGHTS

Table of Legislation

UNITED KINGDOM

INTERNATIONAL TREATIES

1

In Search of Criminal Responsibility

The question of whether an offender is responsible for an offence, along with the rules and institutional mechanisms for defining and proving that responsibility, is crucial to the core modality of criminal justice: to distinguishing guilt from innocence, legitimate from illegitimate conduct. Criminal responsibility encompasses a set of doctrinal rules and principles, and an underlying set of normative ideas in terms of which those rules, doctrines, and practices are interpreted and justified. It also encompasses, though this is less often remarked by criminal law theorists, a set of institutional arrangements for putting them into practice. Since the second half of the twentieth century, the relevant rules and doctrines have often been conceptualized in terms of an overarching 'general part' of criminal law which enunciates the principles of *mens rea*, the defences, provisions for secondary or vicarious liability, criminal capacity, and so on: in short, all the rules which shape how the legal system attributes a particular act or omission to a particular individual or group—indeed, implicitly, how it understands the subject of criminal law.

The proposition that proof of an offender's responsibility for his or her offences is central to the character and legitimacy of contemporary criminal law commands wide consensus. Yet that broad consensus masks substantial disagreement about key features of the concept on which it centres: disagreements about what responsibility 'is'; about what makes it what it is; and about its practical and normative role in and beyond the criminal law. These questions, I shall suggest, are moreover intimately connected—implying that the changing social role of criminal law over time and space directly affects, as well as being affected by, its conceptual structure.

Most of the burgeoning scholarship on criminal responsibility has been occupied primarily with the first of these questions: what it is—its conceptual contours and moral foundations—rather than what it is for—its social roles, meaning, and functions. By contrast, I will argue that we cannot understand what responsibility is, or has been, unless we also ask what it has been 'for' at different times and in different places. My argument sets out from two very simple assumptions. First, I assume that responsibility is best thought of as a set of ideas that play two major roles in the development of modern criminal law: legitimation and coordination. In other words, conceptions and elaborated doctrines setting out the conditions of responsibility serve to legitimate criminal law as a system of state power, this in turn being a condition for criminal law's power to coordinate social behaviour, a task that it accomplishes in part by specifying the sorts of information or knowledge that have to be proven in the trial process precedent to conviction. Second, I assume that three main aspects of its environment shape responsibility: ideas, interests, and institutions. These three contextual aspects affect its conceptual contours and its role or what is required of it.

The relevant *ideas* for the purpose of unraveling the trajectory of criminal responsibility are the prevailing social narratives, knowledges, and understandings of the normative contours and significance of responsibility. As such, ideas form the dominant frame for accounts of criminal responsibility in the philosophy of criminal law and indeed in standard doctrinal histories. Three main sets of ideas have shaped conceptions and practices of criminal responsibility—character, capacity, and outcome—with 'character' standing in for a particular conception of how criminal evaluation attaches to persons and relates to identity; 'capacity' standing in for a concern with agency, choice, and personal autonomy; and outcome standing in for a concern with the social harms which agents cause and/or the risks which they create. These ideas are, however, inadequate in themselves to explicate the trajectory and significance of responsibility because they are in turn shaped by, and have influence on, interests.

Interests—the prevailing structures of power and their dynamics—are themselves often legitimized by ideas. Interests in this sense form the dominant explanatory frame in economic, political, and some legal history. As such, they focus on the key influence on criminal law and criminalization of patterns of social status and the distribution of wealth, resources, social and political voice, and influence. Yet in my account, unlike the theoretical traditions in which the shape of law can be reduced to the play of interests, interests not only shape ideas and institutions, but are themselves both filtered through and shaped by institutions and ideas.

The relevant *institutions* for an understanding of criminal responsibility include the political system, economic institutions, courts, trial processes, and judicial systems more generally (the legal profession, the judiciary, the media, and other relevant professions, e.g., the police, prosecutors, and criminal justice officials of various kinds); the civil service; the penal system; and, increasingly in many countries, corporations. Many, though not all, of these institutions loom large in criminal justice and political histories and in some (but by no means all) legal histories. They both constrain and enable developments emerging from ideas and interests. Yet their independent importance has been poorly incorporated into most criminal law (and indeed other legal) scholarship. This is equally true, moreover, of much comparative scholarship, which has also tended to focus largely on legal doctrines—a puzzling fact, given that the different features of legal procedure that have attracted so much comparative attention are realized through systematically different institutional frameworks, which are themselves embedded in broader institutional features of the relevant social and political systems.

I will therefore argue that what is needed is an account premised on the co-evolution of these three spheres in the production of doctrines and practices of criminal responsibility attribution; one that assumes a mutually constitutive relationship between these three broad spheres rather than privileging any one of them. In other words, the underlying notion of a responsible subject is shaped by an interlocking set of conditions that change over time and place in tandem with factors such as the human situation, prevailing ideas, institutions, and the distribution of power. This implies that, in terms of method, legal scholarship is ideally historical and comparative in outlook, and located within a social, political, and economic framework, so as to build a broad interpretation of the developing relationship between concepts such as responsibility and the factors that explain their shifting influence over time. Drawing on this method, I offer a substantive interpretation of how the respective domains of character, capacity, and outcome—or risk-based patterns of responsibility—attribution have shifted over time, setting out both the implications for the shifting boundaries of criminalization and paying particular attention to recent diagnoses of a period of 'hyper' or 'over-criminalization'. To anticipate, I diagnose the emergence of a distinctive hybrid of character—and risk-based responsibility—attribution: a hybrid which is at once a symptom and a driver of expanded criminalization in recent years. In conclusion, I address some of the normative concerns raised by this substantive interpretation.

Responsibility and Modernity: Historicizing Responsibility

Assumptions about the conditions under which subjects may properly be held responsible are of central importance to a wide range of contemporary social practices. This is most obviously true of those practices—moral blaming, judgments of guilt in criminal law, the operation of disciplinary and regulatory systems in a wide range of fora such as workplaces, schools, families, and the political system—in which individuals or collectivities are explicitly subject to systems of norms. But the significance of responsibility is not restricted to these overtly normative contexts. For the underlying ideas which inform the concept of responsibility—about identity, freedom, voluntariness, choice, agency, self-control—entail that the question of responsibility is of central relevance to political decisions about the design of social institutions more generally. For example, the conceptual structure of civil law and the design of regulatory and administrative institutions, such as systems of taxation, the welfare state, pensions systems, health systems, competition policy, or transport systems, to name just a few, make assumptions about the capacity of the relevant actors—individual or corporate—to act as responsible subjects. In the context of the recent effort in many Western countries to 'roll back the frontiers of the State' in favour of structures of self-regulation, some scholars have spoken of an increasing impulse to 'responsibilize' citizens and corporate bodies: in other words, to draw upon (assumed) capacities for responsible agency as the basis for designing policies of indirect regulation at a distance rather than governance through the direct imposition of norms.[1]

It would, of course, be a mistake to assume that ideas of responsibility, and in particular of individual responsibility, are exclusively a product of modern, post-Enlightenment consciousness. To take just two examples, the discussions of voluntariness and the will to be found in Aristotle's ethics, and the debates about individual conscience and human freedom to be found in the Christian theological tradition, provide two important intellectual ancestors to modern debates about the conditions of responsibility. It is nonetheless the case that most contemporary philosophical analyses of responsibility are grounded in notions of human agency that emerged in Europe in the philosophy of the Enlightenment. The ideas of the self-determining moral agent, equipped with distinctive cognitive and volitional capacities of understanding and self-control, and of a universal human personhood underpinned by these features have been of crucial importance to the gradual development of modern societies in a number of very obvious ways.[2] These ideas are related to the slow movement of modern societies towards democratic political structures; to the development of the (relatively) centralized modern state, along with its increasingly ambitious projects of regulation and concomitant public debates about the proper limits of this regulatory role; to the development of public education; to the spreading institutionalization of human rights. In this sense, even the most steadfastly analytic or conceptual of contemporary philosophical work on responsibility could reasonably be argued to be grounded in an

[1] See Nikolas Rose, *Powers of Freedom* (Cambridge: Cambridge University Press 1999); see in particular p. 64ff, Chapter 7, p. 239ff; cf. the widespread current debate about the diffusion of responsibility for risk management in late modern societies; Ulrich Beck, *Risk Society: Toward a New Modernity* (transl. Mark Ritter, London: Sage 1992); Pat O'Malley (ed.), *Crime and the Risk Society* (Aldershot and Brookfield: Ashgate 1998).

[2] See on this point J. B. Schneewind's argument about the relationship of morality to social change, and about the social significance of the emergence of the idea of morality as self-governance: *The Invention of Autonomy: A History of Modern Moral Philosophy* (Cambridge: Cambridge University Press 1998) pp. 4–6, 419–24. As Schneewind's book shows, the Enlightenment tradition is itself multifaceted: see also Fania Oz-Salzberger, 'New Approaches towards a History of the Enlightenment: Can Disparate Perspectives Make a General Picture?' 29 *Tel Aviver Jahrbuch für deutsche Geschichte* (2000) 171–82; Lindsay Farmer, *Making the Modern Criminal Law* (Oxford University Press 2016) Chapters 2 and 3; Ngaire Naffine, *Law's Meaning of Life: Philosophy, Religion, Darwin and the Legal Person* (Oxford: Hart Publishing 2009).

essentially modern understanding of human being, just as it generally considers responsibility within the context of some particular set of moral or political issues.

The historicization and practical contextualization of philosophical debates about responsibility tends, however, to be weak.[3] For many conceptual analyses of responsibility synthesize from modern philosophical debates to produce a concept of responsibility whose validity or conceptual appropriateness is assumed to transcend place and time and which need not satisfy any particularly rigorous criteria of fit with social practices which deploy ideas of responsibility. On this view, all we need is a clear sense of the conceptual structure of responsibility: there is a 'right answer' to how responsibility should be understood, and this properly delineated concept is either assumed to have, or is treated as if it had, metaphysical status.

For example, in an influential work on responsibility in the context of criminal law,[4] Michael Moore argues that all ascriptions of criminal responsibility which enforce 'strict' liability without proof of fault,[5] or which are applied to corporations, are fundamentally mistaken in that they distort the basic conceptual structure of responsibility, which is analytically tied to concepts of moral blameworthiness that are absent in strict liability and which apply exclusively to individual human personhood.[6] Here, the concept of responsibility has been carved in stone by analytic philosophy, to the extent that practices such as strict liability and corporate responsibility can simply be assumed to be mistaken rather than being capable of generating revised interpretations of the concept. This, of course, makes

[3] Honourable exceptions include Peter Cane, *Responsibility in Law and Morality* (Oxford: Hart Publishing 2002); Lindsay Farmer, *Making the Modern Criminal Law* Chapter 6; see also Darryl Brown, 'History's Challenge to Criminal Law Theory' 3 *Criminal Law and Philosophy* (2009) 271–87; Arlie Loughnan, 'Historicizing Criminal Responsibility', in Z. Hoskins and C. Flanders (eds), *The New Philosophy of Criminal Law* (Rowman Littlefield International 2016), pp. 137–55.

[4] Michael Moore, *Placing Blame* (Oxford: Oxford University Press 1998), see Part II in general and pp. 246–7, 623 in particular; see also John Finnis, 'The Priority of Persons', in Jeremy Horder (ed.), *Oxford Essays in Jurisprudence* (Fourth Series) (Oxford: Clarendon Press 2000) p. 1. For a critique of this kind of approach to corporate responsibility, see Nicola Lacey, 'Philosophical Foundations of the Common Law: Social Not Metaphysical', in Jeremy Horder (ed.), *Oxford Essays in Jurisprudence*.

[5] Strict criminal liability implies the ascription of responsibility independently of any finding of *mens rea* such as intention, recklessness, or negligence.

[6] See Victor Tadros, *Criminal Responsibility* (Oxford: Oxford University Press 2005) p. 11.

the responsibility theorist's life much easier. But we should question whether a method of analysis which so readily dispenses with much of its apparent subject matter can be expected to generate a theory of anything at all.[7] This example also demonstrates, in its insistence on the centrality of human personhood to responsibility, the extent to which its own analysis is grounded in historically and culturally specific understandings—a feature which is confirmed by its own claim to constitute not an exclusively prescriptive theory but rather a middle-order theoretical rationalization of responsibility in criminal law. Note, moreover, the evident tension between a claim to analytical truth or validity and a method focused on the interpretation of legal doctrines which change radically over time.

In addition to this question of 'fit' between concept and social practice, there is an interesting issue about the relationship between philosophy and history. In so far as contemporary philosophers appeal explicitly to the work of earlier theorists of responsibility, they generally do so in what Richard Rorty has usefully called a 'present-centred' way, assuming that the theories developed one, two, or three hundred years ago can be debated, assimilated, or rejected just as if they had been written today.[8] What matters is the structure of the argument, not the context within which, or purposes for which, it was developed. By contrast, issues of context and purpose are central to any 'past-centred' engagement with intellectual history. On the 'past-centred' approach, it is seen as necessary to understand projects of, say, eighteenth-century philosophers in their own terms, before considering their relevance to current moral and political issues. As is evident, these two approaches assume rather different relationships not only between philosophy and the history of ideas but also between philosophy and social history more generally. What is the relationship between what we might broadly call the analytic approach to responsibility in legal, moral, and political philosophy and the interpretive conceptions of responsibility which

[7] On this point, see Nicola Lacey, 'Philosophy, History and Criminal Law Theory' 1 *Buffalo Criminal Law Review* (1998) 295–328.

[8] See Richard Rorty, 'The Historiography of Philosophy: Four Genres', in Richard Rorty, J. B. Schneewind, and Quentin Skinner (eds), *Philosophy in History* (Cambridge: Cambridge University Press 1984); for useful discussion and pursuit of the 'past-centred approach' in relation to Spinoza's theory of responsibility, see Moira Gatens and Genevieve Lloyd, *Collective Imaginings* (London: Routledge 1999) pp. 1–8 and Chapter 6.

have been more prominent in social theory? Clearly, ideas such as responsibility have a history: what we need to understand is the relevance of that history for the conceptual as well as the practical structure of responsibility.[9]

Not all philosophical theorizing about responsibility, of course, assumes an explicitly metaphysical stance. Yet those theories of responsibility which explicitly locate their conceptual analysis in a historical thesis about the centrality of understandings of (particularly individual) responsibility in modernity tend to do so in terms of a very particular, teleological model of historical development. It is generally assumed that, given modern, enlightened understandings of the person and his or her relation to the state, the social order and the natural world, the history of modern Western philosophy has been one of the gradual refinement of conceptions of responsibility. Hence, a few scholars excepted,[10] it is assumed that the modern idea of responsibility is continuous and coherent, emerging slowly but moving surely towards an ever more complete realization of the full, 'enlightened' (the very concept, with its implication of historical progress, is significant) conditions of agency and subjecthood. In either case, the impression is given that there 'is' a conception of responsibility whose structure awaits only historical progress and proper philosophical analysis in order to be fully revealed. This deflects attention from the sense in which practices of responsibility are normative and constructive in that they organize both our practices and our interpretation of the world in distinctive and contingent ways.

From the point of view of interpretive social theory, this influential philosophical approach to the conceptual analysis of responsibility fails adequately to address two crucially important questions. First, can it be assumed that the same idea of responsibility is being mobilized, at the same time, in all the social practices which are shaped, in part, by ascriptions of or assumptions about responsibility?

[9] See, for example, the essays in Peter French (ed.), *The Spectrum of Responsibility* (London: St Martin's Press 1991); Gary Watson (ed.), *Free Will* (Oxford: Oxford University Press 1982); John Martin Fischer and Mark Ravizza, *Responsibility and Control: A Theory of Moral Responsibility* (New York: Cambridge University Press 1998); Ellen Frankel Paul, Fred D. Miller Jr., and Jeffrey Paul (eds), *Responsibility* (Cambridge: Cambridge University Press 1999).

[10] See, for example, Mark Bovens, *The Quest for Responsibility* (Cambridge and New York: Cambridge University Press 1998); Peter Cane, *Responsibility in Law and Morality*.

By this I do not merely mean to ask whether at any one time we need to distinguish, as Hart argued we should, between conceptions such as liability-, role- or capacity-responsibility, though I also believe this to be the case.[11] Rather, I want to suggest that any theorization of responsibility should be open to the possibility that the substantive assumptions which shape what is usually taken to be the core concept of responsibility—assumptions about capacity, freedom, personhood and so on—may be present to radically different degrees in different social discourses of responsibility.

For example, it should not be assumed to be the case that the philosophical foundations of discourses of responsibility in criminal law are identical with those in moral debate, or that either of these map completely onto conceptions of responsibility in citizenship or education. In each of these social practices, it would be safer to start out by making merely the modest assumption that ascriptions of, and ideas about, responsibility are performing distinctive practical/normative roles in relation to various structural problems. These problems include the coordination of expectations; the legitimation of the evaluative base of the practice; the underpinning of such factual judgments as the practice entails; the establishment of the incentive structures which the practice deploys pursuant to its role in coordinating social behaviour. This is not to say that there will not turn out to be important links, at any one time, between conceptions of responsibility in, say, criminal law and moral discourse. But these links should be the object of investigation and not a priori assumptions.

Second, the predominant philosophical approach to responsibility fails to consider the extent to which conceptions of responsibility have shifted over the course of the history of modern societies, and of how in turn these substantive shifts relate to the development of institutions and ideas in their economic, cultural, and political contexts. These, doubtless, are difficult questions to address. It is striking, however, that in recent philosophy and social theory there have been significant attempts to provide historicized accounts of the development of analogous concepts implicated in the development of key social institutions in the modern period. Significant examples include the concept of the person, conceptions of freedom, the

[11] H. L. A. Hart, *Punishment and Responsibility* (Oxford: Clarendon Press 1968) Chapter IX.

concept of law, the idea of human rights, the concept of punishment and associated conceptions such as shame, power, and discipline.[12] Except within very specific fields, however, the history of modern Western conceptions of responsibility remains to be written.

The Existing Literature

Criminal Law Scholarship

There is a large literature on criminal responsibility, most of which falls into one of three categories. First, there are treatises focused on the conceptual analysis of responsibility: for instance, H. L. A. Hart's *Punishment and Responsibility* (1968); Michael Moore's *Placing Blame* (1998); Jeremy Horder's *Excusing Crime* (2004); Victor Tadros's *Criminal Responsibility* (2005); Antony Duff's *Answering for Crime* (2007); and Larry Alexander and Kimberley Ferzan's *Crime and Culpability* (2009). Second, there are treatises focused specifically on the historical development of legal doctrines of criminal responsibility, for instance, George Fletcher's *Rethinking Criminal Law* (1978) and K. J. M. Smith's *Lawyers, Legislators and Theorists* (1998). These two genres of work evince only a limited interest in the relationship between legal and broad social, political and institutional changes. Third, there are social histories of criminal justice and procedure, such as David Garland's *Punishment and Welfare* (1985) and *Punishment and Modern Society* (1990),

[12] See Charles Taylor, *Sources of the Self* (Cambridge: Cambridge University Press 1989) (a book which, given the close connection between selfhood and responsibility in modern philosophy, has curiously little explicit discussion of responsibility); J. B. Schneewind, *The Invention of Autonomy* (a history of modern moral philosophy whose central theme of the emergence of ideas of moral self-governance is highly relevant to the idea of responsibility, yet in which that idea itself does not feature prominently); Nikolas Rose, *Powers of Freedom*; Peter Wagner, *Liberty and Discipline: A Sociology of Modernity* (London: Routledge 1993); Tim Murphy, *The Oldest Social Science?* (Oxford: Clarendon Press 1998); David Garland, *Punishment and Modern Society* (Oxford: Oxford University Press 1990); John Braithwaite, 'Shame and Modernity' 33 *British Journal of Criminology* (1993) 1–18 (reprinted in David Parker, Rosamund Dalziell, and Iain Wright, *Shame and the Modern Self* (Melbourne: Australian Scholarly Publishing 1996)); Michel Foucault, *Discipline and Punish* (transl. Alan Sheridan, Harmondsworth: Penguin 1977); Lynn Hunt, *Inventing Human Rights* (New York: W. W. Norton 2007).

Martin Wiener's *Reconstructing the Criminal* (1991), John Langbein's *The Origins of Adversary Criminal Trial* (2003), Mirjan Damaska's *Evidence Law Adrift* (1997), Peter King's *Crime, Justice and Discretion in England 1740–1820* (2000), and James Whitman's *Harsh Justice: Criminal Punishment and the Widening Divide Between America and Europe* (2003). These, conversely, are relatively little concerned with the specificities of legal-doctrinal conceptions of responsibility.

A fourth literature has begun to emerge which brings, as I suggest we need to do, these bodies of scholarship into dialogue with one another. This literature—still relatively small but highly significant—includes: Jeremy Horder's *Provocation and Responsibility* (1992); Alan Norrie's *Crime, Reason and History* (third edition, 2014) and *Punishment, Responsibility and Justice* (2000); Lindsay Farmer's *Criminal Law, Tradition and Legal Order: Crime and the Genius of Scots Law* (1996); Antony Duff, Lindsay Farmer, Sandra Marshall and Victor Tadros's projects on the criminal trial (*The Trial on Trial I: Truth and Due Process* 2004; *II: Judgment and Calling to Account* 2005; *III: Towards a Normative Theory of the Criminal Trial* 2007) and, with Massimo Renzo, on criminalization (*The Boundaries of the Criminal Law* 2010, *The Structures of the Criminal Law* 2011, *The Constitution of the Criminal Law* 2013), *Criminalization: the Political Morality of the Criminal Law* (2015). Markus Dirk Dubber's *The Police Power* (2005); my own *Women, Crime and Character* (2008); Arlie Loughnan's *Manifest Madness: Mental Incapacity in the Criminal Law* (2012); Peter Ramsay's *The Insecurity State* (2012); Thomas A. Green's *Freedom and Criminal Responsibility in American Legal Thought* (2014), Ely Aaronson's *From Slave Abuse to Hate Crime* (2014); and Lindsay Farmer's *Making the Modern Criminal Law: Criminalization and Civil Order* (2016) also fall into this category of works aspiring to bring different genres of scholarship into productive dialogue[13]

[13] James Q. Whitman has moreover applied similar socio-legal, comparative and historical methods to issues of proof: see *The Origins of Reasonable Doubt* (New Haven: Yale University Press 2008). Susanna Blumenthal's *Law and the Modern Mind: Consciousness and Responsibility in American Legal Culture* (Harvard University Press 2016) will be a further contribution to this emerging literature.

Notwithstanding the contribution of this important emerging literature, our contemporary debate about responsibility as the key legitimating device of the criminal law is dominated by the first group: legal/moral philosophers and scholars of criminal law doctrine, with criminal law scholarship itself dominated by doctrinal scholarship and by philosophical analysis of the foundations of criminal law.[14] These two, very different, paradigms have one big thing in common: they tend to proceed as if the main intellectual task is to unearth the deep logic of existing legal doctrines. Sometimes this goes so far as to read them back onto history, as if things could never have been other than they are. The reasons for this intellectual disposition vary, but to any social scientist it is both a puzzling and an unsatisfactory one. For a serious engagement with historical resources necessarily motivates a more critical examination, which can reveal, first, the contingency of particular legal arrangements and, second, the patterns of development over time which may help us to develop causal and other theses about the dynamics which shape them and hence about the role, function and characteristics of criminal law as a form of power in modern societies. So, in a sense, I shall in this book use history in support of an analysis driven primarily by the social sciences. This is not, evidently, historical scholarship, but it draws on historical research to drive its interpretive project.

The construction of the responsible subject within the rules, principles, and practices of criminal law demonstrates, as I shall argue in detail, three things. First, the story of the evolution of legal understandings of criminal agency and responsibility in the common law demonstrates the relevance to jurisprudence of institutional development, given that institutional as well as cultural and political factors have shaped the uneven reception into legal doctrine of normative ideas more widely diffused in social discourse, and that responsibility in the law is shaped by not only that institutional framework but by the practical and normative tasks which it performs.[15] Second, the story of evolving conceptions of legal responsibility raises vividly and

[14] Unsurprisingly, the division of labour in the field of criminal law scholarship is mirrored in the history of legal theory: see Chapter 6 for discussion of its implications in that context.

[15] For a recent account theorizing criminal law in institutional terms, see Lindsay Farmer, 'Criminal Law as an Institution: Rethinking Theoretical Approaches to Criminalization', in R. A. Duff, Lindsay Farmer, S. E. Marshall, Massimo Renzo, and Victor Tadros (eds), *Criminalization: The Political Morality of the Criminal Law* (Oxford: Oxford University Press 2014), and his *Making the Modern Criminal Law.*

directly what I shall call the 'of' question: in other words, when we talk of a theory or conception *of* a particular idea, what are the criteria of accountability between the phenomenon itself and our conceptualization? Third, and following from the first two points, this approach shows that legal theory must accordingly deploy a reflexive or interpretive methodology which, while engaging with general questions about law and legality, moves constantly back and forth between concepts and social phenomena.[16] This in turn bears on a further question central to recent jurisprudential debate: the sense in which jurisprudence can be general or universal—a question to which I shall turn in the final chapter of the book.

Core Assumptions of the Analysis

The rest of the book is premised on three key conclusions drawn from this preliminary analysis. It will be useful to make those conclusions explicit here.

1: *Responsibility has distinctive structural roles in legitimating and coordinating patterns and practices of criminalization understood as a form of social regulation.* My initial hypothesis about the symbolic and practical role played by responsibility in criminal law can be summed up in the following way. The development of ideas of responsibility for crime are, at root, responses to structural problems of coordination and legitimation faced by systems of criminal law in pursuing its prevailing social functions by both expressive and regulatory means. The content and emphasis of these problems, and of criminal law's social functions, can be expected to change according to the environment in which the system operates, with important factors including the distribution of political interests and economic power, the prevailing cultural and intellectual environment, the organization and relative

[16] I here use the term 'interpretive' in the sense used by Peter Cane, 'Public Law in *The Concept of Law*' 33 *Oxford Journal of Legal Studies* (2013) 649–74, at 652 (sentence including n. 20), rather than in the normative sense developed so influentially by Ronald Dworkin in *Law's Empire* (London: Fontana 1986). Elsewhere in his paper, Cane uses the term 'non-essentialism'—a term which Cane credits to Frederick Schauer (Schauer, 'Hart's Anti-Essentialism', in Luis Duarte d'Almeida, James Edwards and Andrea Dolcetti (eds) *Reading Hart's Concept of Law* (Oxford: Hart Publishing 2013) pp. 237–46—to describe his method, which is similar to the one which I defend in this book; see passage at Cane, *Public Law*, n. 63.

status of relevant professional groups, and the array and vigour of alternative means of social ordering. This starting point implies that the most illuminating approach to criminal responsibility will be both a multi-disciplinary and a cross-institutional one.

We might hypothesize that criminal law, understood more or less as we understand it today, faces four rather general problems of legitimation. The first is a problem of what we might call value coordination: how are the values and substantive judgments which criminal law expresses (and enforces) to be legitimated? The second is a problem of what we might call knowledge coordination: how is knowledge of the facts on which judgments in individual cases are based to be legitimated? The third is the problem of what we might call cultural legitimation: how can the inherently violent and top-down nature of the penal sanction be reconciled with the civilized sensibilities[17] and the ideal of respect for persons characteristic of modern social imaginaries? And the fourth is the challenge of what we might call political legitimation: how can the vastly unequal distribution of the burdens of criminalization be reconciled with the egalitarian ideals and self-conceptions of modern social orders? As we shall see throughout this book, doctrines and practices of responsibility-attribution play a key role in relation to each of these tasks, contributing to both its expressive and its regulatory modes, and structuring the interaction between the two.

2: *Responsibility has to be understood in the context of more general patterns and practices of criminalization, and as functional to criminal law's role as a system of regulation.* My argument makes the assumption—controversial among criminal lawyers, but to my mind absolutely fundamental to any serious attempt to interpret criminal law as a social practice—that the meaning of what goes on in criminal courts can only be understood by tempering our interpretation of legal-doctrinal arguments with socio-legal facts about how cases are selected for trial and processed after conviction, about the operation of rules of evidence and procedure, and about the institutional structure of criminal courts. In other words, my argument assumes that criminal law can and should be understood *as part of an integrated process of criminalization* incorporating all stages from the articulation

[17] On the impact of these developments on punishment, see David Garland, *Punishment and Modern Society* (Oxford University Press 1990) Chapter 10; my claim is that Garland's insight is equally applicable to doctrines of criminal responsibility.

of offences through investigation, diversion, prosecution, trial, sentencing, the royal prerogative, and the execution of punishment. Evaluations of responsibility feed into judgments at each of these stages. Conversely, each stage is structured by assumptions about the nature of responsibility, which may moreover vary as between them.

Criminalization itself must be disaggregated into a number of distinct phenomena: between criminalization as a pattern or outcome, either descriptively or ideally, and either formally (through legislation or case law) or substantively (as enforced); and criminalization as a set of social practices, themselves structured by rules and hence capable of being understood in formal/theoretical or substantive/practical terms. These distinctions are summarized in the simple diagram below (Figure 1.1):

A Criminalization as pattern or outcome (descriptive/normative)

(i.e. what has been or should be criminalized)

Ai Formal Criminalization (legislation, judicial decisions, International treaties)	**Aii** Substantive Criminalization (actual implementation of formal norms)

B Criminalization as a social practice (descriptive/normative)

(i.e. who criminalizes, or should criminalize; on what assumptions and according to what processes and principles)

Bi Formally ('in the books')	**Bii** Substantively ('in action')

Figure 1.1 Varieties of Criminalization.

Criminal law is, of course, one form of regulation—using this term in both instrumental and expressive senses—and this is nicely captured in the concept of criminalization. But, at first sight, the idea that responsibility—generally thought of as a normative, legitimating concept—must be understood in the context of prevailing practices and patterns of criminalization—a positive concept, a practice shaped in good part by power and interests—may seem odd. Yet it is fundamental to my underlying argument that normative concepts are shaped by both their institutional and political (broadly speaking) environment and their practical—hence, in part, regulatory—tasks. The development and survival of key doctrinal and substantive aspects of criminal law is accordingly likely to depend (at least in part) on their direct or indirect contributions to the regulatory objectives of the criminal process. But a key assumption that I shall make in exploring this hypothesis is that the conditions of existence of any regulatory system, such as criminalization, include not only material resources such as economic or physical power, information, and institutional infrastructure but also what we might call symbolic resources such as legitimacy.[18]

Criminal responsibility, therefore, is nested in and shaped by a broader field of regulation which I shall conceptualize as criminalization: a 'regulatory space' populated by a number of distinctive regulatory actors, regulatory modalities, and regulatory tasks: the interaction between these various components constitutes what we might call the *regulatory resources*—material and symbolic, coordinated and fragmented—within a particular regulatory space.[19] The *actors* in the regulatory space of criminalization include, I shall argue, not only legislatures, courts, governments, regulatory agencies, formal criminal justice agencies such as police, prosecution, probation, and prison services but also the full panoply of non-governmental collectivities, such as pressure groups, private security services, other corporations, and indeed—crucially—individual members of society. Drawing on the work of Lawrence Lessig as adapted by Andrew Murray and Colin Scott,[20] we can usefully think of this in terms of a four-fold framework of *regulatory modalities*, consisting of hierarchical, normative or community-based, competition-based, or design-based methods of control, these four methods being deployed variously to three distinctive *regulatory tasks*: standard-setting, information-gathering or monitoring, and behaviour modification or enforcement.

Contemporary criminalization participates in each of the three regulatory tasks and deploys each of the four modalities just delineated. To take some examples, criminal law is involved in both standard-setting and in setting up (through the rules of evidence) the framework for information-gathering; criminal justice agencies such

[18] Cf. John S. Dryzek's analysis of the role of underpinning discourses within institutions: 'The Informal Logic of Institutional Design', in Robert E. Goodin (ed.), *The Theory of Institutional Design* (Cambridge: Cambridge University Press 1996).

[19] Colin Scott, 'Analysing Regulatory Space: Fragmented Resources and Institutional Design' *Public Law* (Summer 2001) 329–53, in turn developing Leigh Hancher and Michael Moran, 'Organizing Regulatory Space', in Leigh Hancher and Michael Moran (eds) *Capitalism, Culture and Economic Regulation* (Oxford: Clarendon Press 1989).

[20] Lawrence Lessig, *Code and Other Laws of Cyberspace* (New York: Basic Books 1999); Andrew Murray and Colin Scott, 'Controlling the New Media: Hybrid Responses to New Forms of Power' 65 *Modern Law Review* (2002) 491–516.

as the police are involved in information-gathering and monitoring; the overall goal of the system is behaviour modification—a task most vividly attempted through practices of punishment. Similarly, criminalization deploys a variety of modalities. The legislation of norms of criminal law is a hierarchical means of standard-setting; social pressure founded in community-based controls is central to the production of compliance with the norms of criminal law; the manipulation of penalties, informed by certain assumptions about the motivations and capacities of the subjects of regulation, could be seen as analogous to competition-based forms of control; and systems of self-regulation backed up by ultimate criminal sanctions in the business area, for example, may create a situation in which standards of compliance and good practice become one aspect of firms' competitive advantage. Design—not only behavioural regulation through architectural design of public spaces or buildings in pursuit of 'situational crime prevention' or the panopticon prison but also normative regulation through the discursive and ritual design of the criminal trial, the choreography of the trial process through courtroom design and rules of evidence—plays various roles in pursuing the regulatory tasks of criminalization. Among these four modalities, however, I shall focus mainly on the role of criminal responsibility in the first two:[21] hierarchical and community-based means of regulatory control; and on the interaction between the two.

It is perhaps one of the most persistent myths about criminalization that it operates, primarily, in hierarchical regulatory mode. This image of criminalization as a hierarchical system is strongly associated with the role of law in the overall regulation of crime. Like most myths, the idea of criminalization as hierarchical has a basis in truth. At the level of standard-setting, courts and legislatures play a leading role, bringing with them the centralizing and top-down aspects of the 'command and control' model. But this is only—indeed less than—half the truth: an image which is itself a product of thinking about criminal law in isolation from the regulatory contexts in which it is interpreted and enforced. The basic point here can be summed up in the old rallying cry of the Realist and law

[21] This is not to say that criminal responsibility is irrelevant to the third and fourth: clearly both competitive and design-based systems of regulation make assumptions about the responsible subject, notably as an agent capable of responding to incentives or an otherwise sentient and reactive being.

in context movements: the law in the books is not the same as the law in action. Moreover, the difference between the two must be explained not merely in terms of limited enforcement resources or the interpretive influence of officials, but in yet broader terms. Take, for example, the fact that (in Britain) the overwhelming majority of suspected offences investigated by the police come to their notice through report by members of the public. It is well known that limited resources—as well as the fact that we would have political objections to living in a panoptically policed society—mean that the proportion of the total amount of social behaviour susceptible to formal criminalization which is actually proceeded against is tiny. What is less often remarked is that a primary gatekeeper between social behaviour which might be defined as criminal and the process of formal criminalization is the ordinary citizen. What this implies, among other things, is that where central, hierarchically defined criminal law standards depart from community standards—as, unfortunately, has often been the case in relation to the application of the law of assault to domestic violence, or, perhaps more positively, in relation to the social use of cannabis, or, in the famous US instance of prohibition of alcohol—or where community standards are themselves contested, the enforcement and, on occasion, interpretation of criminal law will be fundamentally affected by its dissonance with the structures of informal, community-based control.

Lack of alignment with community-based control will, therefore, place limits on the effectiveness with which centrally determined and hierarchically imposed regulatory objectives can be pursued: in this sense, wider social norms themselves regulate formal criminalization. But this is not just a matter of constraint. There is also a story here about regulatory capacity. For, positively, it is the underlying bedrock of social support for criminal law which underpins the widespread voluntary compliance without which the hierarchical regulatory resources of the criminal process at the monitoring and enforcement levels would be entirely incapable of delivering the most modest of regulatory objectives of social coordination.[22] And this is due at least in part to the resonance (or, at the least, lack of dissonance) between the substantive norms of criminal law and prevailing social norms. In this context, the internalization of norms at the social level underpins criminalization in something like the way that trust can facilitate contracting. John Braithwaite's regulatory pyramid sets restorative

[22] Tom R. Tyler, *Why People Obey the Law* (London: Yale University Press 1990).

justice, the preferred option, at the bottom of the pyramid, deterrence through the announcement of standards and threat of penalties in the middle, and incapacitative punishments as the last resort, at the top.[23] In terms of this analysis, one could say that the most important regulatory work in relation to criminalization in fact goes on below the bottom of the pyramid, consisting in the personal internalization of norms, or generalized receptivity to peer pressure, which secures voluntary compliance, rendering resort even to the first level of the regulatory pyramid unnecessary. The pyramid, perhaps, is focused on the tasks of monitoring and enforcement rather than that of standard-setting. And it is here, I argue, that ideas of responsibility play a crucial legitimating and coordinating role.

Particularly in a world of value heterogeneity and moral pluralism, criminal law's distinctive regulatory contribution may, of course, lie not so much in hierarchical standard-setting—a process which has often uncertain outcomes, and ones which depend crucially on alignment with community-based regulation—as in legitimation: an indirect contribution, but a crucial one on the assumption that legitimacy is one of the key symbolic resources of any regulatory system. But just how this legitimacy is to be produced varies over time according to prevailing social, political and institutional conditions. And under modern, democratic, conditions there is a particularly perplexing question as to how criminal law can make a contribution to legitimation in a situation in which there are huge variations in the extent to which its content overlaps with the norms of a conventional morality (which may itself be contested); in which popular attachment to democratic legitimation is an unreliable source given both the perception that governments use criminal law pragmatically; and—in the case of those common law jurisdictions with a powerful but unelected judiciary in particular—in which the judiciary has significant criminal standard-setting power.

To answer this question about legitimation, commentators throughout the twentieth century increasingly turned to the so-called 'general part' of criminal law: the set of rules, principles, doctrines

[23] John Braithwaite, *Restorative Justice and Responsive Regulation* (Oxford: Oxford University Press 2001) Chapter 2, see in particular p. 32; cf. Phillip Pettit's argument for prioritizing 'screening' over 'sanctioning': *Republicanism: A Theory of Freedom and Government* (Oxford: Clarendon Press 1999) Chapter 7; and 'Institutional Design and Rational Choice', in Robert Goodin (ed.), *The Theory of Institutional Design*.

and procedural values which apply across the whole or a substantial part of the substantive terrain of criminal law. It includes, for example: the general defences, underpinned by doctrines of exemption, excuse, and justification; the notions that both a conduct element and a responsibility or fault element should have to be proven, at least in the case of serious offences; the idea that criminal trials should respect certain procedural standards such as a special burden and standard of proof; the broad procedural aspirations often summarized under the heading of 'the principle of legality' or 'the rule of law'. The general part encompasses, therefore, both technical normative and conceptual doctrines and broad procedural values. What is true of each of its features, however, is that they have to do with the *form* of criminal law and not with its *substance*; that is, with the rules addressed to judges in relation to what must be proven, and how it must be proven, to convict someone of a crime, and not with the duty rules addressed primarily to citizens. And it is this focus on form which provides the 'general part' with its legitimating potential in a world in which the substance of criminal law is expanding, and in which the social normative systems underpinning formal criminalization are themselves diversifying and mapping less and less completely onto the special part of criminal law. But the general part itself, as we shall see, has distinctive institutional and historical conditions of existence.

Finally, we need to add to the framework of regulatory actors, tasks and modalities a further set of analytic distinctions having to do with the assumptions which each regulatory modality makes about *the subjects of regulation*: in the case of criminalization, individuals and corporations. First, what assumptions are made about their motivations; second, what assumptions are made about their capacities; and third, what normative limits have the assumptions about their capacities been thought to place on the practice of criminalization? Are the subjects of regulation assumed to be egoists or altruists? Are they assumed to be self-determining agents, capable not only of rational choice but of taking responsibility for their choices, or passive objects of regulatory power? As I seek to show in this book, the changing concept of responsibility is criminal law's primary doctrinal and ideological mechanism for answering these questions about its subjects.

3: *Responsibility as an idea has institutional conditions of existence; it is shaped but not determined by interests. It follows that different conceptions of responsibility can and do co-exist within criminal law at particular times in particular places: their changing balance is key to understanding the broader dynamics of the state's criminalizing power.* The location of criminal responsibility within the broader context of practices of criminalization already implies that the realization of moral/philosophical ideas of responsibility has institutional conditions of existence, and that our analysis of criminal responsibility must, accordingly, be historically and system specific. But this dependence of responsibility on forces shaped both by interests and by institutional arrangements further implies that it is possible, even likely, that multiple ideas of responsibility may be operating in practices of criminalization at any one time. It will therefore be useful to develop a differentiated scheme of possible attribution principles for interpretive purposes. The division of attribution principles into three family groupings, capacity, character, and outcome principles, is familiar in criminal law theory.[24] I shall suggest however that it is useful to make a further subdivision between these overall principles, generating a more sensitive analytic scheme.

The idea that criminal law may most accurately be mapped in terms of a diverse set of co-existing principles of responsibility is hardly novel. In his pathbreaking *Rethinking Criminal Law*,[25] George Fletcher used examples from a broad historical and comparative canvass to identify three distinct 'patterns of criminality'. Within the pattern of manifest criminality, the essence of criminal responsibility is located in acts generally recognizable as threatening to established community interests. Within a conception of subjective criminality, by contrast, criminal responsibility is founded on the particular intentions and other subjective states of mind of the defendant him- or herself. And within a third conception, the pattern of criminality is located in a conception of the risk or harm implied by the relevant criminal conduct. Crucial to Fletcher's account is the claim that these philosophically diverse patterns of criminality might co-exist—indeed have co-existed—within particular systems of criminal law. While the pattern of manifest criminality might certainly be seen as being on the wane from the late eighteenth century on, neither the subjective nor the harm- or risk-based pattern could necessarily pretend to dominance, let alone exclusive jurisdiction,

[24] See, for example, Victor Tadros, *Criminal Responsibility*; Jeremy Horder, 'Criminal Culpability: The Possibility of a General Theory' 12 *Law and Philosophy* (1993) 193–215.

[25] (Boston and Toronto: Little, Brown 1978).

in late modern systems of criminal law, such as those of Britain, Germany or the United States. Indeed, in the case of English criminal law, it is arguable that traces of the pattern of manifest criminality persist, emerging as counters to established doctrines, and as counters with sufficient plausibility to cause significant trouble to the criminal courts.[26]

As Fletcher's account makes clear, broad shifts of influence among these patterns of criminality may be readily identified over long sweeps of space and time. Fletcher generally confines himself to a doctrinal interpretation of the shifts, rather than undertaking a socio-historical analysis of their broader causes or roots in culture, institutional structure or political economy. As we shall see in Chapter 3, he is dismissive of—and has persuasive arguments against—Jerome Hall's famous political-economic explanation of one of the most fascinating creations of the pattern of manifest criminality: the highly technical conception of 'breaking bulk', which allowed for a convenient expansion of the law of theft to cover expropriations beyond those consisting in the outright takings from possession which constituted the original offence.[27] Though Fletcher does not reject outright the broad idea that changes in the criminal law might track the changing needs of economy and society or the changing institutional capacities of the criminal process, his primary focus on the (in his view) relatively autonomous dynamics of criminal law doctrines precludes him from developing any general hypotheses of a socio-legal kind. In this book, by contrast, I want to explore precisely such hypotheses. For while, like Fletcher, I am sympathetic to the idea that legal doctrines do have a certain autonomy, and are not susceptible to the straightforwardly reductive socio-political explanations ventured by some versions of Legal Realism or Law and Economics, it is clear that legal doctrines do not develop in a social vacuum. Therefore, to put the point in the language of systems theory,[28] while legal doctrines are normatively closed, they remain cognitively open; and the environments in

[26] For an elaboration of this argument in relation to the law of theft, deception, and attempts, see Celia Wells and Oliver Quick, *Lacey, Wells and Quick, Reconstructing Criminal Law* (4th ed., Cambridge: Cambridge University Press 2010) Chapters 11–13; see also Lindsay Farmer, *Making the Modern Criminal Law* Chapter 7, and Chapter 3 below.

[27] Jerome A. Hall, *Theft, Law and Society* (2nd ed., Indianapolis: Bobbs-Merrill 1952).

[28] See, for example, Gunther Teubner, *Law as an Autopoietic System* (Oxford: Blackwell 1993).

which they operate create interference which the relatively closed legal system has to incorporate—even though in doing so it translates that interference into (adapted versions of) its own terms. The development of hypotheses about how and under what conditions particular areas of legal doctrine 'translate' the 'interference' from their environment therefore constitutes one of the most interesting challenges for socio-legal scholarship.

In pursuing this project, I have been working in parallel—and in dialogue—with Lindsay Farmer, and I had access to the draft of his fine monograph, *Making the Modern Criminal Law*, during my work on the final draft of this book. Farmer's analysis is referred to and drawn upon at various stages of my text, but it is perhaps useful to highlight both the similarities and the differences between the two works at the outset. Each of us has sought to produce an institutional account of criminal law which is historically contextualized and which acknowledges the interplay between doctrines of criminal law and the social functions of criminal law in differently ordered societies. We both accordingly see the need to analyse criminal responsibility in the light of the changing patterns, functions, and conceptions of criminalization. Farmer's book gives a systematic historical treatment to the subject which I do not attempt in this book. He ranges very widely, addressing both the general and aspects of the special part, and applying—to my mind very productively—the ideas of legitimation and coordination, which I originally framed in relation to responsibility,[29] across the terrain of criminalization. My own approach is more specifically focused on responsibility, drawing on particular areas of legal doctrine so as to illustrate and provide evidence for my interpretive claims, which are driven by an analytic framework rather than worked through in each historical period. While agreeing with Farmer that an account of criminal law cannot be provided through an account of punishment, I see more influence of penal (and indeed prosecutorial) practices on the doctrines of criminal law than he is inclined to acknowledge: in my view, the structure of punishment typically spills over into the institutional logics of criminal responsibility, shaping their meaning. Probably the most important difference between our books, however, is the fact that I try to provide a thesis about the political- economic and social

[29] Nicola Lacey, 'In Search of the Responsible Subject: History, Philosophy and Criminal Law Theory' 64 *Modern Law Review* (2001) 350–71.

drivers of the shifting patterns of responsibility-attribution in criminal law over time, building interests as well as ideas and institutions into my model. In doing so, I provide an account which is necessarily more speculative than Farmer's systematic historical analysis, with the two books complementing one another in their intellectual ambition.

My book's argument proceeds as follows. In Chapter 2, I set out four relatively discrete (yet sometimes overlapping) ideational frameworks within which the conceptions of responsibility have developed: those of capacity, character, outcome, and risk. I then go on to consider the broader cultural and intellectual contexts—such as philosophical understandings of selfhood and of the relationship between individual and state, the psychological and social sciences, religion, understandings of gender—which have provided the broader intellectual environment which has shaped the development of ideas of responsibility. In Chapter 3, I consider the main vectors of power and interest which shape ideas and practices of responsibility-attribution, before moving on in Chapter 4 to consider the main institutions which shape, either directly or indirectly, the development of ideas of criminal responsibility and its attribution. Through each of these chapters are woven case studies illustrating the importance of each of the explanatory factors at particular points in modern English legal history. In Chapter 5, I offer an interpretation of how these interacting forces have co-evolved to produce distinctive—multiple, philosophically conflicting—conceptions of criminal responsibility in early twenty-first-century England. And in Chapter 6, I summarize the methodological upshot of my argument for legal theory and for legal scholarship more generally, as well as confronting some of the normative questions raised by my interpretation in Chapter 5.

2

Ideas

A number of more or less discrete ideational frameworks for the understanding of criminal responsibility can be identified as influencing English criminal law over the last 250 years. Each of them is shaped by assumptions about the nature of human (or corporate, or indeed animal) agency and each has implications for the relationship between that agent and the state or any other body which wields criminalizing power, and, in particular, for the accountability or answerability of that agent and the conditions of that answerability. Two questions in particular arise: what is seen as justifying the calling to account of individuals or other bodies in the name of the criminal process (or the state)—the question of *legitimation*; and what information must be marshalled to invoke that legitimated practice of calling to account—the question of *coordination*, including matters such as rules of evidence and procedure as well as the substantive doctrines of criminal law.[1] This chapter sets out the four principal ideational frames that have underpinned the principles and

[1] As I trust the ensuing discussion makes clear, this task of criminal responsibility in specifying the criteria of relevance of the forms of knowledge which must be brought to bear on the trial's process of proof is one among a much larger set of coordinating challenges which must be met by any criminal justice system. These include the specification of those professionals or lay actors empowered to make authoritative interpretations and to take executive actions, and of the relationships between them—not to mention the very broad sense in which a criminal justice system must aspire to coordinate social understandings and behaviour. My particular focus flows simply from my specific concern with ideas of responsibility; but I hope to draw out the ways in which the coordinating roles of responsibility relate to these broader tasks of coordination implicit in the project of any criminal justice system.

practices of responsibility-attribution in England and Wales over this period. Leaving aside for the moment the question of how we can explain their shifting relationship to one another in the development of English criminal law, the chapter traces each of the relevant pattern's conceptual parameters, considers its varying versions, identifies its underlying justification and its legitimating narratives, and assesses the influence on ideas of responsibility of broader social and political knowledges, drawing some parallels between developing ideas of the responsible subject in criminal justice and in other areas of social practice.

Practices of criminal responsibility-attribution have long exhibited a concern with some combination of character, capacity, and outcome, with 'character' standing in for a particular conception of how criminal evaluation attaches to persons and relates to identity, 'capacity' standing in for the concern with agency, choice, and personal autonomy, and outcome standing in for the concern with the social harms produced by crime. In recent years, a further pattern founded in assessments of risk has also emerged. The underlying justification and legitimating narratives of these four frames are philosophically distinct. The frames draw on different political and social knowledges and they come in varied versions that hold greater or less sway at different times. Yet, they nonetheless can and do co-exist in particular systems of criminal law at particular times. Moreover, the precise configuration of these elements, and the shape which each of them takes, has changed markedly over time. The chapter concludes by considering some case studies which illustrate the way in which conceptually or philosophically distinct ideas of responsibility have been combined in criminal justice practices. The case studies illustrate the interplay of different ideas of responsibility at key moments in the development of modern English criminal law, providing material for the substantive interpretation which will be offered in Chapter 5. Throughout, it is argued that practices of responsibility-attribution must be interpreted in the light of the whole process of criminalization, from law-making through prosecution and law-application at trial to punishment—hence opening up the possibility that multiple and even inconsistent approaches to responsibility are operating not only at different times within a single system but over different institutional spaces of the criminal process at any one time.

Responsibility as Founded in the Engagement of Human Capacity

First, and most obviously, in modern legal discourse we are familiar with the idea that criminal responsibility is founded in capacity. At the heart of this vision of criminal responsibility sits the notion of an agent endowed with powers of understanding and self-control.[2] This notion was most fully developed in post-Enlightenment social philosophy but existed in thicker and thinner versions in earlier and later philosophies. It was developed primarily in relation to human beings but is susceptible of extension to, for example, corporate entities and animals (albeit at the theoretical periphery). Capacity responsibility makes a strong assumption about what it is that we are responsible *for*: we are responsible not for our selves, for who we are, or for our social status, but—on a quasi-contractual basis—for the specific acts which we (choose to) do or (in limited circumstances) refrain from doing.[3] Under this notion of capacity responsibility, respect for agency and individual freedom is central. Capacity theories hence assume either freedom of the will or some version of compatibilism, under which the idea that human conduct is to some degree determined is not inconsistent with genuine responsibility. Capacity responsibility implies a stringent set of legitimating requirements for state criminalization and punishment. Only when criminal law is addressed to human beings as choosing subjects capable of conforming their actions to the criminal law can it be compatible with individual freedom. Conversely, as both Lindsay Farmer and Peter Ramsay have pointed out in relation to recent legal developments, capacity-responsibility makes no claims about the substance of the conduct for which the subject can be held responsible, and hence has the potential to legitimate wide-ranging criminalization wherever these capacities are fully engaged.[4]

[2] See Nicola Lacey, 'In Search of the Responsible Subject: History, Philosophy and Criminal Law Theory' 64 *Modern Law Review* (2001) 350–71 and 'Responsibility and Modernity in Criminal Law' 9 *Journal of Political Philosophy* (2001) 249–77.

[3] Note the resonance with Henry Sumner Maine's idea of a movement from status to contract, *Ancient Law: Its Connection with the Early History of Society and its Relation to Modern Ideas* (1861: London: Oxford University Press 1959).

[4] See Lindsay Farmer, *Making the Modern Criminal Law: Criminalization and Civil Order* (Oxford: Oxford University Press 2016) Chapters 6–9; Peter Ramsay, *The Insecurity State: Vulnerable Autonomy and the Right to Security in the Criminal Law*', (Oxford: Oxford University Press 2012).

Two significantly different legal versions of capacity responsibility need to be distinguished. On the one hand, there is capacity as choice, which generally appears through subjective *mens rea* or fault requirements: legal rules guarantee respect for agency by making intention, knowledge, or foresight the paradigm conditions for criminal liability. On the other hand, there is capacity as fair opportunity, which appears in a broader conception of *mens rea* that includes negligence and 'objective' recklessness: respect for agency is satisfied so long as the agent has a fair chance to conform his or her behaviour to the requirements of criminal law. On each version, the foundation of not only a person's status as a responsible agent answerable to the normative demands of the criminal law[5] but also of an attribution of responsibility for specific actions lies in human capacities of cognition—knowledge of circumstances, assessment of consequences—and volition—powers of self-control. The crucial differentiating factor is the way in which these human capacities—human agency—are engaged in conduct. For the choice-based version of the capacity approach, advertence is key: responsible conduct is conduct which the agent chooses. This notion of capacity-based responsibility naturally issues in a focus on so-called subjective principles of *mens rea*: intention, recklessness or foresight of relevant consequences, knowledge, and so on: forms of *mens rea* which essentially consist in subjective mental states on the part of the defendant. Prime examples in English case law would include *DPP v Morgan* ((1976) AC 182, reversed by the Sexual Offences Act 2003) and *B v DPP* ((1998) 4 All ER 265). Many commentators have noted the increasing emphasis on this form of 'subjectivism', though there is considerable disagreement about the degree of its realization and the timing of and reasons for its ascendancy. On Smith's view,[6]

[5] I am in agreement with writers like Anthony Duff, Jeremy Horder, and Victor Tadros that there is a distinction to be drawn between attributions of responsibility in specific cases and a broader judgment that a subject lacks, in general, the capacities which underpin responsibility. These latter subjects are properly regarded as exempt from criminal responsibility, and this is the most natural way to understand 'defences' such as insanity or infancy. See Duff, *Trials and Punishments* (Cambridge: Cambridge University Press 1986); Tadros, *Criminal Responsibility* (Oxford: Oxford University Press 2005) Chapter 5; Horder, 'Criminal Law: Between Determinism, Liberalism and Criminal Justice' 49 *Current Legal Problems* (1996) 159–86; Nicola Lacey, 'Partial Excuses to Homicide', in Andrew Ashworth and Barry Mitchell (eds), *Rethinking English Homicide Law* (Oxford: Clarendon Press 2000).

[6] K.J.M. Smith, *Lawyers, Legislators and Theorists: Developments in English Jurisprudence, 1800–1957* (Oxford: Clarendon Press 1998).

it is a by-product of utilitarianism, which implies not merely the impropriety but the ineffectiveness of attaching culpability to inadvertent conduct.[7] It has also been argued that it is associated with the increasingly psychologized view of human agency attendant on scientific developments during the course of the nineteenth century.[8] In another account, Alan Norrie has argued that its progress may be explained partly in terms of its ability to provide a legitimating principle which is relatively independent of any evaluation of the relevant conduct. The proof of intention or subjective recklessness being a question of fact, the emphasis is simply on proof of the requisite mental state. This is a feature which may be useful in a system which criminalizes a huge range of conduct, much of it beyond the terrain of 'real' or 'quasi-moral' crime, and in which moral pluralism or value conflict risks tensions which a factual view of *mens rea* may help to keep out of the courtroom.[9]

Whatever the merits of these competing or complementary accounts of the rise of choice-based principles of responsibility, it is clear that, both conceptually and practically, they are not the only show in town when it comes to capacity principles of attribution. For the basic moral intuition underlying the capacity view can be interpreted in another way, with decisive implications for the shape of criminal law. If the basic moral intuition is that it is only legitimate to hold people criminally responsible for things which they had the capacity to avoid doing, we can realize this intuition in one of two ways. We can do so through proof of subjective choice in the sense of intention, awareness, knowledge; or we can ask—as Hart did, for example[10]—whether the defendant had a fair opportunity to conform his or her behaviour to the criminal law standard. This second

[7] Farmer (*Making the Modern Criminal Law* Chapter 6) concurs in Smith's view, but also perceives a shift between the Benthamite importance attached to advertence in the nineteenth-century debates and the emergence of a 'punishable subject' as the twentieth-century era of penal welfarism—itself consistent with a certain reading of utilitarianism—gave way to retributive, moralized understandings of responsibility.

[8] Cf. Roger Smith, *Trial by Medicine: Insanity and Responsibility in Victorian Trials* (Edinburgh: Edinburgh University Press 1981); Joel Peter Eigen, 'Lesion of the Will: Medical Resolve and Criminal Responsibility in Victorian Insanity Trials' 33 *Law and Society Review* (1999) 425–59.

[9] Norrie, *Crime, Reason and History: A Critical Introduction to Criminal Law* (Cambridge: Cambridge University Press 2001); see also my analysis: Lacey, 'In Search of the Responsible Subject'.

[10] H.L.A. Hart, *Punishment and Responsibility* (Oxford: Clarendon Press 1968; 2nd ed., ed. John Gardner, 2008)

approach has the implication that not only subjective mental states but also 'objective' standards like negligence, practical indifference, or the imposition of reasonableness constraints in the specification of defences may be accommodated as paradigm examples of *mens rea*. It also, therefore, offers an account more likely to be able to rationalize the actual shape of systems of criminal law. From the point of view of the argument which Norrie has advanced, this is however at the cost of revealing that a criminal trial is, inevitably, in the business of making a potentially controversial normative evaluation of the defendant's conduct. The question to be proven is no longer the relatively neutral, factual, and dualistic: 'Did the defendant cause the victim's death? If so, did s/he do so with intent to cause death or grievous bodily harm?'; 'Did the defendant have sexual intercourse with the victim? If so, did s/he do so intentionally and aware that victim was not consenting?' It is, rather, 'Did the defendant do these things in circumstances in which we would say that they had had a fair opportunity to avoid them?'. The answer to this question may, of course, be provided by proof of intent or subjective recklessness. But it might also be answered in terms of the defendant's indifference or omission to advert to a risk which would have been obvious to a reasonable person, or to which it would be reasonable for us to expect the defendant to advert, such that we would be inclined to say that the defendant had a fair opportunity to avoid homicide or rape.[11] So long as we are confident that the defendant has the capacities of a reasonable person, this fair opportunity view is perfectly consistent with the moral intuition underlying the capacity principle of criminal responsibility. A further perceived advantage of the opportunity version of capacity-responsibility is that it is less obviously susceptible than the choice version to the truth of determinism, in that the evaluation can be relative to socially pervasive reactive attitudes.[12] The issue, in other words, is not what we 'could' have helped, whether we 'could' have chosen otherwise, but what prevailing social norms judge us to have had a fair opportunity to help or choose.

The philosophical conception of criminal responsibility sketched above is mapped in contemporary criminal law theory and—though to a lesser extent—criminal law doctrines—onto

[11] See Nicola Lacey, 'Responsibility without Consciousness' 36 *Oxford Journal of Legal Studies* (2015 doi: 10.1093/ojls/gqv012).

[12] See P.F. Strawson, 'Freedom and Resentment', in Gary Watson (ed.), *Free Will* (Oxford: Oxford University Press 1982).

an elaborate array of fault or *mens rea* elements such as intention, recklessness, knowledge, belief, and negligence. In their developed form today, both versions of the capacity theory of responsibility also imply a generous panoply of defences encompassing circumstances under which the normal conditions of choice or opportunity-taking are disrupted by external circumstances or the behaviour of third parties (or a combination of the two) and by exempting conditions, such as forms of mental incapacity that deprive the agent of minimum levels of cognitive and/or volitional power. A paradigm example of capacity responsibility would accordingly be the case of someone who intentionally causes grievous bodily harm to another. Excusing conditions, such as duress, or exempting conditions, such as mental incapacity, further refine the compatibility of doctrinal arrangements with the underlying conception of responsibility.

Capacity-responsibility therefore offers a clear answer to the problem of legitimation faced by criminal law under conditions in which respect for individual freedom and agency are strongly held commitments. But note that a practice of responsibility-attribution based on either version of capacity responsibility also implies a particular pattern of coordination—most obviously, a specific evidential focus. On the choice version, the knowledge, intentions, and beliefs of the defendant are central, whereas on the opportunity version, the relevant evidential question rather consists in a counterfactual question about the structure of the world, along with an evaluative judgment about whether the choices available and circumstances surrounding the defendant were such as to afford a 'fair' opportunity to conform to the law. On both versions, however, evidence, or evidential assumptions, about normal or baseline cognitive capacities and capacities of self-direction are central to the notion of the responsible subject of criminal law.

These specific concepts of *mens rea* and defence, along with specifications of criminal capacity and voluntary conduct, have come over the last century to form an increasingly predominant part of what is known as the 'general part' of criminal law, or, in other words, conditions of liability (and of exculpation) which apply across offences. This general part is hence distinguishable from the specific elements of particular offences—the so-called 'special part' of criminal law. In attempting to map the historical development of the responsible subject of criminal law, the obvious strategy would therefore seem to be to look for early modern statements of this 'general part' of criminal law.

This, however, turns out to be an exceptionally difficult thing to do. For, even leaving aside the difficulty that English criminal law of the eighteenth century had neither a comprehensive Code nor even a systematic process of case reporting, such evidence as we have suggests that it lacked anything approaching the sort of 'general part' which is argued to form the doctrinal backbone of criminal law today. The doctrines which we today take as central to capacity-responsibility were gradually developed in cases, treatises, textbooks and, occasionally, legislation over at least 250 years. If we take the best systematic evidence available—influential treatises on the common law of crime in the work of jurists such as Matthew Hale and William Blackstone[13]—we find that it is the rationalization of the special part of criminal law—the ordering of offences in terms of a coherent set of values or interests which they protect or express—which is, as it were, where the theoretical action is. As Lindsay Farmer has argued,[14] this reflects an underlying preoccupation with the articulation of a new rationale of criminal law as a justified tool of modern governance in terms of its capacity to secure a certain conception of civil order: the institution of criminal law, in this vision—exemplified by Adam Smith—becomes a tool of a civilizing process, protecting individual interests in a particular way. As Farmer puts it:

> What we see in this idea of civility is the characteristic twofold formulation of the modern criminalization question. It is, on the one hand, a matter of formulating rules addressed to the individual in order to secure social interests in civil order; it is, on the other, a question of limiting the institution of law so as to secure a particular kind of civil order. What emerges from this reconstruction is the combination of individual and social interests: the individual interest in social order and the social interest in the individual life.[15]

[13] Matthew Hale, *The History of the Common Law of England*, edited by Charles M. Gray (1713: Chicago: University of Chicago Press 1971); William Blackstone, *Commentaries on the Laws of England* Vol. IV (1769: Chicago: University of Chicago Press 1979).

[14] *Making the Modern Criminal Law: Criminalization and Civil Order* Chapters 2 and 3; Farmer's account effectively characterizes criminal law as a key form of public law. See Martin Loughlin, *Foundations of Public Law* (Oxford University Press 2010).

[15] Lindsay Farmer, *Making the Modern Criminal Law* Chapter 2.

But if we look in eighteenth or even nineteenth-century treatises for general statements of the conditions of responsibility, all we find are brief allusions to ideas about intention, malice, or the will, invariably discussed in relation to specific offences such as larceny or homicide. Defences—central to today's conception of the general part—were limited in number and related to specific offences, such as homicide. So it is important to bear in mind that the idea of responsibility as founded in capacity—with its concomitant vision of criminalization as a form of state power which can be justifiably invoked (whether to mete out just deserts or to motivate conformity with the law) only in relation to an agent whose capacities have been engaged in the relevant conduct—has a distinctive history in English criminal law. As we shall see, both later in this chapter and in Chapter 4, general positive doctrines of capacity and *mens rea* emerged as inculpating principles over a long period, at the start of which capacity and, in effect, responsibility, were assumed, with the trial providing an opportunity for exculpation rather than operating on the basis of a presumption of innocence.

Responsibility as Founded in the Evaluation of Character

Second, there is the notion of responsibility as founded in character, itself an idea with diverse philosophical origins as different as Aristotelian philosophy and its intellectual descendant, virtue ethics, Christian doctrines, and the empiricism of David Hume.[16] The idea that an attribution of criminal responsibility is in some sense an evaluation of character has been advanced in radically different guises by Michael Bayles (in Humean form and in relation to criminal responsibility in general), by John Gardner (in Aristotelian form and in relation to defences, conceptualized as mechanisms ensuring that we are not held responsible for things which are 'out of character'),[17] in

[16] See Nicola Lacey, *Women, Crime, and Character: From Moll Flanders to Tess of the D'Urbervilles* (Oxford University Press 2008) pp. 12–40.

[17] See Michael Bayles, 'Character, Purpose and Criminal Responsibility' 1 *Law and Philosophy* (1982) 5–20 (drawing on Hume's philosophy); John Gardner, 'The Gist of Excuses' 1 *Buffalo Criminal Law Review* (1998) 575–98. See also Dan M. Kahan and Martha C. Nussbaum, 'Two Conceptions of Emotion in Criminal Law' 96 *Columbia Law Review* (1996) 269–374; Nicola Lacey, 'Partial Defences to Homicide', in Andrew

my own work, and by Victor Tadros.[18] In its most radical form, it is thought by capacity theorists to be morally unacceptable to the extent that, unless we are held to have capacity for our characters, character responsibility implies holding us accountable for things which we could not, or had no fair opportunity, to avoid; it has also been argued that it is premised on an inappropriately ambitious vision of the moral role of criminal law.[19] Since my purpose in this book is primarily interpretive rather than normative, I shall set these objections aside. It is worth noting, however, that it is also possible for character and capacity notions to be combined, as Martin Wiener has persuasively argued they were in the early Victorian criminal justice project,[20] which aspired not merely to hold people responsible for conduct disclosing bad character, but also to use the penal process to reshape character, in part precisely by engaging the capacity-based agency of subjects.

There are at least three different senses in which assumptions about, or evaluations of, character have informed attributions of

Ashworth and Barry Mitchell (eds), *Rethinking English Homicide*; and essays by Kyron Huigens, ('Homicide in Aretaic Terms'), Kenneth W. Simons ('Does Punishment for "Culpable Indifference" Simply Punish for Bad Character?'), and V.F. Nourse ('Hearts and Minds') in a special issue on *The New Culpability: Motive, Character and Emotion in Criminal Law* (ed. Guyora Binder) 6 *Buffalo Criminal Law Review* (2002) at pp. 97, 219, 361; see also Kyron Huigens, 'Virtue and Inculpation' 108 *Harvard Law Review* (1995) 1423–80; Alan C. Michaels, 'Acceptance: The Missing Mental State' 71 *Southern California Law Review* (1998) 953–1036. On character and responsibility more generally, see Ferdinand Schoeman (ed.), *Responsibility, Character and the Emotions* (Cambridge: Cambridge University Press 1987); Moira Gatens and Genevieve Lloyd, *Collective Imaginings* (London: Routledge 1999) Chapters 3 and 6 (on Spinoza and responsibility); Peter Arenella, 'Character, Choice and Moral Agency: The Relevance of Character to Our Moral Culpability Judgments' 7 *Social Philosophy & Policy* (1990) 59–83; Bernard Williams, 'Persons, Character and Morality' in his *Moral Luck* (Cambridge: Cambridge University Press 1981) p. 1.

18 Nicola Lacey, *State Punishment* (London: Routledge 1988) Chapter 2; Victor Tadros, *Criminal Responsibility*.

19 For criticism of the normative recommendations of various character theories, see R.A. Duff, 'Choice, Character and Criminal Liability' 12 *Law and Philosophy* (1993) 345–83, and 'Virtue, Vice and Criminal Liability: Do we Want an Aristotelian Criminal Law?' 6 *Buffalo Criminal Law Review* (2002) 147–84.

20 *Reconstructing the Criminal: Culture, Law and Policy in England, 1830–1914* (Cambridge: Cambridge University Press 1991); Victor Tadros also sees a place for capacity principles within his primarily character-based theory: *Criminal Responsibility*, in particular Chapters 2, 5, 12. In his view, however, the moral force of the capacity principle is itself parasitic on the more basic sense in which criminal law expresses a judgment of the character displayed in an agent's conduct. Nonetheless, a vision of humans as, under normal conditions of agency, in some sense capacity-responsible for their beliefs, desires, and dispositions underlies Tadros's account.

responsibility in English criminal law, and it is accordingly worth unpacking the variations. First, we have the most fundamental sense of 'character responsibility'—what we might call 'character responsibility proper:' in other words, an attribution of criminal responsibility *is* in some sense a judgment of bad or vicious character, or a wrongful, bad, disapproved character trait—a disregard of human life, indifference to sexual integrity, lack of respect for property rights, and so on. The criminal law, on this view, seeks to convict, label and stigmatize those of bad character or disposition. The principle of responsibility-attribution is merely a function of the overall meaning and purpose of criminal law in its quasi-moral mode, and the criminal conduct is at root a symptom of the underlying rationale for conviction and punishment, namely bad or anti-social character. Note that this sense of character responsibility itself consists of two distinct components: first, there is the component of strong evaluation—of criminal responsibility-attribution as a moral or quasi-moral judgment; second, there is the projection of that moral judgment onto the quality of individual character.

Even though it invites us to condemn not merely the sin but also, and fundamentally, the sinner, character responsibility proper itself occupies a rather wide spectrum. At its most extreme, it exhibits what we might call 'character essentialism' and 'character determinism'. In other words, it proceeds from a view of human character—whether proceeding from theological or, increasingly in an era marked by secularization, scientific or quasi-scientific theories—and of identity as fixed,[21] or at least as relatively stable; and it regards character as determining conduct. Another form of relatively extreme character responsibility would derive from conceptions of criminal responsibility as founded in status formalized in categories such as 'common prostitute' or 'habitual offender'. At the other end of the spectrum, we have character responsibility in the sense of viewing criminal conviction as grounded in the manifestation of a vicious characteristic or character trait, or a disposition hostile to the norms of criminal law—a disposition which might be, as it were, 'out of character', and which does not necessarily mark out a stable propensity

[21] The underlying account of just what fixes character ranges from theological conceptions of evil through to scientific theories of pathology: see my 'Psychologising Jekyll, Demonising Hyde: The Strange Case of Criminal Responsibility' 4 *Criminal Law and Philosophy* (2010) 109–33.

to express such characteristics. Also at this end of the spectrum, we have forms of character responsibility attaching to the qualities of character to be expected of a person occupying a particular social role which they have voluntarily assumed and for which they will have been required to have certain forms of experience or qualification. In its more cautious forms, however, character-responsibility restricts itself to an evaluation of the specific conduct which forms the basis for the present allegation. The relevant question becomes not, 'Is the defendant's conduct evidence of criminal character?' but rather 'Does the defendant's conduct in causing the victim's death or having sexual intercourse with the victim express a settled disposition of hostility or indifference to the relevant norm of criminal law, or at least acceptance of such a disposition?' or, in Tadros's terms, 'does the defendant's conduct qua moral agent display the sort of vice which calls for criminal law's communicative role of expressing moral indignation to be invoked?'.[22] This formulation opens up an obvious path to the elaboration of defences such as duress, provocation, self-defence, or—possibly—mental incapacity. It also preserves the specific allegation of criminal conduct as central to the rationale for conviction and punishment, and is founded on a particular understanding of the defendant's status as a moral agent: a reasoning being responsible for his or her beliefs, desires, emotions, and values. In terms of coordination, while taking a more cautious view of relevant evidence, it would also naturally locate an attribution of responsibility within a broader time frame than that implied by the capacity principles. Between these ends of the spectrum, we have intermediate positions in which criminal conduct expressing vicious characteristics gives rise to a (stronger or weaker) presumption of bad character in the sense of propensity.

Analytically, the distinction between evaluation of an act and evaluation of the character of the actor is clear. But the dynamics which shape the practice of criminal law and criminal justice, and the socially received meaning of criminal conviction, are not necessarily respecters of philosophical integrity. The impulse to move from evaluation of conduct to the sort of evaluation of character which marks the more extreme versions of character responsibility—an impulse which,

[22] For Tadros, actions which are 'out of character' may nevertheless be objects of responsibility, on the basis that D showed a culpable failure to resist, hence accepting, a vicious disposition.

as I shall try to show, surfaces at key points in the history of English criminal justice—is a hugely significant phenomenon. It has large practical and normative implications for the extent to which criminal law exhibits an inclusionary versus an exclusionary temper, and for how far it is seen as addressing free and equal subjects as opposed to managing a threat posed by particular categories of subject. Yet it is one which has received relatively little attention from criminal law theorists (as distinct from criminologists, for whom the question of 'criminal character' has long been central, as well as deeply contested).

The majority of criminal law texts today proceed on the assumption that responsibility in the sense of capacity has dominated modern English criminal law. If we look to legal history rather than criminal law scholarship, however, we see a very different picture. The overwhelming impression one receives from reading eighteenth-century texts such as Blackstone's *Commentaries* is that—unlike for modern judges and commentators—the question of individual criminal responsibility, in the sense of an elaboration of the *conditions under which it is fair for the state to hold a person responsible for a crime*, and, hence, liable to punishment, is not seen as a key question which criminal law has to address. Rather, a rough and ready notion of responsibility for character appears to have been at work: it appears simply to have been assumed that—absent exceptional factors such as insanity (which received no *statutory* recognition through a special verdict in criminal law until 1800)—individuals are to be held accountable for their conduct. In the absence of sophisticated institutions of investigation and proof, reliance on surface appearances was presumably the only practical option available to the criminal process. The absence of a fully articulated 'general part' in commentaries and treatises before the early twentieth century means that they provide relatively thin material for a positive account of how the responsible subject was conceived in the mid-eighteenth century. But this difficulty itself provides an important clue to the changing shape of responsibility in criminal law.[23] There is, furthermore, a wealth of evidence about the operation of the criminal process—the jury system, the role of the Justices of the Peace, the structure and operation of Quarter Sessions and Assizes, the reception of evidence,

[23] Nicola Lacey, 'Contingency, Coherence and Conceptualism', in Antony Duff (ed.), *Philosophy and the Criminal Law: Principle and Critique* (New York: Cambridge University Press 1998) p. 9; see also Lindsay Farmer, *Making the Modern Criminal Law* Chapter 6.

the conduct of investigation and prosecution, the respective roles of lawyers, judges, juries, defendants and victims/prosecutors, the penal system.[24] This evidence offers further clues about the idea of responsible subjecthood which was being assumed and mobilized in mid-eighteenth-century criminal law.

Synthesizing from this material, certain key facts suggest that the understanding of criminal responsibility at the time of Blackstone did not lie in findings about the defendant's cognitive or volitional capacities, let alone in his or her subjective state of mind in the way that psychology has taught us to think about responsibility conditions such as 'intention' today. Rather, it lay in an evaluation of the defendant's conduct judged in the light of evidence about his or her *character and reputation*. Shared understandings of good and bad character compensated for the dilution of the direct knowledge of the earlier, self-informing jury, providing a bridge between a system based on a model of 'manifest criminality' in which criminal responsibility inheres in external conduct, with internal attitude merely an evidential matter, and one based on a model of 'subjective criminality', in which internal attitude is the heart of criminal responsibility.[25]

Certainly, eighteenth-century ideas about age and sanity represent a thin doctrine of capacity as a condition for criminal responsibility: one which was gradually being explored in legal commentaries, and which resonates with Enlightenment conceptions of agency. But capacity in this thin sense was assumed rather than being seen as proper object of investigation by the legal process, which, as we have seen, did not in any case have the resources to undertake such an investigation. From a legal point of view, it would therefore be accurate to say that mid-eighteenth-century criminal law was beginning to formulate an exculpatory doctrine of exceptional incapacity, while its positive ascriptions of responsibility were shaped primarily by evidence about the defendant's character.

To summarize, the mid-eighteenth-century criminal process was geared to identifying, holding responsible, and punishing those whom the local community regarded as of bad character: those who

[24] The most significant features of the process are addressed in John. H. Langbein's important paper, 'Shaping the Eighteenth Century Criminal Trial: A View from the Ryder Sources' 50 *University of Chicago Law Review* (1987) 55–83, at 55.

[25] See George P. Fletcher, *Rethinking Criminal Law* (Boston and Toronto: Little, Brown 1978); for further discussion of this point, see Nicola Lacey, 'In Search of the Responsible Subject'.

lacked support among their peers on the basis of their previous conduct and general reputation.[26] Those whose conduct could be offset by generally positive evidence of reputation and character, conversely, would have been less likely to be held criminally responsible and, if they were, would have a better chance of escaping the more draconian penalties. This would have been true even if an inference of intent or knowledge, *understood as we understand them today*, appears to early twenty-first-century eyes as an obvious one from the facts alleged by the prosecution.

Under certain conditions, then, an evaluation of the defendant's character has been seen as legitimating a finding of criminal responsibility. But, as in the case of responsibility as founded in capacity, character responsibility also has implications for coordination. To grasp these implications, we have to look beyond the forms of *mens rea* and the structure of defences, and focus on two further mechanisms which occupy a particularly important place in practices of responsibility-attribution based on character: character evidence, and the criminalization of status. For as legal arrangements structuring the admissibility of evidence of bad character become more expansive, the practical line between character responsibility proper and bad character as probative becomes blurred. In this context, the creation and enforcement of status offences assumes a particular significance.

The rationale for allowing evidence of bad character is obvious enough: it is that past manifestations of bad or vicious character are relevant to the *proof* of responsibility. In the attributive practice of character responsibility proper, criminal conviction is, as it were, irrebuttable evidence of bad character: it is a judgment of bad character, based on the premise that criminal conduct amounts to the expression of vicious characteristics. The evidential character mechanism, rather, addresses the process leading to conviction. Bad character as manifested in previous offending behaviour or, perhaps, undesirable behaviour more generally is seen either as indicative of a propensity towards such behaviour, and hence as tending towards proof of guilt, or as tending to undermine the credibility of a defence or a

[26] This reference to community and peer judgment should not be taken to imply that the standards invoked were either simple or unitary. Clearly, judgments of character would have been relative to prevailing social structures such as class and gender, with the positive testimony of, for example, a defendant's master or employer weighing particularly heavily in the trial and pardoning processes.

plea of not guilty, with the same result. A commitment to the more extreme forms of character responsibility would seem to imply a wide embrace of the relevance—indeed the centrality—of character evidence. Conversely, a responsibility principle strongly focused on proof of engaged capacity at the time of the offence would be likely to take a more modest view of the relevance of character evidence.[27]

Character evidence needs in turn to be distinguished from a second mechanism that has been influential in facilitating the character-based attribution of responsibility. This is the idea that being a certain kind of person—or bearing a certain sort of status—itself grounds criminal responsibility. In this sense, criminality might be seen as inhering in a type or group rather than in an individual. Within the logic of status offences, a group membership or a given status is, presumptively or absolutely, criminal: we know criminals from the company they keep, or from the kind of person that they are. Like character evidence, status offences expand the time frame in relation to which a putatively criminal act is interpreted, attaching the offender to some part of his or her history. In some forms, status offences further impose a form of guilt by association. These mechanisms of history and association—what we might call the 'bad apple' mechanism and the 'knowing an offender by the company s/he keeps' mechanism—reinforce one another: a judgment of guilt by association becomes a part of the history in relation to which a person is judged in the future, while a history of bad character may be indicative of the likelihood of guilty association. These mechanisms are, I shall suggest, of great importance in interpreting the varying fortunes of character responsibility in criminal law.

At the other end of the spectrum from character responsibility proper, there is character responsibility as a view of criminal conviction grounded in the manifestation of a vicious characteristic, or character trait, or a disposition hostile to the norms of criminal law, which might be out of character and which does not necessarily mark a propensity to express such characteristics. Between these two ends of the spectrum, there are intermediate positions in which criminal conduct expressing vicious characteristics gives rise to a (stronger or

[27] On the relevance of character evidence under modern conceptions of responsibility, see Mike Redmayne, 'The Relevance of Bad Character' 61 *Cambridge Law Journal* (2002) 684–714; 'The Ethics of Character Evidence' 61 *Current Legal Problems* (2008) 371–99; and *Character in the Criminal Trial* (Oxford: Oxford University Press 2015).

weaker) presumption of bad character in the sense of propensity. The impulse to move from an evaluation of conduct to the sort of evaluation of character that marks the more extreme versions of character responsibility has surfaced at key points in the history of English criminal justice. It has large implications for the extent to which criminal law exhibits a stigmatizing temper and for how much it is seen as addressing free and equal subjects as opposed to managing a threat posed by particular categories of subject, whether identified in terms of past behaviour, neuroscientific or psychological evidence, or otherwise. And the different versions of character responsibility have, of course, different implications in terms of the doctrinal preconditions of guilt (as well as for how it might be proven): the mental states and choices that are central to the capacity notion of responsibility continue to matter as evidence of, or proxies for, features of character, expressed dispositions, neural conditions, or attitudes hostile to the norms of criminal law. Thus, patterns of attribution founded in character are concerned with judging the defendant within a distinctive evidential and temporal frame. One might also argue that the more robust forms of character responsibility lend themselves rather naturally to either a purely retributive view of the rationale of punishment or to practices of punishment oriented to degradation or incapacitation rather than to reform or reconciliation.[28]

Responsibility as Founded in the Causation of Harmful Outcomes

Third, criminal law has not infrequently invoked a notion of outcome responsibility, attributing responsibility primarily or purely on the basis of the defendant having caused an outcome proscribed by the criminal law. Here, the underlying philosophical frame is consequentialist: criminal law is conceived as a distinctive system of regulation oriented to public harm-reduction. Again, outcome responsibility comes in more and less stringent forms. For example,

[28] Nicola Lacey and Hanna Pickard, 'From the Consulting Room to the Court Room? Taking the Clinical Model of Responsibility Without Blame into the Legal Realm' *Oxford Journal of Legal Studies* 33: 1–29 (2013) and 'To Blame or to Forgive? Reconciling Punishment and Forgiveness in Criminal Justice', 35 *Oxford Journal of Legal Studies* (2015), 665–96: 10.1093/ojls/gqv012.

pure causal responsibility, as in a doctrinal system of absolute responsibility, has founded its legitimating narrative not only in the moral significance of causing harm, but also in the idea that the effects we cause in some sense become part of our identity.[29] Even if we are less responsible in one sense for an accidentally caused harm, such as injuring someone after being jostled and losing one's balance, most of us would find it strange if a person who had inadvertently caused harm in this way simply shrugged his or her shoulders and said, 'That has nothing to do with me.' In practice, however, most outcome responsibility in criminal law is less stringent than this, mitigating absolute liability by means of the application of general defences and/or of a specific 'due diligence' or 'no negligence' defence. Alternatively, there is outcome responsibility in terms of the special duties that attach to particular roles or to particularly dangerous activities, such as driving vehicles and engaging in potentially harmful industrial processes and other commercial activities. And constructive liability—liability which attaches to the causing of a certain outcome while in the course of committing a different offence—as under the felony murder rule[30] or in cases of constructive manslaughter—provides another form of outcome responsibility.

The emergence of strict liability is generally associated with the idea of criminal law as oriented to harm-reduction, with utilitarian theories of punishment, and with the development of these ideas at the hands of the nineteenth-century regulatory, legislative state and the mid-twentieth-century welfare state. Yet, as systematic codes and commentaries on English criminal law developed, they concerned themselves with only part of criminal law: essentially with that part which had constituted the long-standing common law of crime, as gradually amended or collated by consolidating legislation. It is of course generally acknowledged that statutory law-making had become a central force in the development of the boundaries of formal criminalization by the nineteenth century, and, in particular, that the middle of that century saw an increasing resort to criminalization through the expansion of the summary jurisdiction

[29] See Tony Honoré, 'Responsibility and Luck: The Moral Basis of Strict Liability', in his *Responsibility and Fault* (Oxford: Hart Publishing 1999) pp. 14–40.

[30] The felony murder rule was abolished in England and Wales by the Homicide Act 1957, section 1, but retains a place in several other common law jurisdictions, notably many US states; see Guyora Binder, *Felony Murder* (Stanford: Stanford University Press 2012).

in response to the expanding regulatory needs of the nation state and an industrializing and urbanizing economy.[31] But the shape of the nineteenth-century commentaries—indeed, even of the early twentieth-century textbooks—reflects this change to a remarkably modest degree, if at all. Moreover, summary offences have continued to be marginalized in criminal lawyers' and philosophers' accounts of formal criminalization: not until 1990 did an English criminal law text accord a central place to a wide range of regulatory offences.[32]

Furthermore, the dearth of systematic historical accounts of the development of summary offences raises questions about whether this standard account of the mid-nineteenth century explosion of the summary jurisdiction has a firm basis. Can we even be confident, as Ashworth and Zedner have argued, that '[O]ffences of strict liability ... did not appear in English law in significant numbers until the mid-nineteenth century'?[33] For example, reaching as far back into the origins of English capitalism as the fourteenth century, criminal law, administered by local justices but created by legislation, was used to regulate the relationship between master and servant.[34] An early example of a hybrid civil/administrative/criminal genre, master and servant laws regulated not only wages and the supply of labour, but also labour discipline and, indirectly, social order and economic stability. Penalties included loss or reduction of wages, dismissal, fines, whipping and, in a substantial minority of cases, imprisonment in Bridewells, Houses of Correction, and local Gaols. Whipping had declined as a penalty by the nineteenth century, but prison sentences by this stage tended to be with hard labour, that is the treadmill. The eighteenth century, moreover, saw a profusion

[31] See Lindsay Farmer, *Criminal Law, Tradition and Legal Order: Crime and the Genius of Scots Law, 1747 to the Present* (Cambridge: Cambridge University Press 1997) Chapters 1 and 4.

[32] Nicola Lacey, Celia Wells and Dirk Meure, *Reconstructing Criminal Law* (London: Weidenfeld and Nicolson 1990); Smith and Hogan's *Criminal Law*, first published in 1965, devoted a chapter to road traffic offences, Lindsay Farmer, *Making the Modern Criminal Law* Chapter 5.

[33] Andrew Ashworth and Lucia Zedner, 'Defending the Criminal Law: Reflections on the Changing Character of Crime, Procedure, and Sanctions' 2 *Journal of Criminal Law and Philosophy* (2008) 21–51, at 32. In making this assertion, they are reflecting a judgment widely shared by both lawyers and historians.

[34] For a comprehensive analysis of this fascinating field, see Douglas Hay and Paul Craven (eds), *Masters, Servants and Magistrates in Britain and the Empire, 1562–1955* (Chapel Hill: University of North Carolina Press 2004). The broad findings on which I rely here are drawn from the introductory essay.

of such statutes, leading to confusion about overlap and interpretation, which foreshadows the problems of which commentators like Husak understandably complain today.[35] Nor were these master and servant laws insignificant as compared with 'regular' criminal law. On the contrary, they were very substantial in number in relation to criminal offences, and they were regularly enforced by Justices and, in the nineteenth century, as Justices' status declined, by the King's or Queen's Bench. In another striking analogy with contemporary aspects of 'overcriminalization', many of the relevant offences did not require proof of fault in the sense of malice.

Moreover, localities, in their various constitutionally recognized forms, long enjoyed legislative powers extending to regulation akin to or amounting to criminalization. And even as these local jurisdictions gradually lost power in the course of modernization, the legislature often stepped in to facilitate law enforcement by summary means. As Bruce Smith has shown,[36] from the mid-seventeenth century, Parliament was already busy enacting summary offences. The number of summary offences on the statute book rose from 70 in the 1660s to over 200 by the 1770s. Not only were they triable before magistrates, but—in another parallel with some of today's developments[37]—they often featured formal presumptions against the defendant. Many of these statutes were concerned with possession of valuable substances such as coal, lead, or wood, cut from forests. Smith argues that they were intended as mechanisms to resolve some key difficulties of proof in larceny cases—notably in cases where it was hard to prove that the allegedly stolen goods were in fact feloniously taken (for example where the goods were not readily identifiable, as would have been the case with many valuable commodities in the eighteenth century)—and in cases of carriers or outworkers

[35] Douglas Husak, *Overcriminalization* (New York: Oxford University Press 2008)

[36] Bruce Smith, 'The Presumption of Guilt in the English Law of Theft, 1750–1850' 23 *Law and History Review* (2005) 133–71. On the lengthy history of regulatory offences in English criminal law, with its origins in the gradual process of royal appropriation of power from the church courts, see Jeremy Horder, *Ashworth's Principles of Criminal Law* (8th edition Oxford University Press, 2016) Chapter 2.

[37] Andrew Ashworth and Meredith Blake, in their 'The Presumption of Innocence in English Criminal Law' *Criminal Law Review* (May 1996) 306–17, estimated that, at the time of their study, 40 per cent of offences triable in the Crown Court in England and Wales featured burdens operating against the defendant. See also Law Commission of England and Wales, *Criminal Liability in Regulatory Contexts* (Consultation paper no. 195: 2010).

who had got possession lawfully but then embezzled or appropriated without breaking bulk.[38] In effect, Smith argues that these summary offences were easy ways of proving what would otherwise have been charged as a felony, and that they—like their close summary cousins, vagrancy and police offences—constituted a seriously intrusive form of state power. In 1836—even before the supposed explosion of summary offences—Smith records 903 such charges before the Thames Police Office alone, with an 80 per cent conviction rate.

The extensive provisions comprehended by the summary jurisdiction, whether in the service of securing property and the conditions for flourishing local commerce, or geared to ensuring public order, should, surely, be part of any historical picture of formal (and indeed substantive) criminalization. Yet they seldom are. The 'police power', though—as Markus Dubber has argued—never formally distinguished from criminal justice in the development of modern English criminal justice, has all too often been written out of the history of English criminal law.[39] But the fact is that various forms of 'outcome responsibility' have in fact dominated certain areas of criminal law for centuries, with the causation of harmful outcomes regarded as legitimating the imposition of criminal liability. And, like capacity and character responsibility, outcome responsibility has implications for the coordination of the facts which must be assembled by the criminal process. Quite simply—and given a baseline of criminal capacity—the proof of outcome responsibility depends on the establishment of a causal link between the defendant's act or omission and the proscribed outcome. (The straightforwardness of this proposition does not, of course, imply that establishing this link

[38] 'Breaking bulk' connoted tampering with the entirety of a package or parcel, for example in this case by opening the bales. Further technical difficulties of proof evaded by these statutes were the question of whether things detached from land, or wild animals, were legally capable of being stolen. On the technical complexity of the early law of larceny, see Jerome Hall, *Theft, Law and Society* (2nd ed., New York: Bobbs-Merrill 1952); George P. Fletcher, *Rethinking Criminal Law* Chapters 1–3.

[39] Markus D. Dubber's *The Police Power: Patriarchy and the Foundations of American Government* (New York: Columbia University Press 2005) is an honourable exception; see also Lucia Zedner, 'Policing Before and After the Police: The Historical Antecedents of Contemporary Crime Control' 46 *British Journal of Criminology* (2006) 78–96; Lucia Zedner and Ian Loader, 'Police Beyond Law' 10 *New Criminal Law Review* (2007) 142–52; Andrew Ashworth and Lucia Zedner, *Preventive Justice* (Oxford: Oxford University Press 2014) Chapter 2.

Markus D. Dubber and Mariana Valverde (eds), *The New Police Science: The Police Power in Domestic and International Governance* (Palo Alto, CA: Stanford University Press 2006).

is always easy: issues of causation often turn up exceptionally difficult conceptual and empirical questions.[40])

Responsibility as Founded in the Apprehension of Risk

Finally, and overlapping with both outcome responsibility and character responsibility, there is responsibility as founded in risk. Again, responsibility as risk comes in several different versions, with risk being conceived in either clinical or actuarial terms. Moreover responsibility as risk overlaps in interesting ways with both outcome and character responsibility. The idea of attaching responsibility to clinical risk or pathology shades into the more extreme versions of character responsibility. Risk-based responsibility also equates to a more inchoate version of outcome responsibility and might indeed be regarded as a product of the emergence of disciplines such as statistics or of a range of medical techniques that enable, or purport to enable, the prediction of outcomes. A pattern of risk-based responsibility-attribution is accordingly particularly evident in the practices of preventive criminalization which have arguably enjoyed a distinctive manifestation in the late twentieth and early twenty-first century.[41] Grounding responsibility-attribution in findings of risk appears to have particular legitimating appeal under conditions of widespread insecurity or fear.[42] Yet it also relates to a certain—perhaps unstable—reliance on the power of technologies to manage risk—engendering in the penal sphere the practices which Feeley and Simon have associated with a 'new penology', which shifts attention from individuals to the risks posed by aggregate groups.[43] In terms of coordination, risk-based responsibility raises particularly complex causal or quasi-causal questions relating not only to courts' abilities to evaluate complex scientific or statistical evidence, but also in terms of uncertainty about the confidence to be placed in risk

[40] See Jane Stapleton, *Disease and the Compensation Debate* (Oxford: Clarendon Press 1986).

[41] Andrew Ashworth and Lucia Zedner, *Preventive Justice*.

[42] See Peter Ramsay, *The Insecurity State: Vulnerable Autonomy and the Right to Security in the Criminal Law*.

[43] Malcolm Feeley and Jonathan Simon, 'The New Penology: Notes on the Emerging Strategy of Corrections and its Implications' (1992) 39 *Criminology* 449–74

assessments and about the propriety of, in effect, 'fixing the future' by basing an attribution of responsibility in a forward-looking as opposed to a past-oriented judgment.[44]

Of course, preventive measures arguably based on evaluation of risk and a concern with its minimization have long been a central tool of policing, of pre-trial procedure, and of sentencing. Stop and search powers, the institution of remand in custody, and various forms of preventive sentence are longstanding features of the English criminal process, with binding-over powers and vagrancy laws being yet more venerable English legal arrangements.[45] And, as we shall see, both below and in Chapter 5, it might be argued that the criminal classification statutes of the end of the nineteenth and early twentieth centuries constituted a form of criminalization based on attributed responsibility for risk. But it is incontrovertible that the mechanisms for criminalization on the basis of risk have both expanded their scope and diversified their form over the last quarter century. In their analysis of these recent phenomena of preventive justice, Ashworth and Zedner distinguish between several different kinds of preventive measure across the pre-trial, post-trial, and sentencing processes, as well as in areas such as the regulation of mental ill health and of immigration. First, there are civil preventive orders such as the Anti-Social Behaviour Order (ASBO) and its successor, the injunction to prevent anti-social behaviour under Part I of the Anti-Social Behaviour, Crime and Policing Act 2014. These attract, in effect, criminal sanctions on breach. In the case of the ASBO, this was explicit; in the case of the new measure, the sanction will be achieved via civil proceedings for contempt of court. Ashworth and Zedner list twelve families of such measures, the vast majority of them introduced over the last twenty years.[46]

Second, there are preventive offences in the criminal law itself. Many of them, like attempts, possession offences and endangerment offences, are of long standing, but others, particularly in the area of

[44] Lucia Zedner, 'Fixing the Future? The Pre-emptive Turn in Criminal Justice', in Bernadette McSherry, Alan Norrie, and Simon Bronitt (eds), *Regulating Deviance: The Redirection of Criminalization and the Futures of Criminal Law* (Oxford: Hart Publishing 2009).

[45] Ashworth and Zedner, *Preventive Justice* Chapter 3.

[46] Ibid. 75–6; for figures on the use of these orders, see p. 82. Further, such orders, as well as reforms of the ASBO, have been introduced by the Anti-Social Behaviour, Crime and Policing Act 2014, as discussed in Chapter 5 below. See also Peter Ramsay, *The Insecurity State.*

counterterrorist legislation, are of more recent genesis. Moreover, a significant number of these new offences draw the boundaries of responsibility-attribution at an earlier stage, inviting a characterization of them as not merely inchoate, but pre-inchoate offences. The offence of engaging in any conduct in preparation for giving effect to an intention to commit acts of terrorist or assist another to do so under section 5 of the Terrorism Act 2006 would be a good example. Note that this tendency to push back the boundaries of responsibility-attribution in time is far from being restricted to areas such as counter-terrorism or drug regulation. As Lindsay Farmer has shown, developments in offences against the person and sexual offences—the extension of the conception of psychological assault, the creation of a sex offender register—as well as in property offences—notably in the example of money-laundering—also move in this pre-inchoate direction.[47]

Third, there are criminal preventive orders handed down by a criminal court supplementary to a conviction. A key example would be a further successor to the ASBO, the Criminal Behaviour Order, which can include any prohibition or requirement that will help in preventing further behaviour likely to cause harassment, alarm or distress where a court has found that an offender convicted of another offence has engaged in such behaviour. This is, evidently, a very broad power, backed up by a maximum penalty of five years' imprisonment and, strikingly, attracting a standard of proof of the relevant behaviour to only a balance of probabilities.

CASE STUDIES

The Broad Intellectual and Cultural Environment in which Ideas of Criminal Responsibility Develop

As we have seen, each of these four overlapping yet distinctive ways of thinking about criminal responsibility—as founded in character, capacity, outcome, or risk—have had a place in English criminal law over the last 250 years. But they themselves have shifted in

[47] Lindsay Farmer, *Making the Modern Criminal Law* Chapters 7–9.

tone and substance over time, while the relative influence that they hold within the criminal law, have also been shaped by broader cultural ideas that make up the environment in which ideas of responsibility develop. Among these, the most salient include: attitudes towards the proper relationship between individual and state and towards the proper ambitions of the state; ideas about democracy and forms of governance; beliefs about human nature, specifically social Darwinism, eugenics, and early criminology, and theories about sex and gender; changing attitudes to violence amid the 'civilizing process'; and the process of secularization and the accompanying decline in the significance of religious symbols in legitimating criminalization and punishment. Legal ideas about responsibility are the product of a much broader set of ideas about the self and about relations between the self and society that significantly affect both the legitimation challenges faced by criminal law and the opportunities for legitimation and coordination that are available.[48] Hence they need to be contextualized within intellectual and social history. A sketch of some of the most important factors underpinning the development will serve to highlight the significant but complex links between understandings of responsibility in criminal law and criminal justice and those informing or assumed by other important social practices. I will focus on a number of these broader ideas and practices: those about the nature of individual agency and the role of environment in shaping subjectivity, including assumptions about sex and gender; the relationship between individual and state; the growth of the psychological and social sciences since the mid-nineteenth century (alongside the concomitant impact of religion and secularization); and the emergence of utilitarian thinking. These are, of course, just some among many factors which might have been selected as examples.

The Nature of the Self and Ideas about Human Nature

First, ideas about the nature of individual agency and the role of environment in shaping subjectivity shift over time and are at issue in prevailing understandings of responsibility. In his exploration of the 'sources of the self,'[49] Charles Taylor shows how the key elements of

[48] See Lacey, *Women, Crime, and Character* pp. 25–34.

[49] Charles Taylor, *Sources of the Self: The Making of Modern Identity* (Cambridge, MA: Harvard University Press 1989); see also Charles Taylor, *Modern Social Imaginaries* (Durham, NC: Duke University Press 2004).

modern individual selfhood—notably, the idea of selfhood as involving a sense of inwardness—were assembled over many centuries, with marked developments associated with Augustine, Descartes' *Cogito*, and Locke's sensational psychology.[50] Glimpses of a reflexive human self focused on its own interior are visible in Shakespeare's plays, in Montaigne's essays, and in innumerable diaries and letters of the early modern period. But, Taylor argues, it continued to develop up to the philosophies of the Enlightenment and indeed beyond.

Taylor's focus is on the development of ideas of selfhood within philosophical texts—a focus which, as he acknowledged, omitted any assessment of the social institutions within which these ideas evolve. Filling this gap, historian Dror Wahrman has investigated the institutional context of Taylor's argument, analyzing the 'making of the modern self' through a mesmerizing array of cultural practices, including beekeeping manuals, novels, theatre, fashion, portraiture, and translations of the classics.[51] Wahrman argues that the Enlightenment philosophies of the seventeenth century, most notably Locke's view of the individual as a '*tabula rasa*' (to be shaped by experience) and the decline of faith in an essential human nature located in a divinely ordered universe, gave birth to a new and fluid conception and social practice of identity, whose defining feature was that identity had to be created and assumed. As a social construct, an individual could be modified through the adoption of different clothes, different manners, or different associates. In the 1780s, this external, socially constructed notion of selfhood began to be displaced by the 'modern regime of identity', in which individual personhood is believed to inhere in the unique and stable inner self that ultimately found its most complete expression in Romanticism. While the older ideas of identity resonated with the idea that responsibility attribution

[50] Taylor's is not a radically relativist position. In his account, core aspects of selfhood were already in place in ancient Greek philosophy and have been in a process of development from this core across the centuries.

[51] Dror Wahrman, *The Making of the Modern Self: Identity and Culture in Eighteenth-Century England* (New Haven: Yale University Press 2004). For other important works historicizing selfhood and exploring the conditions under which emerging ideas of selfhood operate and by which they are enabled, see Roy Porter (ed.), *Rewriting the Self: Histories from the Renaissance to the Present* (London: Routledge 1997); Nikolas Rose, *Governing the Soul: The Shaping of the Private Self* (London and New York: Routledge 1990); Richard Sennett, *The Fall of Public Man* (Cambridge: Cambridge University Press 1977); Patricia Meyer Spacks, *Imagining a Self: Autobiography and Novel in Eighteenth-Century* (Cambridge, MA: Harvard University Press 1976).

resides primarily in the assessment of visible indices of character, the idea that identity resides in an authentic psychological self implied a need to investigate the interior world of the defendant as a means of assessing responsibility. Only then did an investigation of the psychological interior become generally important to the legitimation of criminal law. Conversely—and by the same token—any notion of fragmentation in the self would become threatening to the integrity of the responsible subject: the unity and rationality of the modern self became central to projects of governance, in part as a result of utilitarian ideas, through the nineteenth century.

The Growth of the Psychological and Social Sciences

Second, the growth of the psychological and social sciences since the mid-nineteenth century has been a key factor in the development of the late modern idea of criminal responsibility as founded in cognitive and volitional capacity. The idea that criminal responsibility can be enunciated in terms of states of mind—intention, foresight, belief, and so on—is premised on a dualistic vision of a human being that can be traced to Descartes and on the idea that the interior world of human individuals can be the object of social knowledge and, indeed, of proof in a criminal court. In this context, the development of what we now call psychology was of general assistance to the development of the subjective theory of *mens rea* that is so influential in English criminal law today. Conversely, these developments went hand in hand with a decline of faith in the religious symbols and doctrines, eroding a mechanism which had underpinned confident evaluations of criminal wrongdoing, as we shall see in our case study below.

This development pulled in different directions, however, which helps to explain the slow, uneven, and incomplete development towards a subjective notion of capacity responsibility. For example, the idea that the subjective mental states of human beings could be the object of investigation in a criminal court promised a 'factualization' of criminal responsibility that would make it less dependent upon local knowledge or shared evaluations and hence, crucially, less controversial.[52] On the other hand, it also threatened to undermine the project of developing a discrete and technical, legal conception of criminal responsibility because it appeared to assume a

[52] See Alan Norrie, *Crime, Reason and History* pp. 15–32.

privileged position for medical and psychological evidence. The well-documented turf wars between the judiciary and the nascent psychiatric profession throughout the nineteenth century,[53] the continued place of older discourses of madness as manifest in the sense of being recognizable to lay observers,[54] and the persistence of value-laden *mens rea* terms such as 'maliciously' well into the twentieth century[55] are eloquent testimony to the courts' concern with establishing their own autonomous professional expertise and to their continuing commitment to and confidence in the idea of legal judgment as evaluative rather than factual or scientific. Moreover, the development of the social and human sciences,[56] most obviously those genetic or social-Darwinian arguments that appeared to undermine the idea of individual freedom and hence, potentially, that of the capacity-based responsibility for crime, prompted another interesting accommodation of character and capacity models in criminal policy, as well as intimations of the emergence of a new model based on risk. It underpinned the frequent attempts, from the 1860s on, to identify and subject to special, character-based policies certain groups of offenders—habitual inebriates, habitual offenders, the weak-minded, the vagrant, and the juvenile delinquent[57]—while assuming the existence of freedom and hence capacity responsibility for other offenders.

Utilitarianism

Third, the emergence of utilitarian thinking, in both its pure Benthamite form and in the modified form developed in John

[53] See, e.g., Norrie, ibid.; Roger Smith, *Trial by Medicine*; Joel Peter Eigen, 'Lesion of the Will: Medical Resolve and Criminal Responsibility in Victorian Insanity Trials'.

[54] See Arlie Loughnan, *Manifest Madness: Mental Incapacity in Criminal Law* (Oxford: Oxford University Press 2012).

[55] *See* Jeremy Horder, 'Two Histories and Four Hidden Principles of Mens Rea' 113 *Law Quarterly Review* (1997) 95–119 (discussing the historical and continuing importance of the principle of malice in English criminal law); see also Nicola Lacey, 'In Search of the Responsible Subject'.

[56] See Martin Weiner, *Reconstructing the Criminal* pp. 185–306; see also Markus D. Dubber, 'The Right to be Punished: Autonomy and Its Demise in Modern Penal Thought', 16 *Law and History Review* (1998) 113–46 (arguing that Enlightenment conceptions of autonomy have been lost from criminal law's discourses of responsibility since the turn to rehabilitation and scientific models).

[57] See Leon Radzinowicz and Roger Hood, *The Emergence of Penal Policy in Victorian and Edwardian England* (Oxford: Clarendon Press 1990) pp. 172ff.; see also Mariana Valverde, *Diseases of the Will: Alcohol and the Dilemmas of Freedom* (Cambridge: Cambridge University Press 1998) (discussing shifting Victorian conceptions of the individual will in the context of alcohol policy); Lucia Zedner, *Women, Crime, and Custody in Victorian England* (Oxford and New York: Oxford University Press 1991) pp. 219–64 (discussing women specifically).

Stuart Mill's famous essay, *On Liberty*, had a key influence on conceptions of criminal responsibility. As has been widely discussed, it became a powerful impetus for law reform,[58] but it also underpinned the powerful model of rational agency that informed the emerging doctrines of capacity responsibility and an intensifying focus on proving the advertent psychological states that underpin the mechanism of deterrence. Additionally, it provided a harm-reduction framework to legitimate the regulatory offences that were emerging as key solutions to the problems of rapid urbanization and industrialization. The ambitions for rationality, completeness, and system encapsulated in Benthamite utilitarianism moreover fed directly into the unfinished project of codification through its key influence on the various Criminal Law Commissions of the first part of the century, as well as feeding into the legislative consolidations of mid-century onwards, and the imperial projects of codification.[59] Conversely, utilitarian rationalism had its own effect on the attachment to religious doctrines and symbols which had underpinned older ideas of criminal law authority and bad character, lending weight to a more systematic and professional approach premised on a model of bureaucratic authority.

Changing Relations Between Individual and State

A fourth factor of obvious relevance to the genesis of ideas of criminal responsibility has been the development of the nation state during the nineteenth and early twentieth centuries—a period during which the modern project of governance grew in both complexity and intensity.[60] On the one hand, the growth of centralized state power, and the increasing ambition of the state's governance of its population, appears to have given rise, from the early nineteenth century onwards, to a certain confidence in the possibility of shaping the habits and dispositions of citizenhood through the development

[58] Coleman Phillipson, *Three Criminal Law Reformers: Beccaria, Bentham, Romilly* (London: J. M. Dent and Sons 1923); K. J. M. Smith, *Lawyers, Legislators, and Theorists.*

[59] See Lindsay Farmer, *Making the Modern Criminal Law* Chapter 5.

[60] See S. E. Finer, *The History of Government III: Empires, Monarchies and the Modern State* (Oxford: Oxford University Press 1997) Book 5. In relation to the administrative apparatus of the British state (and for an instructive corrective to the view that its development is mainly to be attributed to the influence of Benthamite ideas), see Oliver MacDonagh, 'The Nineteenth Century Revolution in Government: A Reappraisal' 1 *Historical Journal* (1958) 52–67.

of institutions such as criminal justice, the poor law, and, later, education and health systems. As Martin Wiener has shown, this at first effected an interesting compound of moralism and utilitarianism in criminal policy, and of character and capacity as bases for criminal responsibility.[61] In the early nineteenth century, the English state explicitly thought of criminal law as a key character-building institution, with its subjects being assumed, within both utilitarian and evangelical traditions, to be capable of shaping their characters according to the secular or religious incentive system provided by a reformed, rationalized criminal law and the disciplinary framework of the modern prison, and hence become law-abiding citizens. This was, one might say, a project of modernization in the service of moralization (and one, which, as we shall see in Chapter 4, was importantly premised on the formation of a raft of new governmental competences and institutions.) On the other hand, changing social and political structures posed new challenges for the criminal process. In an increasingly—albeit tentatively—democratic political culture, with its slow movement towards the idea of universal citizenship, the question of whether the conviction and punishment of the free individual could be justified became increasingly pressing through the century, as the liberal ideas most vividly expressed in J. S. Mill's *On Liberty* infused political sensibilities and hence altered the structure of legitimation problems facing government.[62] Both the expansion and the increasing secularization of governmental authority[63] might be expected to have accentuated the legitimation problems faced by the criminal justice system. Moreover, these legitimation problems gradually took on new forms as the ideas of freedom and the relationship between individual and state was further modified by the evolution of welfare states and new forms of state regulation in the twentieth century.[64]

[61] See Martin J. Wiener, *Reconstructing the Criminal* Chapters 1–3; Lindsay Farmer, *Criminal Law, Tradition and Legal Order* pp. 119ff; on the notion of character informing the penitentiary movement, see John Bender, *Imagining the Penitentiary* (Chicago: University of Chicago Press 1987); on the role of character in the shaping of social policy more generally, see Radzinowicz and Hood, *The Emergence of Penal Policy in Victorian and Edwardian England* pp. 35–6.

[62] J. S. Mill, *On Liberty* (1859: Harmondsworth: Penguin 1974).

[63] On secularization and its implications for criminal law, see Jeremy Horder, *Ashworth's Principles of Criminal Law* Chapter 2.

[64] Thomas A. Green, *Freedom and Criminal Responsibility in American Legal Thought* (New York: Cambridge University Press 2014).

Responsibility and Gender

Finally, it is worth noting the significance of changing ideas about sex and gender for the concept of responsibility. In the present day, it is one of the most striking and pervasive features of criminal justice in all developed countries that the practice of criminalization is heavily gendered. In England and Wales, for example, women make up less than a fifth of those convicted of criminal offences each year;[65] moreover, their offences are on average significantly less serious than those of men.[66] From this perspective, the—admittedly patchy—evidence available for the mid-eighteenth century is striking, for it shows that women at that time made up a far higher proportion of those appearing before the criminal courts. For example, the proportion of women tried at the Old Bailey fell from 45 per cent at the end of the seventeenth century to 12 per cent in the early twentieth century.[67] By the time that sexually differentiated official statistics were being collected in the late nineteenth century, the figures already show a pattern relatively close to that with which we are familiar today.[68]

[65] Frances Heidensohn and Marisa Silvestri ('Gender and Crime', in Mike Maguire, Rod Morgan, Robert Reiner (eds), *The Oxford Handbook of Criminology* (5th ed., Oxford: Oxford University Press 2012) Chapter 12 pp. 336–69) analyse the relatively low participation of women in crime in England and Wales today, while noting important qualitative differences between men's and women's offending. Detailed gender-differentiated figures on criminal justice are published by the government each year in accordance with section 95 of the Criminal Justice Act 1991: see, for example, https://www.gov.uk/government/uploads/system/uploads/attachment_data/file/380090/women-cjs-2013.pdf (accessed 7 August 2015). In June 2015, women made up just 4.5 per cent of the prison population in England and Wales: http://www.prisonstudies.org/country/united-kingdom-england-wales (accessed 16 July 2015).

[66] For an analysis of the late-twentieth-century statistics on female crime in England and Wales, see Dorothy Wedderburn et al., *Justice for Women: The Need for Reform: The Report of the Committee on Women's Imprisonment* (London: Prison Reform Trust 2000) Chapter 1; for a more general assessment of the relationship between gender and crime, see Ngaire Naffine, *Feminism and Criminology* (Oxford: Polity Press 1997).

[67] Clive Emsley, *Crime and Society in England, 1750–1900* (2nd ed., London and New York: Longman 1996), Chapter 6 and in particular p. 152; for further discussion of these figures and their interpretation, see Malcom M. Feeley and Deborah H. Little, 'The Vanishing Female: The Decline of Women in the Criminal Process, 1687–1912' 25 *Law and Society Review* (1991) 719–57.

[68] See Radzinowicz and Hood, *The Emergence of Penal Policy in Victorian and Edwardian England* Chapter 5, showing that, in the first year in which judicial statistics were differentiated by gender (1893), women committed fewer than 10 per cent of the recorded convictions for felonious or malicious woundings; 15 per cent of the thefts, and 25 per cent of convictions for drunkenness; David Philips' data for the Black Country in the mid-nineteenth century, which indicate that women made up about one third of those appearing before the Assizes, appear to show that the change must have accelerated during the latter

Theories have abounded about why it is that women today commit fewer offences than men and/or are less often prosecuted for the offences which they do commit. Everything from biological explanation, through the writing off of offending women as 'feeble-minded' or the zoning of such women into the mental health system, to arguments about the disciplinary aspects of modern femininity have been propounded as explanations for the male-domination of crime.[69] The eighteenth century figures provide, of course, a piece of counter-evidence to the idea that low rates of female offending are based in biology. But they also raise some interesting questions for the social constructionist.

Clearly, the invention and cultivation of a highly disciplinary conception of sexual difference in the nineteenth century—a conception according to which, as Zedner puts it, crime was 'the very negation of the ideal of femininity'[70]—and its gradual expansion outwards from the bourgeoisie, would have had significant implications for the criminalization of women. It would be likely to have been influential in the production of social norms of acceptable female behaviour, in shaping individual subjectivities, in affecting perceptions of female behaviour and the degree of danger it poses, and hence in shaping decisions to report and prosecute.

As I have argued in more detail elsewhere,[71] the move from criminalization founded in character to a more capacity-based approach constituted a further basis for the decreasing formal criminalization of women from the early nineteenth century onwards. If the main basis for criminalization in the middle of the eighteenth century was the local character and reputation of the offender, this probably applied

part of the nineteenth century. Such figures must, of course, be treated with caution: on the need for a careful use of statistics in historical research, see V. A. C. Gatrell, 'The Decline of Theft and Violence in Victorian and Edwardian England', in V. A. C. Gatrell, Bruce Lenman, and Geoffrey Parker (eds), *Crime and the Law: The Social History of Crime in Western Europe Since 1500* (London: Europa Publications 1980) p. 239. Gatrell's own figures show women constituting about 30 per cent of those committed for trial for indictable offences in 1805; Emsley's data (Emsley, *Crime and Society in England, 1750–1900*) puts the equivalent figures as 27 per cent in 1857 and as 19 per cent in 1890. Furthermore—see ibid. p. 153—women made up only a relatively constant 20 per cent of summary offenders.

[69] See, for example, Lucia Zedner, *Women, Crime, and Custody in Victorian England* Parts I and III; Frances Heidensohn, *Women and Crime* (London: Macmillan 1985); Ngaire Naffine, *Feminism and Criminology* (Oxford: Polity Press 1997).

[70] Lucia Zedner, *Women, Crime, and Custody in Victorian England* p. 19; see more generally Michel Foucault, *The History of Sexuality* (London: Peregrine 1976); and in relation to France, Ruth Harris, *Murders and Madness: Medicine, Law and Society in the Fin de Siècle* (Oxford: Clarendon Press 1989).

[71] See Lacey, *Women, Crime, and Character.*

just as readily—albeit, doubtless, in rather different ways—to women as to men. By contrast, the development during the course of the nineteenth century of an idea of responsibility as founded in freedom and capacities, coinciding as it did with an increasingly medicalized view of female deviance[72] and an understanding of women as less rational, more feeble-minded, less autonomous, less fully citizens—indeed, less persons—than men, may have had the ironic consequence that women became less often subject to criminal justice controls.

Conversely, the persistence of character-based judgments in the identification of special groups for criminal justice intervention—the habitual offender, the inebriate or, most recently, the 'dangerous'—might also help to account for the disproportionately high representation of multiply socially disadvantaged women in the courts and prisons of not only the late nineteenth century but also the late twentieth.[73] Furthermore, the criminalization of prostitution constitutes a vivid example both of a survival of character-responsibility in criminal law itself and of the distinctive way in which sexuality continues to be implicated in social judgments of women's character.[74]

The Co-existence of Competing Ideas of Responsibility: Character, Capacity, Outcome, and Risk in Modern Criminalization

Mens Rea and Defences

The main debates about criminal responsibility have been focused on the stage of criminal law doctrine and its application in the

[72] See on this point Roger Smith, *Trial by Medicine* Chapter 7, detailing the gradual pathologization of female crime during the nineteenth century as weakening self-control, particularly in relation to pregnancy, menstruation, childbirth, and lactation.

[73] A fascinating statistic in this regard is that women made up *a majority* of habitual offenders convicted over 20 times in the late nineteenth century—see Clive Emsley, *Crime and Society in England, 1750–1900* p. 153. This presumably ties up with the fact that only one third of the women proceeded against in 1890, as opposed to half of the men, were of previous good character (see Lucia Zedner, *Women, Crime, and Custody in Victorian England* pp. 306–7).

[74] See Judith Walkowitz, *Prostitution in Victorian Society: Women, Class, and the State* (Cambridge: Cambridge University Press 1980); Clive Emsley, *Crime and Society in England, 1750–1900* pp. 153–4; Carol Smart, *Women, Crime, and Criminology* (London: Routledge and Kegan Paul 1976). For the legal position in England and Wales, see Celia Wells and Oliver Quick, *Lacey, Wells and Quick, Reconstructing Criminal Law* (4th ed., Cambridge: Cambridge University Press 2010) Chapter 14.

courts, notably in terms of the *mens rea* principle and the elaboration of defences. The assumption of most criminal law theorists is that criminal law is, or at least should be, based on one coherent principle of responsibility; the majority of contemporary British (and north American) criminal law theorists see this as being one of the two capacity principles sketched above, albeit both character theories and theories seeking to integrate character and capacity have attracted some interest. But, at an interpretive level, it is relatively easy to demonstrate that English criminal law moves between the two capacity principles, and moreover applies principles of liability in some areas which resonate with aspects of the outcome and character principles. Let us focus on the capacity principles first. The existence of offences such as manslaughter, which can be committed through negligence—a form of objective *mens rea*—as well as the reasonableness threshold applied to elements of most of the defences, affords substantial evidence of the operation of the opportunity principle. Does this mean that the fair opportunity theory is a better account of English criminal law than the choice theory? I would argue that it does not. To establish this argument, we would have to be sure that the offences to which entirely subjective principles of *mens rea* apply—murder, for example—count as instances in which the 'choice' guaranteed by proof of intention or subjective recklessness *amounts in itself* to proof that the defendant had a fair opportunity to act otherwise than he or she did. This, however, can be disputed. The limited scope of the defences, as well as the restricted time frame in terms of which the defendant's choice is set, prevents the court from making the sort of overall assessment of the fairness of the defendant's opportunity which is invited by the application of an open-ended 'reasonableness' test. In subjective *mens rea* cases, the law is interested, in other words, not so much in the fairness or otherwise of the circumstances in which the defendant made his or her choice, but rather in the choice itself. Of course, the defences do some moral fine-tuning here. But it remains the case that application of a subjective *mens rea* test does not itself invite an assessment of fair opportunity. Hence it may be argued that criminal law is pluralistic even across capacity principles.

Furthermore, the existence of many offences of strict liability to which no due diligence offence applies, as well as the persistence of instances of constructive liability such as constructive manslaughter, show that contemporary English criminal law also espouses principles of outcome-responsibility to a significant degree. The applicability of the general defences to most of these offences means, however, that it is outcome-responsibility of the hybrid kind: if not guaranteeing fair opportunity, the law is at least ruling out liability in certain particularly egregious instances of lack of fair opportunity. Diversifying the picture yet further, a range of offences such as offences of the possession of a variety of prohibited goods or substances such as firearms or dangerous drugs, along with endangerment offences (such as driving under the influence of alcohol, or dangerous driving) and inchoate or preparatory offences (such as attempts, conspiracies, incitements and offences of pure preparation such as that under recent counterterrorism legislation, discussed in Chapters 3 and 5) introduce and expand a clear element of risk-based responsibility attribution, albeit often combined with aspects of capacity-based responsibility founded on mental states such as knowledge.

Can it be argued that any aspects of criminal law's liability standards lend themselves to interpretation as based on character rather than capacity or outcome or risk principles? I would argue that there are indeed significant traces at least of the more cautious version of the character approach in contemporary English criminal law. My reason for arguing this lies both in substantive law and in the law of evidence. Victor Tadros has made a powerful case that only a version of what I have called the 'cautious' character theory can capture the essentially evaluative and communicative nature of criminal condemnation.[75] Tadros argues that both *mens rea* requirements and many defences represent the criminal law's attempt to restrict responsibility-attribution to those who, *qua* agents, have displayed a morally vicious character through the relevant conduct.[76] Indeed, he argues that the operation of the prevailing, open-ended, reasonableness tests may under certain circumstances invite inappropriately broad character inferences, punishing for vices such as ignorance rather than restricting criminal punishment to appropriate moral terrain such as wilful blindness, indifference, and so on. (This is a symptom, perhaps, of the curious difficulty which contemporary criminal law theorists have had in coming up with an agreed rationalization or substantive theory of criminalization, itself a product of

[75] Victor Tadros, *Criminal Responsibility*.

[76] Ibid. pp. 23–43. An agent acts, on Tadros's view, *qua* agent, when he or she is motivated by reasons which cohere with his or her more general set of values and dispositions.

the 'factual/scientific' orientation of the subjectivist capacity theory, and of a certain discomfort with the morally controversial nature of criminal judgment.[77])

In addition, the large number of evidential presumptions operating in English criminal law, as well as a smaller number of conclusive, legal presumptions, operating against defendants, give further reason for thinking that character principles operate at the level of formal conviction. Presumptions may or may not leave room for a capacity interpretation. If someone is, for example, conclusively presumed to have raped a person whom they have defrauded as to the nature and quality of the act of sexual intercourse under the Sexual Offences Act 2003, the law might be interpreted as saying that this person's conduct has conclusively expressed an indifference to the law's anti-rape norm, or it could be argued that the basis for the attribution of responsibility for rape lies in the choice to defraud and/or the fair opportunity not to have defrauded. But the evidential presumption that someone who has sex with a person who is very inebriated or unconscious does so without either consent or a reasonable belief in consent seems to put the capacity aspect of responsibility onto the back foot: this behaviour is assumed to express indifference to the anti-rape norm *unless* the defendant can produce evidence rebutting the inference. It may be argued, of course, that such presumptions—like the many presumptions operating in the area of drug offences—are designed to overcome the problems of proving the advertent forms of responsibility associated with the choice version of the capacity principle crafted in dualist terms. But the selection of the specific circumstances around which the presumptions operate is informed by judgments about behaviour which may be assumed to express anti-social or criminal practical attitudes or character. Once again, therefore, we

[77] Ibid. Chapter 13. On the lack of any convincing account of where we draw the boundary between criminal and non-criminal conduct, see Leo Katz, 'Villainy and Felony: A Problem Concerning Criminalization', 6 *Buffalo Criminal Law Review* (2002) 451–82. Recent years have seen a revival of interest in the rationale for criminalization, with important contributions, including Douglas Husak, *Overcriminalization*; Antony Duff, Lindsay Farmer, Sandra Marshall, Mario Renzo, and Victor Tadros (eds), *The Boundaries of the Criminal Law* (Oxford University Press 2010), *The Structures of the Criminal Law* (Oxford University Press 2011), *The Constitution of the Criminal Law* (Oxford University Press 2013), *Criminalization: The Political Morality of the Criminal Law* (Oxford University Press 2015). On the reasons why the rationale of criminalization became problematic as criminal law modernized, see Lindsay Farmer, *Making the Modern Criminal Law* Chapters 2 and 3.

seem to be confronted with a hybrid rather than a pure approach to responsibility in criminal law doctrine. This conclusion is strengthened by the fact that English law has recently changed in such a way as markedly to expand the forms of character evidence admissible in criminal trials. This broadened admissibility of character evidence[78] will inevitably shape the practices of attributing criminal responsibility in the trial process, changing the structure of knowledge-coordination at the trial by providing material from which judge and jury may form evaluative, character-based assumptions which will supplement legal capacity-based tests wherever—as is usually the case—they are sufficiently open-ended to admit of character-based inferences.

Pre-trial Practices: Policing and Prosecution When we broaden our focus from the moment of attributing formal responsibility in criminal law doctrine to the earlier and later moments in the practice of criminalization, the evidence of multiple principles of responsibility increases markedly, and includes, unfortunately in my view, marks not only of the cautious but also of the 'overall' character approach. Take, for example, the plentiful evidence from many jurisdictions of differential policing and prosecution practices structured around the social axes of race, ethnicity, class, gender. The process of selecting the pool of people to whom formal attributions of criminal responsibility will be applied is inevitably affected not only by police and prosecution judgments about choice or fair opportunity but by assumptions about character or disposition—themselves, unfortunately, sometimes based on inaccurate and prejudiced stereotypes about the kinds of people likely to be involved in criminal conduct. The extent and nature of such character-based judgments is, of course, a matter for empirical investigation; but such evidence as we have, particularly about police attitudes, suggest that they are pervasive.[79] Historians of English criminal justice have noted that the locally based practices of filtering cases for prosecution up to the reforms of the early nineteenth century were heavily structured by local knowledge of character and reputation: local Justices of the Peace and Grand Juries were decisively

[78] Criminal Justice Act 2003 ss. 98–101; see further Chapter 5 below.

[79] For a summary of the evidence in the UK, see Coretta Phillips and Ben Bowling, 'Racism, Ethnicity, Crime and Criminal Justice', in Mike Maguire, Rod Morgan, and Robert Reiner (eds), *The Oxford Handbook of Criminology* (3rd ed., Oxford: Oxford University Press 2002) p. 579.

influenced by such information, while character evidence was hugely important to the conduct of criminal trials.[80] In relation to a world in which 'manifest' rather than 'subjective' criminality was the order of the day,[81] it comes naturally to make the link between these pre-trial and evidential practices and the overall shape of the principles of responsibility being applied to criminal defendants. Practices of policing and prosecution in colonial societies provide yet more vivid instances of decision-making shaped decisively by generalized assessments of character, generally structured on racial lines.[82] In criminal justice today, the widespread practice of plea-bargaining demonstrates at once continuity in substance—facilitating as it does the selection of cases for prosecution on the basis of judgments based on assumptions about character or dangerousness, often based on age, class and/or race; and a shift in form—towards professionalized, procedurally regulated mechanisms.

Today, particularly in Britain and America, where criminal justice scholarship has until recently been marked by a curiously unproductive division of labour between criminologists, criminal lawyers, and students of the criminal process and punishment, criminal law scholars have trained their focus on the substance of criminal law (supplemented to some extent by the law of evidence). This has diverted attention away from the consequences of pre-trial practices, such as plea-bargaining, for the patterns of responsibilization *as realized in criminalization practices as a whole*. Among other things, this has led to an under-developed legal debate about the consequences of even formal pre-trial developments that are based on or invite character-based responsibility attributions—some of them distinctly of the overall rather than the cautious variety.

80 See Lacey, 'Responsibility and Modernity in Criminal Law' pp. 258ff; for an important corrective to the view that these practices were not state-directed, see Bruce P. Smith, 'The Myth of Private Prosecution in England, 1750–1850', in Markus D. Dubber and Lindsay Farmer (eds), *Modern Histories of Crime and Punishment* (Stanford: Stanford University Press 2007).

81 Fletcher, *Rethinking Criminal Law*; see also Guyora Binder, 'The Meaning of Killing' and, on the related concept of 'manifest madness', Joel Peter Eigen, '"An Inducement to Morbid Minds": Politics and Madness in the Victorian Courtroom', both in Markus D. Dubber and Lindsay Farmer (eds), *Modern Histories of Crime and Punishment*.

82 See the papers by Elizabeth Kolsky, 'Crime and Punishment on the Tea Plantations of Colonial India', Wendie Ellen Schneider, '"Enfeebling the Arm of Justice": Perjury and Prevarication in British India', and Martin Wiener, 'Criminal Law at a Fault Line of Imperial Authority: Interracial Homicide Trials in British India', in Markus D. Dubber and Lindsay Farmer (eds), *Modern Histories of Crime and Punishment*.

Perhaps the most obvious example here would be the creation in both the UK and US of sex offender or paedophile registers, which in effect mark out a certain group of people as presumptively criminal in character.[83] Another example would be various anti-terrorism laws on both sides of the Atlantic, which use nationality or citizenship as rules of thumb for potential terrorist criminality.[84] A further instance is the diffusion of preventive detention for those suspected of involvement in terrorism—the links here with crude assumptions about character are all too evident in former US Vice-President Dick Cheney's defence of detention without trial at an offshore camp: 'The important thing here to understand is that *the people that are at Guantánamo are bad people*.'[85] In England, there was also the amazing survival, until recently, of the (female-) gender-specific status, 'common prostitute'.[86] Beyond this, the rapid advance of genetic technology opens up the real possibility of a pre-trial criminal process significantly shaped by genetically-based assumptions as to character—or more accurately, character-based risk—in the sense of likelihood of engaging in criminal conduct. In the face of this genetic revolution, the principles of responsibility so central to criminal law doctrine may quickly become marginal unless vigorously defended in the context of an understanding of the potential relevance of DNA evidence to traditional practices of legal responsibility-attribution. As all these examples show, it is impossible to grasp how practices of responsibility-attribution work except within the context of the broader practices of criminalization.

Post-Conviction Practices: Sentencing and Punishment In England and Wales, the moment of conviction has long heralded a significant dilution in the defendant's process rights, not least in relation to constraints on the sort of evidence taken as admissible and relevant to decisions about sentence and execution of sentence. Whether

[83] See, for example, Sex Offenders Act 1997, Sexual Offences Act 2003.

[84] See, for example, the Anti-Terrorism Crime and Security Act 2001 section 23, successfully challenged on human rights grounds in *A v Secretary of State for the Home Department* [2004] UKHL 56: see further Chapter 5 below.

[85] As quoted in Associated Press, 'Cheney Says No To Closing Prison', *The New York Times*, 13 June 2005 p. A14 (my emphasis).

[86] See Celia Wells and Oliver Quick, *Reconstructing Criminal Law* Chapter 16; *Director of Public Prosecutions v Bull* [1994] 158 J. P. 1005. The term was finally removed from the Street Offences Act in 2009.

in the guise of pleas in mitigation, pre-sentence reports, psychiatric reports, reports by probation officers or prison staff, a welter of information about the convicted person's character becomes central to the decision-making process. This stretches well beyond past criminal record, encompassing judgments or information about lifestyle, attitudes, and compliance with probation or prison discipline. At a formal level, in significant developments in both the UK and the US, legislation and policy structuring sentencing has in recent years added impetus to character-based attributions: 'three strikes' laws; other mandatory sentences for certain kinds of offences; 'dangerous offender' policies of one kind or another all provide examples. These arrangements amount not only to punishment for bad character but also define that character in inflexible terms at the legislative level, thus removing the possibility of an individualized judgment, which is arguably central to the very idea of treating defendants as agents.[87] Again, this does not, of course, show that character-based principles shape the attribution of formal criminal responsibility. But it does show that even to the extent that formal criminal responsibility is based on a precondition of choice or fair opportunity, the full implications of that formal responsibility will be decisively shaped by character-based judgments which modify the practical realization of criminal responsibility in the sentencing and penal processes. Different conceptions of responsible subjecthood may be operating at the prosecution, trial, and punishment stages—and each contributes to the overall construction of the subject of criminal law.

The Evolution of Mental Incapacity Defences in the Eighteenth to Nineteenth Centuries: Can Character and Capacity be Separated Completely, Even at the Level of Ideas?

The treatment of what we would today call mental incapacity defences, in which what would become the psychiatric profession was emerging as an authoritative witness to the 'facts of the mental matter', is a particularly instructive case study in the complex interrelationship between conceptions of responsibility as founded in capacity, character and, most recently, risk. In principle, the field of

[87] Samuel H. Pillsbury, 'A Problem in Emotive Due Process: California's Three Strikes Law' 6 *Buffalo Criminal Law Review* (2002) 483–524.

mental incapacity should reflect the most fully developed aspect of the 'inner' or 'psychological' model of criminal responsibility. To the extent that it does not do so, raises interesting questions about the decline of an evaluative/character-based practice during the era of modernization.

How were matters of specifically mental incapacity dealt with before eighteenth-century English criminal courts? Their handling is striking to the modern legal gaze. Though rules excluding the testimony of witnesses on grounds of incompetency were already developing in the eighteenth century,[88] there was no statutory recognition of an insanity defence until 1800, and no elaborated common law definition of insanity until the M'Naghten rules were formulated in 1843.[89] Of course—as remains the case today—many potential insanity cases would have been filtered out of the criminal process long before they came to trial. But, as records show, significant numbers of putatively insane defendants nevertheless reached the courts: Joel Peter Eigen has identified 331 cases before the Old Bailey between 1760 and 1843 in which issues of mental derangement were raised as possible defences.[90]

When such cases did reach the courts, their disposal was shaped by common-sense jury assumptions about madness and its implications for the vicious will that underpinned culpability. That there is little sign of any analysis of the definitions of insanity discussed by treatise writers like Hale or Blackstone in most of the run-of-the-mill cases reported in the Proceedings of the Old Bailey should come as no surprise given the usual absence of defence lawyers. And while medical testimony was gradually emerging as a relevant matter, it was in its early forms itself closely articulated with various forms of lay knowledge and understanding, as indeed was to be expected given that the formal organization of the medical profession was far

[88] See Elizabeth P. Judge, *Character Witnesses: Credibility and Testimony in the Eighteenth Century Novel* (D.Phil. thesis, Dalhousie University 2004, http://dalspace.library.dal.ca/handle/10222/54642) Chapter 4.

[89] *M'Naghten's Case* (1843) 10 *Clarke and Finnelly* 200.

[90] Joel Peter Eigen, *Witnessing Insanity* (New Haven: Yale University Press 1995) p. 6; the annual rate grew slowly from 33 in the 1760s to 71 in the 1830s, by which time the insanity defence had already undergone some formalization. The overall rate, however, was low, amounting to between 4 and 8 cases per 1000. On the gradual rise of insanity pleas, and on the history of the insanity defence in general, see also Nigel Walker, *Crime and Insanity in England*: Volume One, *The Historical Perspective* (Edinburgh: Edinburgh University Press 1968) Chapters 3–4.

from having gained a monopoly over broadly medical practice.[91] As Arlie Loughnan has argued,[92] the prevailing pattern here—echoing George Fletcher's notion of 'manifest criminality'[93]—was a pattern of 'manifest madness': insanity was simply what a jury recognized as such, and the system worked on the basis of a deep implicit confidence in the institutional capacity of the trial to 'read' criminal responsibility from character and conduct.

In this rather fluid legal context, as Dana Rabin has shown, prevailing cultural influences had a decisive and direct effect upon legal practices.[94] Rabin marshals evidence that the emerging culture of sensibility in the latter part of the eighteenth century prompted defendants to push the boundaries of what had conventionally been understood as insanity to embrace a wide variety of states of emotional distress, gradually introducing into the courtroom a mind-body distinction which was quite new, and which reflected both the emerging idea of human identity as residing in a mental interior, and an institutional confidence in the capacity of the trial process to investigate that interior. This process was ultimately seen as threatening to the integrity of the law's prohibitions, and was accordingly closed off through the increasingly technical specification of the conditions for the insanity defence being developed in case law from the early nineteenth century on.[95]

How does this story continue, as we trace its path through the nineteenth century? In Rabin's account, we see the interest in subjective

[91] Eigen, *Witnessing Insanity* Chapters 4–6.

[92] Arlie Loughnan, 'Manifest Madness: Towards a New Understanding of the Insanity Defence' 70 *Modern Law Review* (2007) 379–401 and *Manifest Madness: Mental Incapacity in the Criminal Law* (Oxford: Oxford University Press 2012); see also Roger Smith, *Trial by Medicine* Chapter 7, which illustrates that even in the nineteenth century, non-technical assumptions about female insanity continued to inform the trial process, with infanticide cases in particular often tried without medical evidence being led; see also Lacey, *Women, Crime, and Character* pp. 20–3.

[93] Fletcher, *Rethinking Criminal Law.*

[94] Dana Y. Rabin, *Identity, Crime, and Legal Responsibility in Eighteenth-Century England* (Basingstoke: Palgrave Macmillan 2004) Chapter 3.

[95] As Rabin also notes, the eighteenth-century cases often display what is to our eyes a strange blurring of the concepts of criminal intention and character. Indeed, the idea that intent simply *was* a matter of character underpinned the seventeenth-century willingness to contemplate poverty as an excuse for crime: ibid. pp. 87–9. Not until a case of 1787 does her sample of mental incapacity cases feature a decisive judicial attempt to separate, analytically, the question of character from that of mental state: ibid. p. 160. The case is that of Francis Parr, Old Bailey Sessions Papers t17870115–1. For an early example, see the judgment of Chief Justice Holt in *Mawgridge* (1707) *Kel* 119. My point, however, is that such examples were isolated. I am grateful to Jeremy Horder for alerting me to this case.

experience—in what we would today call psychology—pressing its way onto the trial's agenda. This was only to be expected: John Locke's 'sensational psychology', after all, dated back to the late seventeenth century, and found expression in cultural forms such as the novel from at least the 1720s onwards; while the image of selfhood as residing in an authentic inner depth marked by not only experience but also a level of continuity and integration was gaining currency from the latter part of the eighteenth century.[96] But ironically, as Rabin shows, the increasing cultural acceptance of the power of psychological experience, and of its relevance to individual responsibility, which legitimated a more expansive terrain of defences, simultaneously posed coordination problems for criminal law: problems about both the trial's capacity adequately to assess lay and expert evidence of such states, and consequently about the capacity of the recognition of 'psychological' excuses to undermine the law's prohibitions. The law's response was to try to focus mental incapacity defences exclusively onto *cognitive* as opposed to *volitional* incapacities: the undoubted power of emotional forces was sidelined in an insanity test focused on radical cognitive defects, finally concretized in the M'Naghten Rules' test of a failure to 'know the nature and quality of [the] act'.[97] This, surely, epitomized the psychological world-view, and, in widening the already opened doorway to the 'alienist' witness, further undermined the process of lay evaluation which had underpinned the practice of mental incapacity exculpation for the past centuries.

Or did it? In fact, it may readily be seen that the matter was very much more complicated. We can begin to see why when we remind ourselves of the fact that the cognitive failure which had to be proven under the M'Naghten rules could take one or two forms: it could be an inability to know the nature and quality of the act *or*, if the defendant did know it, an incapacity to 'know right from wrong'. The idea of 'knowing right from wrong' is, of course, an inextricable mix of fact and evaluation. So it is hardly surprising that the latter nineteenth century was marked by a persistent debate about the concept of 'moral insanity'—the key point at which pressure for the expansion of the defence, to cover, in effect, cases of volitional defect, failures of self-control, was applied. Undaunted—and assisted by the emerging doctrines of *mens rea*—medical witnesses made repeated

[96] Dror Wahrman, *The Making of the Modern Self*; Lacey, *Women, Crime, and Character* Chapter 1.

[97] *M'Naghten's Case* (1843) 10 CL; Fin 200.

attempts to establish a defence of 'irresistible impulse' and, where unable to frame a defence of insanity cast as a 'lesion of the will', took their campaign into the terrain of *mens rea* as a whole, arguing that a damaged will undermined criminal responsibility.[98] If, to quote one medical witness, 'a person in a state of acute mania would not think about the moral quality of her acts',[99] and if the inability to 'know right from wrong' itself flowed from a deranged judgment, the gap between someone who 'just couldn't help themselves' and someone who 'failed to understand what they were doing' is perilously fine.

It is therefore important not to exaggerate the apparent shift from an evaluative to a scientific world-view. The late Victorian discourses of criminal pathology were, like the discourse of 'mind doctors' of the era, themselves imbued with evaluations of moral character.[100] This is vividly exemplified in the famous debate about so-called 'moral insanity', a pseudo-medical concept which, as Lucia Zedner puts it, 'equated mental health with virtue ...'[101] and which was applied with particular intensity to women. It is true that by the very end of the century, there was a tendency to regard habitual offenders in terms of pathology: women 'less as "bad" than as "mad"',[102] men as falling into a number of quasi-biological groupings which found statutory expression (for both sexes) in the late nineteenth and early twentieth century.[103] But for most of the nineteenth century, the tendency was to rely on open-textured concepts such as 'moral insensibility', and hence to locate criminality in the failings of properly moral character rather than in psychological incapacity.[104]

Throughout the second half of the nineteenth century, the concept of 'moral insanity' was drawn on to conflate capacity, conduct,

98 Joel Peter Eigen, 'Lesion of the Will: Medical Resolve and Criminal Responsibility in Victorian Insanity Trials', see in particular p. 442.

99 Case of Emily Walmsley, Old Bailey Sessions Papers t18830430-550, testimony of Charles Wheeler, surgeon.

100 As Ruth Harris has shown (*Murders and Madness: Medicine, Law and Society in the Fin de Siècle*) much the same *mélange* of medicine and moralism characterized debates about criminal responsibility in late nineteenth-century France.

101 Lucia Zedner, *Women, Crime, and Custody in Victorian England* p. 270.

102 Ibid. p. 46.

103 See Leon Radzinowicz and Roger Hood, *The Emergence of Penal Policy in Victorian and Edwardian England* Chapters 8–12.

104 In passing, it is worth noting that the persistence of concepts such as 'moral insanity' puts a different spin on the 'turf wars' between doctors and lawyers charted by Roger Smith in his influential account of criminal insanity in nineteenth-century England (*Trial by Medicine*). Smith argues that medicine and law were in competition

and character, focusing on external signals of danger or degeneracy rather than internal features of psychology and intentionality. And this continuing focus on character is reflected in a number of other tangible institutional arrangements. For example, the impressionistic category of 'the criminal classes'—those of bad reputation and/or with previous convictions—was regarded as hugely important to the identifiability of those thought to be 'vicious in character'.[105] Here we have a classic example of character-based assumptions shading into those shaped by assessments of risk.

These findings from the criminal process are strongly reinforced by Roger Smith's study of the historical journey of the concept of 'inhibition'—a usefully ambiguous idea, which was central to the Victorian project of regulation precisely because of the way in which it spanned scientific and evaluative resonance. The relationship went in two directions: while 'the social value of the self-regulated person—someone with a "good character"—was a coherence condition for any scientific theory of mental or bodily control,' 'the evaluation of human conduct was constitutive in comprehending the bodily or mental conditions making organized activity possible.' Hence, as Smith puts it, '[p]hysiology was not in conflict with ethics. If physiological science provoked a "crisis" about what it was to be human, this was as much a crisis of coherence within science as between science and wider culture.'[106] The highly contested nature of scientific theories of mind and brain rendered them exceptionally fragile legitimating sources for criminal law. So the body—or more accurately, bodies—of knowledge which the emerging sciences were producing did not stand against common sense and lay evaluation. Rather, they found their force when grounded within a shared

because while law sought to make an evaluative judgment based on an assumption of responsibility, medicine sought to make a factual judgment on the basis of determinist assumptions. The moral insanity debate suggests that what was at issue was rather a pair of competing evaluations. On the role of 'moral insanity', and the resonance with James Cowles Prichard's influential 1835 text on insanity in Robert Louis Stevenson's *Jekyll and Hyde*, see Robert Mighall, 'Diagnosing Jekyll: The Scientific Context to Dr Jekyll's Experiment and Mr Hyde's Embodiment', in Robert Louis Stevenson, *The Strange Case of Dr Jekyll and Mr Hyde and Other Tales of Terror*, edited by Robert Mighall (London: Penguin 2002) pp. 147–8.

[105] See Lucia Zedner, *Women, Crime and Custody in Victorian England*.

[106] Roger Smith, *Inhibition: History and Meaning in the Sciences of Mind and Brain* (London: Free Association Books 1992) pp. 231, 237–8.

discourse, and found much of their ground of legitimation and practical mobilization within those co-existing social resources.[107]

Smith's argument gives further depth to our understanding of why volitional defects were so threatening to the law. 'Inhibition', understood as the capacity for self-control, and as a concept with both scientific and evaluative dimensions, was the condition for the very project of Victorian governance. But the ambiguity of 'inhibition' further suggests the precise nature of a re-articulation of older ideas of character with the newer psychologized discourse of self-control: good character simply *became* the capacity for self-mastery—entailing the 'characteristic ' of not posing a risk—which dominates the moral discourse of the novel from the late eighteenth century,[108] and which underpinned the criminal justice projects of nineteenth century England until the sway of social Darwinism somewhat eroded it in the latter part of the century. On this worldview, failures of self-control are seen as fundamentally moral failures.

It therefore appears that the nineteenth century conception of criminal responsibility—and, by implication, conceptions of non-responsibility, epitomized by the legal conception of insanity—represented a complex mix of evaluation and factual assessment; of evaluations of character and investigations of engaged psychological capacity. At the level of legitimation, social conditions as various as the diversification of criminal law, inchoate democratization, and the growth of the 'sciences of mind and brain' gave a new spin to conceptions of criminal responsibility as founded in the factual condition of mental, inner states of individual human beings. Similarly, at the level of coordination, the modernization of criminal procedure, the growth of legal representation and hence of legal doctrines, and the rise of expert witnesses created new resources for the investigation of the 'factual' aspects of criminal responsibility. Evaluations of character had not disappeared, but their balance with the new psychological discourse was changing. Yet—as is hardly surprising given the contested nature of the early sciences

[107] Cf. Stephen Shapin, *A Social History of Truth: Civility and Science in Seventeenth-Century England* (Chicago: Chicago University Press 1994).

[108] I am thinking here, in particular, of the work of Jane Austen, Frances Burney and Maria Edgeworth: see Lacey, *Women, Crime, and Character* pp. 85–9.

of mind and brain—there was anxiety about the robustness of the psychological model.

One particular manifestation of this anxiety further serves to illustrate the bearing of wider social knowledges, understandings, and attitudes on the development of responsibility doctrines. As Eigen has shown, the late Victorian period was marked by a curious 'new' phenomenon, which found its way with increasing frequency into the criminal courts.[109] This was a genre of defendants who, though not obviously displaying the classic marks of insanity, such as mania, delusion, or radical cognitive dysfunction, claimed exculpation on the basis that they were mentally absent from the scene of the crime. 'Unconscious crimes' did not fall squarely within the M'Naghten rules' definition of insanity as founded in cognitive failures rooted in 'disease of the mind'.[110] These, rather, were failures of volition or cases of suspended consciousness which were not obviously related to disease.

In his analysis of the social history of multiple personality, Ian Hacking traces this phenomenon back to the case of Mary Reynolds in England in 1816, and follows the development of the idea along its rise and gradual decline over the following century.[111] Importantly, Hacking shows that ideas of double or multiple consciousness were not only historically but also spatially specific (as well as being hotly contested in each time and place).[112] In France, the history of dual personality remained associated with physicalist conceptions such as hysteria, and was associated—as in the article which Robert Louis Stevenson's wife recalled as his inspiration for the plot of his literary classic, *Jekyll and Hyde*[113]—with a dual memory as well as dissociated consciousness. In England and, particularly, America, the ultimate triumph of Freud's psychoanalytic theory ensured the demise of double personality by

[109] Joel Peter Eigen, *Unconscious Crime: Mental Absence and Criminal Responsibility in Victorian London* (Baltimore and London: Johns Hopkins University Press 2003).

[110] Ibid. pp. 6ff.

[111] Ian Hacking, *Rewriting the Soul: Multiple Personality and the Sciences of Memory* (Princeton, NJ: Princeton University Press 1995); see in particular Chapters 9 and 10. Mary Reynolds is discussed on p. 142.

[112] Ibid. pp. 134, 142.

[113] Robert Mighall's essay, 'Diagnosing Jekyll: The Scientific Context to Dr Jekyll's Experiment and Mr Hyde's Embodiment' (at p. 145) suggests that Stevenson's wife recorded that the tale was inspired by his reading of a French scientific article about sub-consciousness.

relocating 'the second self', theoretically, within the subject as repression, thus rendering the memory as, in principle, recoverable.[114]

Eigen has traced the genesis and disposal of cases in the criminal courts which represent the pervasive Victorian preoccupation with absent-mindedness of double consciousness—a preoccupation which realized itself in a public obsession with mesmerism, hypnosis and sleepwalking, phenomena which find vivid literary expression not merely in the 'double consciousness/second self' genre already discussed but also in nineteenth century novels as diverse as George Eliot's *Daniel Deronda*, Wilkie Collins' *The Moonstone*, and Thomas Hardy's *Tess of the d'Urbervilles*.[115] Such popular interest—epitomized by the mania for public displays of hypnotism—discloses a fundamental tension in Victorian society. As Eigen puts it, 'Given Victorians' well-documented preoccupation with the will and the era's paramount goal of fostering an ethic of self-mastery among all British citizens, such morbid fascination with unconscious and uncontrollable behaviour reminds one of someone with an abject fear of snakes who, upon entering a zoo, makes his way immediately for the reptile house.'[116]

[114] As indeed it readily is in Stevenson's story, with acute implications for Jekyll's moral agony. Nancy K. Gish has persuasively suggested that the scientific source of Stevenson's 'case' was Pierre Janet's theory of hysteria as grounded in split personality caused by dissociated consciousness: 'Jekyll and Hyde: The Psychology of Dissociation', 2 *International Journal of Scottish Literature* (2007) pp. 1–10: ISSN 1751-2808; www.ijsl.stir.ac.uk p. 155.

[115] For a small selection of Victorian novels featuring significant incidents of absence or duality of mind, see George Eliot, *Daniel Deronda* (1876: London: Penguin Classics 1995) (Gwendolen Grandcourt's dissociated state implies that she is unsure whether her husband's death was an accident); Wilkie Collins, *The Moonstone* (1868: London: Penguin Classics 1998) (a 'theft' committed during a laudanum-induced trance); Thomas Hardy, *Tess of the d'Urbervilles* (1891: New York: Bantam Classics 2004) (Tess's mind is 'dissociated' from her body at the time of Alec's murder, while Angel acts out some of his desires during an episode of sleepwalking); Charlotte Brontë, *Jane Eyre* (1847: London: Penguin Classics 2006) (Jane is able to hear Rochester's call from many miles away); Wilkie Collins, *The Woman in White* (1860: London: Penguin Classics 1999) (Laura Fairlie loses her identity to the 'mad' Ann Catherick); Oscar Wilde, *The Picture of Dorian Gray* (1891: London: Penguin Classics 2000) (Dorian Gray's dissipated life is etched onto his portrait while leaving his body and face intact). Though it is an autobiographical essay rather than a novel, mention must also be made of Thomas De Quincey's *Confessions of an Opium Eater* (1821: London: Signet Classics 1966), which gives a vivid account of the experience of laudanum-induced hallucinations. The relationship between responsibility and consciousness is discussed further in Lacey, 'Responsibility without Consciousness'.

[116] Eigen, *Unconscious Crime* pp. x, 15.

In unravelling the causes of this preoccupation, Eigen's starting point is the assumption that knowledge and consciousness were seen as central to criminal responsibility, which took off from a Lockean notion of the unified subject as capable of being known to itself, and one whose consciousness included 'an intuitive capacity to know right from wrong'.[117] It was the very threat which states of absent or multiple consciousness posed to Victorian notions of social control which underpinned the fascination with these phenomena. Focusing on examples such as sleepwalking, irresistible impulses, or unconsciousness, Eigen examines a sample of cases from the Old Bailey which posed a challenge to that model by developing '[a] vocabulary that embraced somnambulism and absence, amnesia and passion, [drawing] the courtroom defendant further away from the centuries-old conception of "the person": a consequences-perceiving, conscious and remembering being'.[118] He finds that medical testimony was often sought in these cases, and that juries not infrequently went beyond the M'Naghten rules to bring in verdicts such as 'not guilty on grounds of unconsciousness'.[119]

While, clearly, neither our late-twentieth-century psychiatric vocabulary of 'multiple personality disorder' nor the Freudian framework of the unconscious were available to nineteenth century defendants, this did not prevent defendants from deploying available cultural resources—notably 'the language of memory and consciousness, of horror at learning of the deed and despair at learning of one's own contribution' to distance their responsibility[120]. As Eigen puts it, 'Here was ample evidence that actual courtroom persons were anything but a unity. not only might they be unconscious during the crime, they could not conceive of a reason why anyone would have contemplated that action.'[121] From the point of view of the integrity

[117] Ibid. p. 117.

[118] Ibid. p. 179.

[119] See Elizabeth Carr's case, OBSP (Old Bailey Sessions Papers) 1875–6, Case 413, 11th sess.

[120] See, for example, the case of Julia Spickernell *Proceedings of the Old Bailey* t18890204-214.

[121] Eigen, *Unconscious Crime*; this and the quotation in the previous sentence, p. 179. Doctrinally, these sorts of arguments led to the development of a (highly restricted) defence of automatism: the first automatism defence resulting from a plea of somnambulism did not occur until 1878, in Scotland—see Walker, *Crime and Insanity in England* Chapter 4.

of both criminal law's proscriptions and the legitimacy of punishment this thought was deeply disturbing. Eigen suggests that, in the light of psychoanalytic theory, 'Today's reader of the OBSP begins to wonder whether the supposed discontinuity reveals different persons, or irreconcilable emotions within the same person. Most of the crimes appear to have been premeditated, all involved victims and defendants well known to each other, and most featured the use of a lethal weapon or poison, suggesting a deliberate choice of means to effect a specific, envisioned end.'[122] But even this interpretation is hardly reassuring from a criminal law point of view.

Indeed, it is precisely this disturbing phenomenon to which Robert Louis Stevenson's 'case' of *Jekyll and Hyde*—a huge literarary phenomenon of the late nineteenth century—speaks.[123] Like defendants relying on states of absence of mind, double consciousness or possession by the devil, Jekyll seeks to displace not only his desires but his responsibility onto Hyde, whom he himself then diagnoses as suffering from 'moral insanity'.[124] But the story also makes swingeing moral evaluations, many of them with strong biblical associations: Jekyll describes Hyde as 'wicked' and 'evil'; as 'the slime of the pit ... that insurgent horror [that] was knit to him [Jekyll] closer than a wife, closer than an eye; lay caged in his flesh'. Yet when he sees his evil alter ego in the mirror, 'I was conscious of no repugnance, rather of a leap of welcome. This, too, was myself. It seemed natural and human. In my eyes it bore a livelier image, it seemed more express and single, than the imperfect and divided countenance, I had been

[122] He continues: 'If this defendant was "missing" at the time of the crime, the perpetrator was certainly no stranger to the victim. Over the years 1843 to 1876 ... the concept of the unconscious itself ... underwent the greatest change in court. Originally merely the repository of forgotten knowledge and innumerable connections among ideas, the unconscious took on a new function, storing the resentments and hostilities not expressed within the victim and the offender's day-to-day interaction'. Eigen, *Unconscious Crime* pp. 33–4.

[123] In 1886, *The Strange Case of Dr Jekyll and Mr Hyde* burst onto the literary scene, selling 40,000 copies in the first six months after publication alone; entering the 'collective consciousness', and, in doing both of these things, catapulting the thirty-five-year-old Robert Louis Stevenson to fame: Robert Mighall, 'Introduction', in *Stevenson, Jekyll and Hyde* pp. ix, xxxiii.

[124] Stevenson, *Jekyll and Hyde* p. 64: 'no man morally sane could have been guilty of that crime'; cf. the clerk's assumption that whoever committed the Carew murder was 'mad' (p. 29). Similarly, Lanyon assumes that Jekyll is 'insane' when he receives his strange letter (p. 49), just as he earlier inferred from Jekyll's unorthodox researches that he was 'wrong in mind' (p. 12).

hitherto accustomed to call mine.'[125] Hyde resides within Jekyll—and hence represents the ultimate crisis of judgment: the unitary subject is split asunder, negating a straightforward attribution of 'factual' responsibility; that split also undermines the older discourse of evaluation of character by representing character, too, as ambivalent and as split. And the hope that new scientific knowledges—of both medical science and evolutionary biology—would provide new technologies for identifying criminality to replace the older model of character is shown, in Stevenson's horror story, to be a chimera.

This problem of grounding and legitimating attributions of responsibility within a stable human subject was not, of course, entirely new. In the era in which criminal responsibility attributions were driven by, and underpinned by a confidence in, evaluation of character, Henry Fielding was already raising questions about how it might be resolved. Of the world's judgments on *Tom Jones,* the likeable rogue whose criminal and dubiously lawful adventures enliven the eponymous novel, Fielding averred that 'A single bad act no more constitutes a villain in life than a single bad part on the stage. The passions, like the managers of a playhouse, often force men upon parts without consulting their judgment,

[125] Ibid. pp. 69, 58; cf. Chris Danta, 'The Metaphysical Cut: Darwin and Stevenson on Vivisection' 36 *Victorian Review* (2010) 51–65, and discussion of Hyde as representing the 'animal' side of human nature—surely a Darwin-shaped theme, and one absent from the other examples of the 'double consciousness' genre which I have cited. The human/animal/evil axis is also an aspect of Bram Stoker's *Dracula* (1897: Oxford: Oxford World's Classics 1998), a book which shares with *Jekyll and Hyde* the pitching of a fact-recording lawyer and a doctor against evil; the representation of the boundary between evil and insanity as blurred (pp. 100ff., 186); and depictions of sleepwalking (pp. 72, 86), hypnosis (p. 44), 'unconscious cerebration' (p. 69), and other out of body experiences (pp. 160, 201). By contrast, *Dracula* presents its readers with a further twist to the horror of criminality's immanence in respectable urban life: that of criminality as contagious. The trope of dual personality, and the questions of its implications for responsibility, and for the possibility of distinguishing character from capacity responsibility, continues to echo in literature. Cf. John Banville: 'There is no moment in this process of which I can confidently say, there, that is when I decided she should die. Decided?—I do not think it was a matter of deciding. I don't think it was a matter of thinking, even. That fat monster inside me just saw his chance and leaped out, frothing and flailing. He had scores to settle with the world, and she, at that moment, was world enough for him. I could not stop him. Or could I? He is me, after all, and I am he. But no, things were too far gone for stopping. Perhaps that is the essence of my crime, of my culpability, that I let things get to that stage, that I had not been vigilant enough, had not been enough of a dissembler, that I left Bunter to his own devices, and thus allowed him, fatally, to understand that he was free, that the cage door was open, that nothing was forbidden, that everything was possible.' (*The Book of Evidence* (London: Secker & Warburg 1989) p. 151). My thanks to Peter Ramsay for this reference.

and sometimes without any regard to their talents. Thus the man, as well as the player, may condemn what he himself acts ... few characters were so absolutely vicious as not to have the least mixture of good in them ...'[126] Even here, we see a forerunner of Jekyll's discovery that 'man is not truly one, but truly two',[127] and a consequent uncertainty about the grounds of moral evaluation of character. And this presages a centuries-long introspection on whether character is a matter of nature or nurture which also finds expression in *Jekyll and Hyde*: Dr. Jekyll's friend and colleague, Dr. Lanyon, for example, finds himself wondering, as he looks at Hyde, not only about his 'nature and character' but also about his 'origin, his life, his fortune and status in the world'.[128] In a world yet more complex and mobile than the one confronting Tom Jones' contemporaries, Hyde therefore represents a nostalgia for an earlier—perhaps mythic—world of confident moral evaluation, where 'Satan's signature upon a face'[129] is manifest; as well as a deep perplexity about the implications for individual responsibility—and hence for the very project of modern governance—of the multiplicity of human subjectivity.

This sense of the crucial importance of being able to *recognize* criminality was of course about to realize itself in statutory form in the many late Victorian provisions classifying groups of offenders such as the 'weak-minded' and the 'inebriate'.[130] And it was finding contemporary scientific expression in the statistical and photographic researches of Charles' Darwin's cousin, the early eugenicist Francis Galton, who hoped (but, unsurprisingly, failed) to identify the essence of criminal personality by superimposing multiple photographic images of offenders

[126] Henry Fielding, *The History of Tom Jones, A Foundling* (1749: Oxford: Oxford World's Classics 1996) at pp. 286, 794; Fielding nonetheless continued for most of his life to place some confidence, or perhaps hope, in character as a basis for social judgment: see his 'Essay on the Knowledge of the Characters of Men', in his *Miscellanies* Vol. 1, edited by Henry Knight Miller (1743: Oxford: Clarendon Press, 1972); see also Arlene Fish Wilner, 'Henry Fielding and the Knowledge of Character' 18 *Modern Language Studies* (1988) 181–94.

[127] Stevenson, *Jekyll and Hyde* p. 55.

[128] Ibid. p. 52.

[129] Ibid. pp. 7–8, 10, 13, 16. Throughout the tale, Stevenson emphasizes that everyone who sees Hyde instantly recognizes his evil or deformity: a clear echo of 'manifest criminality', but one which is hard to sustain in the rationalist discourse of individual responsibility, though it was about to have a new revival in the form of the criminal classifications on which the late Victorians became so keen—a development which could be read as a new twist in the history of 'external' patterns of responsibility-attribution.

[130] See Leon Radzinowicz and Roger Hood, *The Emergence of Penal Policy in Victorian and Edwardian England* Chapters 8–12.

to distil a common essence.[131] We see here the emerging modern preoccupation with identifying and managing risk—an impulse which may readily be projected onto evaluations of character. Hence, perhaps, Stevenson's reversion to an older vocabulary of manifest evil: of Hyde as a 'hellish but inorganic' 'fiend'.[132] The reversion held little comfort, however, in an age which aspired to ascribe individual responsibility, yet which had begun to question the location of responsibility for 'evil'.

Equally striking is Stevenson's anticipation of Freud, not merely in his model of split subjectivity with shared, or at least recoverable, memory, but specifically in his observation that Jekyll's weakness of will in keeping Hyde at bay is prompted by an 'unconscious reservation' about whether he really wants to do so. Decades before the widespread reception of Freud's theories,[133] defendants in the criminal courts, and writers like Stevenson,[134] Wilde, Collins, and Eliot, were posing the question of responsibility for conduct beyond consciousness. It remains a puzzle that neither legal doctrine nor—with a few honourable exceptions, notably the pioneering work of Herbert Fingarette[135]—criminal law theory have been keen to explore the resolution to this problem offered by Freudian theory which, in relating the subject structurally to its unconscious, provides a framework within which one can begin to comprehend that subject's responsibility for conduct generated by its unconscious states.[136] As for double consciousness, while 'multiple personality disorder' gradually established itself as an object of theoretical and clinical interest in psychiatry, psychology and, somewhat later, philosophy, a systematic analysis of its normative and practical implications for mechanisms

[131] Robert Mighall, 'Diagnosing Jekyll' pp. 152–4.

[132] Stevenson, *Jekyll and Hyde* pp. 69, 11.

[133] Freud's early work with Josef Breuer, *Studies in Hysteria*, was published in 1895, while his elaborated theory of the unconscious unfolded in further publications over the next five decades. *Studies in Hysteria* (1895: London: Penguin Books 2004).

[134] Stevenson, *Jekyll and Hyde* p. 63.

[135] Herbert Fingarette, *Self-Deception* (2nd ed., Berkeley and Los Angeles: University of California Press 2000); Herbert Fingarette and Ann Fingarette Hasse, *Mental Disability and Criminal Responsibility* (Berkeley: University of California Press 1979); see further Richard Wollheim (1985), 'Crime, Punishment and Pale Criminality' *Oxford Journal of Legal Studies* (1988) 8 (1): 1–16.

[136] If this can be explained by the gradual decline of defences of 'absence' or 'duality' of mind, which so preoccupied late Victorian courts, we can perhaps speculate that the issue will arise again shortly as a result of recent developments in the psychiatric understanding of multiple personality. Whether or not this is a plausible speculation, it is a topic for another paper.

of responsibility-attribution in criminal law did not, as far as I am aware, appear until the publication of Elyn Saks' *Jekyll on Trial* in 1997.[137] Whatever the explanation, *Jekyll and Hyde* stands for a world in transition: juxtaposing evolutionary biology, psychological medicine and biblical judgment; informed by modern 'science' yet deeply preoccupied with moral conventions, it leaves the reader perplexed about the proper way in which to attribute responsibility for Jekyll's imperfectly realized self-control and Hyde's manifestly criminal acts.

In this chapter, I have tried to show that, even in the substantive criminal law, and even at the conviction stage, multiple conceptions of responsibility have co-existed at various times in England and Wales. Today, capacity responsibility is salient, but not exclusive, while risk, outcome and character-based assessment have tremendous sway at the prosecution and sentencing stages, producing a hybrid pattern of responsibility-attribution in the overall practice of criminalization. For each of these patterns, we can moreover discern a broader intellectual and cultural context, and an understanding of this context helps us to relate developments in criminal law to those in political, literary, and scientific spheres. But the evolution of criminal responsibility cannot be understood entirely in terms of the history of ideas. For, as we shall see in the following two chapters, the context which shapes patterns of responsibility-attribution also includes shifting interests and power relations, as well as the institutional frameworks which provide a framework within which ideas of responsibility are actualized.

[137] Elyn R. Saks with Stephen H. Behnke, *Jekyll on Trial: Multiple Personality Disorder and Criminal Law* (New York and London: New York University Press 1997); on the development of 'multiple personality' in the medical sciences, psychoanalysis, philosophy, and popular culture see also Hacking, *Rewriting the Soul*. Despite the title of Saks' book, Jekyll would not, strictly, come within the definition of multiple personality disorder, which typically depends on a radical failure of integration which implies separate memories: see Saks, *Jekyll on Trial* Chapters 1 and 2. See also Herbert Fingarette, *Self-Deception* (Berkeley and Los Angeles: University of California Press 1969, 2000); Herbert Fingarette and Ann Fingarette Hasse, *Mental Disability and Criminal Responsibility* (Berkeley: University of California Press 1979); and Michael S. Moore, *Law and Psychiatry: Rethinking the Relationship* (Cambridge: Cambridge University Press 1984).

3

Interests

Each of the ideational frames discussed in the previous chapter will be familiar to any student of criminal law. But what determines which of these ideas prevails or dominates? Or when they prevail? And over which aspects of criminal law? The legitimation of criminal law depends on a discourse of justice, right, or appropriateness, which, increasingly, in democratic times, has come to involve the idea that all are equal before the law. Yet the reality is that criminal law is generally shaped by powerful interests: it is made by elites, while it is disproportionately enforced against non-elites. The structure of these patterns of interest and power has changed over time, however, with decisive consequences for doctrines and practices of criminal law. Hence some discussion of the influence of these factors, and of the legitimation problems which they pose for criminal law, is key to the project of this book.

Of the three broad dynamics which I have argued are fundamental to our understanding of law in general and of criminal responsibility in particular, interests have probably caused the greatest methodological controversy. Evidently, broad interpretations of law—including criminal law—as shaped by underlying power structures have surfaced regularly in social theories of law. Probably the most influential—as well as the most controversial—tradition reaches back to Marx and Engels, and finds expression in a variety of legal, criminological, and penal analyses. Key examples would include: Rusche and Kirchheimer's argument, in *Punishment and Social Structure*,[1] that the roles of criminalization and

[1] Georg Rusche and Otto Kirchheimer, *Punishment and Social Structure* (first published, in German, 1939; New York: Russell Sage 1969); see David Garland, *Punishment and Modern Society* (Oxford: Oxford University Press 1990) pp. 83–130.

punishment are functional to elite control of the economy through the discipline of surplus labour; Pashukanis's analysis of the form of bourgeois law as expressing commodified social relations through the mechanism of the formally equal contracting legal subject;[2] and Alan Norrie's productive application of Pashukanis's ideas to criminal law in *Law, Ideology and Punishment*,[3] which emphasized the contribution of the construction of the responsible subject in the modern general part of criminal law as ideological: as legitimating the repressive and unequal system of criminalizing power through the form of the capable, choosing responsible subject.

As one of the most influential and searching analysts of the power dynamics of criminal law, the historian and social theorist, E. P. Thompson, himself acknowledged in his classic work, *Whigs and Hunters*,[4] there are, however, some obvious drawbacks to interest-based analyses of law. First, they tend to be reductive in that they simply assume that phenomena such as law have no autonomy, in the process interpreting those who have aspired to use law to resist power as, in effect, the dupes of ideology. As Thompson famously observed, things are more complicated than this[5]—and can be seen to be so even from the perspective of an interest-based analysis: if law were no more than a cover for underlying interests, and served them consistently even when announcing safeguards or entitlements capable of being used in opposition to those interests, it would lack the credibility and legitimacy which are in fact key to its power. The very deployment of law and legal concepts in the service of interests is premised, therefore, on law's relative autonomy: hence understanding the distinctive forms and modalities of legal power remains important. Law cannot be reduced to a crude matter of interest alone.

Second, interest-based analyses such as Marxian theories of law tend to assume a rather monolithic structure of power, with economic power mapped onto a class structure typically understood as the main determinant of legal arrangements. Relevant though the

[2] Evgeny Pashukanis, *Law and Marxism: A General Theory* (1924: transl. Barbara Einhorn, London: Pluto 1978)

[3] Alan Norrie, *Law, Ideology and Punishment* (Dordrecht: Kluwer 1991); see also Peter Ramsay, 'Pashukanis and Public Protection', in Markus D. Dubber (ed.), *Foundational Texts in Modern Criminal Law* (Oxford: Oxford University Press 2015).

[4] E. P. Thompson, *Whigs and Hunters* (Harmondsworth: Penguin 1975).

[5] Ibid. pp. 262–3.

distribution of economic power has been to the development of criminal law and ideas of criminal responsibility, it is in fact fragmented by other vectors of power which have a distinctive importance: gender, race, and social status to name but the most obvious.

Finally, interest-based analyses are often either vague or unconvincing when it comes to the explication of the causal links between interests and outcomes in the law or legal arrangements. In the case of Marxist analysis, these arguments take the form either of an implausible form of class instrumentalism, which itself assumes unified and organized classes which are rare and in any event contingent; or of a rather vague assertion of the way in which 'material forces' are 'reflected' in the structures of allegedly superstructural phenomena such as law and ideology.[6]

These are real difficulties with interest analyses of law—from Marxist legal theory to the cruder versions of legal realism. But these difficulties have, unfortunately, occasioned a significant over-reaction, which is itself problematic. This is the reaction of more or less evacuating the analysis of interests from the study of law and legal development, resulting, in criminal law, in the evacuation of questions of power and interest to the fields of criminology, penology, and criminal justice studies. Following on from my claim that the development of criminal responsibility must be interpreted in the light of patterns and practices of criminalization, I would argue that, notwithstanding the methodological problems just canvassed, we need to reinsert a concern with interests into criminal law scholarship. For as long as we keep in view the fact that interests are mediated by institutional structures and realized and rationalized in terms of ideas, often themselves realized in the institutional form of legal doctrines, the problem of reductivism can be avoided. (Indeed, as we shall see in the close relationship between this chapter and the next, however clear the distinction is conceptually, it is difficult to prise apart the analysis of interests and of the institutions through which they are realized in our interpretive analysis of particular developments.) Moreover the origins of modern criminal law in political decisions render it not merely strange, but intellectually problematic, to evacuate the study of interests from the study of criminal law.

In this chapter, I therefore set out a conceptual map of the interests which we might expect to have been most influential in the

[6] For a general discussion, see Hugh Collins, *Marxism and Law* (Oxford: Clarendon 1982).

development of criminal law, before presenting some case studies which illustrate the force of interests in shaping particular developments over the history of modern English criminal law.

Interests and Forms of Power Shaping the Development of Criminal Responsibility

Economic Power

Both directly and indirectly, the distribution and scope of economic power has important implications for patterns of criminal responsibility-attribution. During the last 250 years, formal distinctions of status hierarchy based on class, gender, and, later, ethnicity have gradually been eroded, with important implications for the distribution of symbolic or cultural power, and for the problems of political legitimation faced by criminal law. Yet economic inequality, after (on most measures) declining significantly in the decades after the Second World War, has been growing steadily since the early 1970s.[7] Moreover the persistence—and, in recent years, acceleration—of the gap between those in the top and middle thirds of the distribution of wealth and those in the bottom third, many of them trapped in intergenerational cycles of low education, poor housing, and poverty, has arguably created a new form of status hierarchy: radical inequality is closely associated with a *de facto* differential social status that sits ill with contemporary ideals of legality. On the other hand, the massive expansion of what is in effect a middle class, with levels of education and wealth which increased markedly in the second half of the twentieth century, has had an impact on political preferences: as the Blair government's embrace of so-called 'Left Realism' in criminal justice policy demonstrated, the existence of an electorally decisive middle class concerned to protect its own comparative advantage, and preoccupied with its own security

[7] Income inequality started to decline after 1945; on Thomas Piketty's measure of capital output, the period of equalization reaches back to 1914. But on either measure, the 1970s mark a change. See Thomas Piketty, *Capital in the 21st Century* (transl. Arthur Goldhammer, Cambridge, MA and London: Harvard University Press 2014). For discussion of the close links between patterns of economic inequality and political dynamics, see David Soskice, '*Capital in the 21st Century*: A Critique' 65 *The British Journal of Sociology* (2014) 650–66.

and with the way in which an excluded underclass may threaten it, has lent salience to criminal justice as an electoral issue.[8] This development has, ironically, blunted the potential political legitimation problem deriving from the unequal impact of criminal law in an era strongly attached to the formal value of equality before the law.

Let us note immediately the fact that power-based patterns of social structure have implications for the salience of particular ideas of responsibility. For example, a combination of middle class electoral power and the structural economic exclusion of a significant minority arguably renders patterns of attribution based on stereotypes of bad character appealing, while also making those less securely placed in the socio-economic order an object of perceived risk to the better off.[9] So, while economic inequality has been a persistent feature of British society over the period we are interested in, the changing distribution of inequalities has had enormous importance for criminal responsibility, principally because this distribution has had decisive implications for political power, which, as we shall see, is of comparable significance to economic power.

Professional Power

The growth of professions and the attendant emergence of professional power during the nineteenth century had a key impact on criminal responsibility. Most notably, the growth and increasing organization and power of the legal profession—an issue whose institutional dimensions will be examined in the following chapter—provided both the incentive and the mechanism for the development of refined legal doctrines of responsibility. Likewise, the growing power and organization of a range of other professions (including the medical profession, the 'psy' professions, and the civil service)—each of which drew on new knowledge in science, criminology, medicine, statistics, demography, and other disciplines—has fundamentally changed the conditions under which ideas of responsibility are formed and put into practice. It has affected coordination by mandating new forms of evidence, and creating new interests

[8] See Nicola Lacey, *The Prisoners' Dilemma: Political Economy and Punishment in Contemporary Democracies* (Cambridge: Cambridge University Press 2008); and 'Political Systems and Criminal Justice: The Prisoners' Dilemma after the Coalition' 65 *Current Legal Problems* (2012) 203–39.

[9] Peter Ramsay, *The Insecurity State: Vulnerable Autonomy and the Right to Security in the Criminal Law* (Oxford: Oxford University Press 2012).

shaping the design and implementation of the criminal process quite generally and of the criminal trial in particular.[10] Specialized criminal justice professionals also emerged in this period: the police in the late eighteenth and early nineteenth centuries; the welfare-oriented criminal justice professions, such as probation officers and social workers, in the early twentieth century; and the experts in assessing various kinds of risks, using increasingly sophisticated technologies, in the latter part of the twentieth century.[11] Albeit in different ways, each of these organized and influential professions formed interest groups, which had an impact on the development and implementation of conceptions of responsibility.

Cultural or Symbolic Power and the Power of the Media

The proposition that relative powerlessness is associated with vulnerability to (substantive) criminalization is a commonplace of interest-based analysis of criminal justice. But this proposition must be complicated by any consideration of cultural or symbolic power, which itself demonstrates the interplay between interests and ideas. For while the cultural aspects of racial, ethnic, or religious discrimination—the lack of voice or status as much as the lack of political clout or money—seem likely to be relevant, significant differences in the patterns of criminalization of different minority groups, as well as the relatively low levels of criminalization of women, disrupt any simple claim about the association between cultural powerlessness and vulnerability to criminalization.[12] Nonetheless, any sensitive interpretation of the development of patterns of responsibility-attribution will have to be attentive to the interactions between symbolic and other forms of powerlessness.

[10] See, for example, Roger Smith, *Trial by Medicine: Insanity and Responsibility in Victorian Trials* (Edinburgh: Edinburgh University Press 1981); Joel Peter Eigen, 'Lesion of the Will: Medical Resolve and Criminal Responsibility in Victorian Insanity Trials' 33 *Law and Society Review* (1999) 425–59; Arlie Loughnan, *Manifest Madness: Mental Incapacity in Criminal Law* (Oxford: Oxford University Press 2012); Nikolas Rose, *The Psychological Complex: Psychology, Politics and Society in England, 1869–1939* (London: Routledge and Kegan Paul 1985); W. T. Murphy, *The Oldest Social Science* (Oxford: Oxford University Press 1997).

[11] See Andrew Ashworth and Lucia Zedner, *Preventive Justice* (Oxford: Oxford University Press 2014); Mike Redmayne, *Character in the Criminal Trial* (Oxford: Oxford University Press 2015) Chapters 6, 8, 12.

[12] By contrast, there is considerable evidence of the links between cultural powerlessness and a lack of real protection from the criminal law: see, for example, Ely Aaronson, *From Slave Abuse to Hate Crime* (New York: Cambridge University Press 2014).

In terms of patterns and principles of responsibility-attribution, a particular issue here will be the ways in which these are effective in underlining, expressing, or perpetuating race, class, or gender stereotypes—with assumptions about women's agentic capacities highly relevant to the interpretation of their capacity responsibility at various times.[13] A range of racial and class stereotypes—most vividly reflected in differential policing practices[14]—are also of relevance in the implementation of character responsibility. Note, too, the ways in which available symbolic repertoires can express and stabilize distinctive models of legal, political, and social authority.[15] Hence cultural resources underpin the power to construct particular practices of responsibility-attribution as well as shaping the mentalities and capacities of those subject to them. For example, popular culture is replete with messages about what it is to be a responsible subject or indeed a person, and with images of abjection and authority; all of these form a key part of the context in which legal practices emerge and take meaning and significance.[16]

The power of the news media and other media of mass communication has grown exponentially with the creation of the internet, increasing the reach and speed with which images of crime, criminality, and criminal justice are diffused. This has undoubtedly had an impact on ideas of criminal responsibility and patterns of responsibility-attribution, particularly in the media's capacity to legitimize and delegitimize

[13] See Nicola Lacey, *Women, Crime and Character: From Moll Flanders to Tess of the d'Urbervilles* (Oxford: Oxford University Press 2008); Carol Smart, *Women, Crime and Criminology* (London: Routledge 1976); Ngaire Naffine, *Feminism and Criminology* (Oxford: Polity Press 1997).

[14] See, for example, Coretta Phillips and Ben Bowling, 'Ethnicities, Racism, Crime and Criminal Justice' in Mike Maguire, Rod Morgan, and Robert Reiner (eds), *The Oxford Handbook of Criminology* (5th ed., Oxford: Oxford University Press 2012); and see more generally, Paul Gilroy, *There Ain't No Black in the Union Jack* (2nd ed., London: Routledge 2002).

[15] See Nicola Lacey and Hanna Pickard, 'The Chimera of Proportionality: Institutionalising Limits on Punishment in Contemporary Social and Political Systems', (2015) 78(2) *Modern Law Review* 216–40.

[16] This argument is key to the theoretical framework of successive editions of *Reconstructing Criminal Law*: see in particular the first edition (Nicola Lacey, Celia Wells, and Dirk Meure, London: Weidenfeld and Nicolson 1990) Chapter 1.I. In *Women, Crime and Character*, I explored in depth one such example: the ways in which eighteenth and nineteenth century British novels tracked the shift from a system of social authority based on honour to one based on legislative authority, and from a model of responsibility as founded in external markers of character to one founded in inner psychological capacity.

particular ideas of responsibility in the criminal process, as well as sharpening the political salience of criminal law and criminal justice by raising the profile (often in an alarmist or misleading way) of crime.[17]

Political Power

Economic, cultural, and professional power is therefore of real significance to criminal law. But perhaps the most obviously important form of power relevant to the development of criminal law is political power. The modern period was, after all, an era in which there was a decisive shift in the distribution of political power, and with it a panoply of changes in the form of governance, which had major implications for criminal law. Most obviously, this transition entailed a steady growth of legislation as a source of English criminal law and of the resort to criminalization as a tool of governance. As Lindsay Farmer has recently argued, it also prompted a rethinking of criminal law as an elaborate modality of governance oriented to a distinctive conception of civil order.[18] With the further development of the nation state in the UK during the nineteenth and early twentieth centuries, the modern project of governance has grown in both complexity and intensity.[19] As democratic institutions gradually emerged and widened their scope, there was a decisive shift of power from landowners to merchants and the emergence of an urban bourgeoisie. And in the hands of an

[17] See, for example, Robert Reiner, 'Media-made Criminality: The Representation of Crime in the Mass Media', in Mike Maguire, Rod Morgan, and Robert Reiner (eds), *The Oxford Handbook of Criminology* (4th ed., Oxford: Oxford University Press 2007) 302–37; Chris Greer and Robert Reiner, 'Mediated Mayhem: Media, Crime and Criminal Justice', in Mike Maguire, Rod Morgan, and Robert Reiner (eds), *The Oxford Handbook of Criminology* (5th ed., Oxford: Oxford University Press 2012) 245–78; Robert Reiner, Sonia Livingstone, and Jessica Allen, 'Casino Culture: Crime and Media in a Winner-Loser Society', in K. Stenson and R. Sullivan (eds), *Crime, Risk and Justice: The Politics of Crime Control in Liberal Democracies* (Cullompton: Willan 2001); Richard Sparks, *Television and the Drama of Crime* (London: Sage 1992); Stanley Cohen, *Folk Devils and Moral Panics* (1972: London and New York: Routledge Classics 2011); Richard V. Ericson, Patricia M. Baranek, and Janet B. L. Chan, *Visualizing Deviance: A Study of News Organizations* (Toronto: University of Toronto Press 1987).

[18] See Lindsay Farmer, *Making the Modern Criminal Law: Criminalization and Civil Order* (Oxford: Oxford University Press 2016).

[19] *See* S. E. Finer, *The History of Government from the Earliest Times III: Empires, Monarchies, and the Modern State* (Oxford: Oxford University Press 1997). For an account of the development of the administrative apparatus of the British state and for an instructive refutation of the view that its development is mainly to be attributed to the influence of Benthamite ideas, see Oliver MacDonagh, 'The Nineteenth-Century Revolution in Government: A Reappraisal' 1 *The Historical Journal* (1958) 52–67.

increasingly bourgeois, urban legislature, including a significant number of lawyers, the 'age of reform' was born. Many of the institutional innovations to be discussed in the next chapter were a product of the reorganization of government and the state in the hands of a new elite. At the turn of the twentieth century, with the development of the party system (itself driven by changes such as the increasing importance, and organization, of industrial labour from the late nineteenth century and, ultimately, changes in the distribution of economic power, already discussed), these political interests became yet more organized: capable of both strategic action and the coordination of support within a relatively stable popular base. With the emergence of the Labour party, new interests entered the political arena, adding to the gradually changing demographics of the legislature.

Given the rising salience of electorally driven political power to the development of criminal law, both criminal law and criminal justice have been liable throughout this modern period to become objects of political contest. This occurred with particular intensity in the last decades of the twentieth century, fostered by the system of 'winner takes all', adversarial, majoritarian politics dominated by two main parties, yet in which settled partisan affiliation is declining, leaving a significant group of decisive middle class voters 'floating' between the two main parties, or indeed between them and a third, smaller party holding the balance of power.[20] Under conditions in which this decisive group of 'median' voters become concerned with crime and security—as was undoubtedly the case in England and Wales in the last decades of the twentieth century—'tough' criminalization policy became attractive to legislators.[21] In other words, criminalization became itself a route—and was perceived as a route—to political power. The politicization of criminal law through legislation's domination over common law has also implied shifting power relations between judges and politicians, while the gradual emergence of criminal law as an object of electoral competition has rendered politicians' approach

[20] See Nicola Lacey, *The Prisoners' Dilemma* (discussing the implications of political systems for criminal justice); see also Nicola Lacey, 'Political Systems and Criminal Justice: The Prisoners' Dilemma after the Coalition'. As these sources indicate, there is evidence that this effect is greater in systems with more diffused and intensive practices of electoral competition: see also Nicola Lacey and David Soskice, 'Crime, Punishment and Segregation in the United States: The Paradox of Local Democracy', *Punishment and Society* (2015) Vol. 17(4) 454–481.

[21] See Lucia Zedner, *Security* (London: Routledge 2009); Robert Reiner, *Law and Order: An Honest Citizen's Guide to Crime and Control* (London: Polity Press 2007).

to criminal responsibility more and more relevant to how they attain and keep power. In these intersecting forces, we see how various forms of power interact to shape the balance of interests and their impact on institutions, ideas, and practices of responsibility-attribution.

CASE STUDIES

Outcome Responsibility, Summary Jurisdiction, and the Legitimation of Corporate Power

The changing distribution of governmental power as shaping the modernization of criminal law and the criminal process. It is widely agreed that the mid nineteenth century saw a significant expansion of summary jurisdiction, enabling the streamlined and relatively inexpensive enforcement of a range of new statutory offences, many of them oriented to the regulatory needs of a rapidly urbanizing and industrial economy.[22] This development also effected a shift in practices of responsibility-attribution, giving a new practical importance within the criminal law to the principle that a subject may be responsible for the production of harmful outcomes, even absent proof of responsibility in the sense of bad character or engaged capacity.[23] This willingness to accept a wider practice of outcome-based responsibility was also associated with the diffusion of utilitarian ideas, in which prime moral importance is attached to consequences. And it had an intrinsic institutional component: as Lindsay Farmer has shown,[24] it was the expansion of the summary police courts which made it possible to implement an expanded role for outcome responsibility.

But a full understanding of the emergence of a large area of criminal law dominated by strict liability must also include a grasp of the various interests that shaped the relevant legislative developments. And the scale and significance of two important forms of responsibility—responsibility

[22] See, in particular, Lindsay Farmer, *Criminal Law, Tradition and Legal Order: Crime and the Genius of Scots Law, 1747 to the Present* (Cambridge: Cambridge University Press 1996); *Making the Modern Criminal Law: Civil Order and Criminalization*.

[23] See further, Nicola Lacey, 'Space, time and function: intersecting principles of responsibility across the terrain of criminal justice' *Criminal Law and Philosophy* Vol. 1 (2007) 233–50.

[24] Farmer, *Criminal Law, Tradition and Legal Order.*

for outcomes and corporate responsibility—can readily be shown to have been driven, to a significant extent, by interests of various kinds. It is generally acknowledged that the dismantling of the early modern, *ancien régime* in criminal justice, and its gradual replacement from the end of the eighteenth century, was driven by the triumph of bourgeois, merchant interests which had established a firm parliamentary base with considerable political power in addition to its commercial power. This emerging political elite had an overriding interest in the success and stabilization of cities as locations for a growing urbanized industrial and mercantile economy. But the scale and speed of both industrialization and urbanization presented considerable challenges to government, with existing institutional mechanisms for regulation, which had largely lain in the hands of local justices of the peace, inadequate to provide order in increasingly populous urban areas. Moreover social problems in London and the northern industrial cities were exacerbated by the instabilities of the early capitalist economy. Problems of potential social disorder, like questions of health and safety in areas such as workplaces, roads, and railways, prompted new mechanisms for licensing and regulation, originating in national legislation, and for making centralized provision for institutional mechanisms for enforcement. As both Lindsay Farmer[25] and Alan Norrie[26] have shown in detail, the expansion of the summary jurisdiction and the multiplication of summary offences were key to this project of modern governance. The middle decades of the nineteenth century accordingly saw the creation of large numbers of strict liability offences, many of them engaging in the regulation of specific activities impinging on the public interest, health, or welfare, oriented to the orderly coordination of life under industrial capitalism. Clearly, much of this legislation was driven by an increasingly centralized and ambitious government's need to regulate urban and industrial life, with health and public order being prime considerations. Moreover, criminalization was a useful tool for central government in its efforts to coordinate standards amid a system of local government through parish vestries, which remained highly fragmented and dominated by parochial interests for most of the nineteenth century.[27]

[25] Lindsay Farmer, *Criminal Law, Tradition and Legal Legal Order* and *Making the Modern Criminal Law* Chapters 3 and 6.

[26] Alan Norrie, *Crime, Reason and History: A Critical Introduction to Criminal Law* (3rd ed., Cambridge: Cambridge University Press 2014) Chapter 2; see also his *Law, Ideology and Punishment*.

[27] Lee Jackson, *Dirty Old London: The Victorian Fight with Filth* (New Haven and London: Yale University Press 2014).

Note, however, that while this phenomenon was evidently inspired in part by utilitarian notions of order and efficiency, it was by no means a crudely instrumental process. Rather, the legislative strategy was alive to the needs of legitimation. Since many of the new legislative obligations fell precisely upon those responsible for directing the engines of capitalist growth, this imposition might have risked economic interests had it been framed in terms of moralized criminalization. As Alan Norrie has pointed out,[28] the creation of large numbers of statutory offences targeted at middle rather than working class people—factory owners, shopkeepers, and so on—created a potential legitimation problem for a government whose own power derived from the bourgeois interests newly subject to such regulation. In Norrie's view, the enactment of these new offences through the distinctive summary process served to solve this legitimation problem by zoning the new offences outwith the category of 'real crime', hence enhancing their acceptability to the relatively privileged people subject to them. The expansion of the summary jurisdiction accordingly created a mechanism whereby criminal law gained the capacity to deliver a form of regulation free of moral connotations, which would be acceptable to the powerful interests subject to its disciplines. In doing so, the Victorian legislature further embedded an elusive distinction between 'real' and 'regulatory' crime—the latter realized through a parallel system of summary jurisdiction generally focused on outcome responsibility—which haunts English criminal law to this day. This important feature of English criminal law, which is thrown into relief by a historical reading, is further illuminated by a comparative understanding of the European systems, which effected a very different settlement: a formal distinction between administrative infractions and criminal law which has underpinned a rather different pattern of responsibility attribution in the civilian systems.[29]

One important and distinctive aspect of the increasing deployment of criminal law as a tool of modern regulatory governance had to do with the emerging legal framework governing corporations. Once again, the gradually emerging doctrines of corporate criminal capacity strongly reflected the distribution of both economic and political interests, with strict liability offences serving the regulatory interests of political elites as well as serving legitimation functions

[28] *Crime, Reason and History* Chapter 5.

[29] See James Q. Whitman, *Harsh Justice* (New York: Oxford University Press 2003).

in relation to corporate power. This is evidenced by the contrasting approach to corporate responsibility for serious crime. The identification doctrine of the early twentieth century was narrowly drawn in terms of a fully psychologized doctrine of *mens rea* which marginalized corporations as lacking a 'soul to damn':[30] it limited corporate responsibility for serious crime to the unusual situations in which it could be pinned on someone sufficiently highly placed in the company to be 'identified' as its controlling mind and will. The increasing power and reach of corporations, as well as the growing reach of news media, which raised public consciousness of the significance of corporate activities, somewhat altered the balance of political interests as the twentieth century wore on, with considerable social pressure occasioned by some spectacular tragedies occasioned by corporate negligence—the sinking of the Herald of Free Enterprise in Zeebrugge harbour in 1987 being the obvious example. Twenty years, several relevant public inquiries, and a great deal of litigation later, the growing public perception of the need for greater corporate responsibility had further shifted political elites' apprehension of legitimation needs, prompting a modest expansion of corporations' liability for serious crime in the form of the Corporate Manslaughter and Corporate Homicide Act 2007.[31]

From Manifest to Subjective Criminality in the Law of Theft

Interests and the legitimation of property crime

Few would challenge the ideas that property relations are central to how any social order works, and that they have always been a key concern of the criminal law. Yet these general propositions mask

[30] The idea of a corporation lacking body and soul originates with Edward, 1st Baron Thurlow (1731–1806) who was remarking, even before corporate capitalism had established itself, on corporations' inability to have a conscience. The identification doctrine was introduced in *DPP v Kent and Sussex Contractors* [1944] KB 146; *R v ICR Haulage* (1944) 30 Cr. App. Rep. 31. See Celia Wells, *Corporations and Criminal Responsibility* (2nd ed., Oxford: Clarendon Press 2001); C. M. V. Clarkson, 'Kicking Corporate Bodies and Damning their Souls' (1996) *Modern Law Review* 59 (4): 557.

[31] See Celia Wells, *Corporations and Criminal Responsibility*. Nicola Lacey, 'Philosophical Foundations of the Common Law: Social Not Metaphysical', in Jeremy Horder (ed.), *Oxford Essays in Jurisprudence* (Fourth Series) (Oxford: Clarendon Press 2000).

both the fact that conceptions of property have changed radically over the last 400 years, and the fact that criminal law's construction of property interests has shifted alongside these changing social conceptions. These shifts provide a further illustration of the influence of changing interests on the shape and significance of criminal law's conception of responsibility.

Looking back to the early modern forms of criminal law which prevailed up until the late eighteenth century, we can see that the key importance which they attached to property crimes—in particular to theft and forgery[32]—reflected the importance of property as a source of social power and of status differentiation. As mercantile and then industrial capitalism gradually developed, eroding the centrality of feudal relations and bringing with them new forms of valuable property and property relation, private property emerged as a key concern within liberal conceptions of political entitlement, generating the liberal idea of property ownership originating in the self-ownership of the free individual, whose choices would determine the legitimacy of proprietary transactions based on bargaining and agreement. Moving yet further forward to the twentieth century, new forms of property emerge: welfare rights; intellectual property; computer software; and other intangible forms of property with particular value in a knowledge economy. They challenge criminal law's constructions of property, bringing them far from the idea of property as simply divided into real property (land) and personal property (chattels, 'things').

How criminal law attributes responsibility for violations of interests in property is therefore a useful case study in how changing social ideas about property affect the development of criminal law. It also illuminates the shifting boundary between criminal and civil law, not least because property interests are the creature of civil law and are protected by legal institutions such as contract, land law and equity. So questions constantly arise about how the line is being drawn between criminal and civil protection and about how it should be drawn. Should criminal law always deploy the same concepts of property as the civil law? What are the respective functions of criminal and civil law in this area? And finally, changing conceptions of responsibility for property crime raise questions about the relationship between how criminal law attributes responsibility and changing

[32] See Lindsay Farmer, *Making the Modern Criminal Law* Chapter 7.

ideas of the individual, civil society, and the state, which in turn raises questions about the historical contingency of basic elements of liability, such as *mens rea*. A brief survey of the law of theft—a central offence against property throughout the modern history of English criminal law—reveals both the contingency of particular conceptions of property crime and the contribution of a number of factors—social and economic conditions, prevailing political interests, influential legal doctrines, the imperatives of procedural forms, historical accident—to the development of conceptions of criminal responsibility.

A useful starting point is George Fletcher's classic analysis of the history of theft in the common law, already introduced in Chapter 1. Fletcher sets out from a distinction between three basic kinds of general property crime: larceny; embezzlement; and false pretences.[33] Larceny, as defined by Blackstone in the mid eighteenth century—and hence in a period when common law had already begun to change—consisted in a felonious taking and carrying away of the personal goods of another. It had to be felonious in the sense of being done with an *animus furandi*—theftuous spirit or intent—but, as we shall see, this was not really equivalent to contemporary *mens rea* or intent. Larceny was essentially a crime against possession—hence physical taking—which entailed that those in possession could not be guilty of larceny. Embezzlement, by contrast, consisted in appropriating goods which had been entrusted to the defendant's possession to her or his own use; while false pretences consisted in gaining possession of goods by means of some pretence or cheating. Hence, as Fletcher explains, the difference between these three kinds of offence had centrally to do with the nature of the victim's participation: in larceny, the victim in no way voluntarily participates; in embezzlement, the victim agrees to the initial taking but not to the later appropriation; in false pretences, the victim agrees to the transfer of possession, but only because he or she is the victim of a deception. This illustrates the variety of interests or wrongs which criminal laws about property can express. Whilst larceny is about possession, embezzlement is about trust, and false pretences is about the integrity of transactions.

33 George Fletcher, *Rethinking Criminal Law* (Boston and Toronto: Little, Brown 1978) pp. 1–122.

Significantly, embezzlement and false pretences developed late in the common law, as statutory innovations coming much later than larceny (innovations themselves, one might surmise, driven by new interests emerging amid changes in economic and social relations, which necessitated a firmer legal enforcement of the conditions for trust). To summarize, Fletcher's argument is that in the development towards contemporary law, the distinction between these three forms of separate property violation becomes blurred. Furthermore, he argues that this blurring expresses a deeper change in the underlying conception of criminality—a change which Fletcher identifies in terms of a move between two different conceptions of what justifies the ascription of criminal responsibility: a move from the manifest to the subjective patterns of liability discussed in Chapter 1 above.

As we noted in Chapter 2, when we look at eighteenth century analyses of crime, such as that in Blackstone's *Commentaries*,[34] we find that, as compared with modern treatments, relatively little time is spent on the conceptual framework. Blackstone instead elaborated the idea of larceny by means of lots of exemplary hypothetical cases, which illustrate difficult issues. Procedural, substantive, and penal issues are moreover interwoven in his account. The last point is particularly significant, because in Blackstone's time, larceny was divided into grand and petit larceny—theft of goods worth above a shilling and up to a shilling: the former was a capital offence, the latter attracted benefit of clergy. Because the essence of larceny was a taking, the consent of the owner had to be wanting: and because it had to be a taking from possession, someone legally in possession could not be a thief. Hence anyone in lawful possession of property was immune from prosecution for theft. This meant that uncertainties in the civil law of property—especially the law of possession, and in particular the line between possession and mere use or custody—were of central importance in the law of larceny. For example, was a domestic servant in legal possession of cutlery or linen, or did she only have 'care and oversight'? If the latter, she could be guilty of larceny if she took the goods away; if the former, she could not—it was merely a private or civil matter for the property owner to resolve on the basis of his or her own social

[34] William Blackstone, *Commentaries on the Laws of England* Vol. IV (1769: Chicago: University of Chicago Press 1979).

authority. Further difficult doctrinal issues had to do with what constituted a carrying away. Blackstone cites the case of a guest stealing goods from an inn, and being caught on his way out; this was thought to be a sufficient taking away.

Of particular interest for my concerns in this book is the summary way in which Blackstone deals with *animus furandi*. He simply observes that, apart from its role in 'excusing those who labour under incapacities of mind or will', it 'indemnifies also mere trespassers and other petty offenders', and he goes on to cite examples of temporary deprivation, clarifying that the paradigm example of *animus furandi* is that of the person found taking 'clandestinely' (though he goes on to say, not entirely helpfully, that 'this is by no means the only criterion of criminality: for in cases that may amount to larceny the variety of circumstances is so great, and the complications thereof so mingled, that it is impossible to recount all those, which may evidence a felonious intent, or *animum furandi*; wherefore they must be left to the due and attentive consideration of the court and jury').[35] I therefore want to linger on the role of *animus furandi* in grounding Fletcher's argument that the early common law's conception of larceny was based on a very different pattern of criminality from the modern law of theft. And—of key importance to this book's argument about the historical contingency of conceptions of responsibility—we need to understand something about how the common law constructed different forms of violation of proprietary interest—what we would today call *actus reus*—in order to grasp the very different role which *animus furandi* played in the constitution of criminal liability, as compared with states of *mens rea* today, such as an intention permanently to deprive.

Blackstone was writing on the cusp of the era of modernization, after several of the most significant steps towards the development of a capitalist economy had taken place. The nature of these social and economic changes is well exemplified by Fletcher's analysis of the emergence of a number of 'points of stress' in the early law of larceny. As he points out, the basic idea of theft as a felonious taking from possession meant that there were a number of problematic cases that did not fall within the conception. The examples he points out are those of the person who comes into possession with

[35] Ibid. p. 232.

a felonious purpose unknown to the owner; the person who finds goods which he later appropriates; the person to whom goods are mistakenly delivered, and who then appropriates them; and the person to whom goods are delivered by a third party and who appropriates them rather than passing them on to the owner. Each of these cases poses a problem for common law larceny because each encounters the barrier of possessorial immunity: in each case the putative thief has got possession, and hence cannot become a thief by his or her later appropriation.

These problems are exemplified by the *Carrier's Case*, decided by the Star Chamber in 1473. A foreign merchant had entrusted some bales of dyeing weed to a carrier. During the transport, the carrier broke open the bales and appropriated some of the contents. The contents came into the hands of the sheriff of London, who, when sued by the original owner, claimed that they were forfeit to the King as products of a felony, and that they were therefore lawfully in his possession. The problem was that as the carrier was in possession of the goods, it could be argued that he had not committed the felony of larceny because there was no trespassory taking. Lord Chokke, whose argument prevailed, argued that the carrier's 'breaking bulk' constituted such a trespass, and that therefore there could be a felony. This idea of breaking bulk remained until the mid nineteenth century, when fraud and embezzlement encompassed such behaviour, as the major exception to the law of possessorial immunity, adding to the array of other techniques for avoiding its effect (such as by arguing that certain kinds of bailees did not get lawful possession in the first place).

What explains the decision? On the face of it, the rule about possessorial immunity may seem an obscure technicality, and the argument about breaking bulk a clever judicial fiction designed to get around it. But this explanation of the case begs the question of why the judges would have wanted to get round it from the late fifteenth century on. One tempting explanation is based on economic interests. Jerome Hall[36] has argued that the decision was driven by the imperatives of commerce and the desire, in particular, to protect foreign merchants: as international trade began to develop more quickly, it was important that foreign traders felt properly protected by local laws, otherwise they might be

[36] Jerome A. Hall, *Theft, Law and Society* (2nd ed., Indianapolis: Bobbs-Merrill 1952).

put off developing trade links. But, as Fletcher points out, this is not an entirely convincing argument, because the contrary decision on the point would have protected the merchant just as well. If there were no felony, there would be no reversion of the goods to the King under the laws on waif—goods found, but not claimed—therefore allowing their recovery by the merchant. So, in fact, the decision that it was a felony then necessitated the further innovation that the ordinary law of waif would not apply to goods of foreign merchants, to protect them and their incentives to engage in trade with English clients. But even if Hall's explanation were convincing, it begs a further question: what was the rationale for the original rule, and why did this apparently rather technical modification of it—along with the other ways the common law found around Fletcher's other problem cases—last for so long?

Fletcher's argument here is that the original form of larceny reflected an idea of manifest criminality, and that the subsequent modifications were designed (though with increasing dilution) to retain the law of larceny within that framework. What he means is that the essence of criminality is an act which is obviously or manifestly threatening or damaging to the community—it can be recognized as such by any observer. Hence the rather visual image of 'taking and carrying away'. Essentially, he diagnoses here a throwback to early conceptions of *furtum manifestum* from Roman law, in which manifest theft—catching a thief red-handed, as it were—entailed the immediate right of justified killing on the part of the discoverer. This contrasted sharply with non-manifest theft, which was treated basically as a civil matter pertaining to compensation. He suggests that the doctrine of possessorial immunity in common law was doing much the same thing: it was identifying the line between those relationships which were and were not properly within the ambit of the criminal courts. For example, if domestic servants had possession of the household chattels with which they worked, then they could not be prosecuted for theft from their employers. From the point of view of manifest criminality this made sense: domestic servants' appropriations were not larcenies unless they related to goods manifestly outside their normal sphere of work (marked by possession)—even after the Carrier's case—because these were ongoing relationships which could constitute a discrete framework of social control in relation to property. Commercial relationships between strangers, by contrast, were gradually moved into the public sphere and regulated by criminal as well as civil law.

What Fletcher identifies here is a particular conception of the nature of the private: the assumption is that criminal law should not intervene until there is an unequivocal manifestation of danger to the community. At this point, he also notes that the *animus furandi* does not operate, as in the case of modern *mens rea*, as evidence of a subjective state of mind which confirms the interpretation of an equivocally criminal act and underpins the need for social protection or the ascription of culpability. There is no dualistic, mind–body, *mens rea–actus reus* analysis here, but rather an integrated reading of an action, as one which could be recognized by any observer as a crime. Whereas in contemporary law, *mens rea*—such as an intention permanently to deprive under section 1 of the Theft Act 1968—is a substantive question, a separate question going to liability—in the earlier common law, the idea of *animus furandi* was simply part of the evidence from which manifest criminality could be inferred.

Fletcher then goes on to argue that in the nineteenth century we see the emergence of a competing—or perhaps complementary—pattern of liability, which he calls subjective liability. This he allies with Benthamite utilitarianism and Beccaria's classicist penology, in other words, the idea that the essence of criminality is the subjective intent of the offender to violate a legally established and socially recognized interest. In terms of penal ideology, this brings an emphasis on social protection and deterrence. In terms of substantive law, it engenders over time a focus on the conceptual distinction between *mens rea* and *actus reus*, an elaboration of excuses, and a movement towards inchoate offences such as attempt. In terms of the larger narrative of this book, the history of theft shows us that the shift of emphasis from manifest to subjective criminality was driven not only by the changing ideas about human selfhood discussed in Chapter 2, but also by the changing needs of an emerging mercantile and capitalist economy under conditions of urbanization and industrialization, in which the identification of manifest criminality, or bad character, became increasingly problematic. In the specific area of property law, the shift entailed the gradual blurring of the boundaries between the later offences of embezzlement and false pretences and the original conception of larceny—a blurring which finds its most extreme expression in the Theft Act 1968, but which was already evident in the Larceny Act 1916. Hence, theft today is defined not in terms of a taking from possession but in terms of *an appropriation of the rights of an owner*—something which could cover both dealing in an unauthorized way with what you have possession of and even getting something with the owner's consent (e.g. where you have lied to the owner to get it). So all three conceptions of property crime—larceny, embezzlement, and false pretences—are comprehended by the modern law of theft, implying a more comprehensive and flexible protection for property rights in a fully capitalist economy. Hence the conceptual as well as the material contours of criminalization have tracked the changing interests of a capitalist economy to a remarkable degree.

The Politicization of Law in the Late Twentieth Century: Expanded Criminalization; New Forms of Risk and Character-based Responsibility

A persistent theme in criminal law scholarship of the last twenty years has been the phenomenon of 'overcriminalization' The increasing scope of criminalization, I shall suggest, has been driven by political interests, and is productive of a new degree of pluralization in the range of practices of responsibility-attribution. A full analysis will be provided in Chapter 5; here, it will be sufficient to give some indication of the development which I have in mind, and of its main consequences for criminal responsibility. Note that one of the key implications of any increase in the scope of criminal law is a consequent increase in the discretionary power of police and prosecutorial authorities, notably through the practice of plea-bargaining. Hence, that form of professional power has significant implications for practices of responsibility-attribution.

The proposition that criminalization has increased in both scope and intensity in countries like the UK and the USA over the last twenty years is widely accepted. But how can we actually assess this purported growth in criminalization? Even in relation to formal criminalization—the law in the books—this is in fact more complicated than it seems. The most obvious approach is to look at legislation—the outcome of political power. And here, certainly, we see a hugely changed landscape over the last thirty years. Until the late 1970s, there persisted a lively debate, stretching back to the nineteenth century, about the difficulty of getting criminal law rationalized in codified statutory form, with the main block being regarded as a lack of parliamentary time for criminal law matters. But the world has changed. There have been thirty major pieces of criminal legislation over the twenty-one years since 1994.[37] Moreover, this leaves aside more specialist legislation incorporating significant criminal offences, for example: the Children Act 2004; the Education Act 2005; the Financial Services and Markets Act 2000; and—for a little light relief—the Fireworks Act 2003.

So criminalization now occupies a very prominent place on the parliamentary agenda. But this in itself cannot tell us all we need to know. These statutes are of different lengths, not all of their provisions enact criminal offences, and some of their provisions replace previously existing offences; moreover, criminal offences are tucked away in ostensibly non-criminal statutes and they are often created in the regulatory sphere by secondary legislation. So we need to try to work out how many criminal offences exist, and how this number has changed over time. This turns out to be harder than one might think, for a number of reasons—notably, the difficulty of agreeing upon criteria for what counts as a single offence (e.g., do aggravated forms of offence such as assaults motivated by racial hatred, count as separate offences?).[38] There have, however, been some credible estimates.

[37] Criminal Justice and Public Order Act 1994 (c.33); Crime (Sentences) Act 1997; Crime and Disorder Act 1998; Criminal Justice (Terrorism and Conspiracy) Act 1998 (c.40); Criminal Justice (International Co-operation) (Amendment) Act 1998 (c.27); Youth Justice and Criminal Evidence Act 1999; Criminal Justice and Court Services Act 2000 (c.43); Terrorism Act 2000; Regulation of Investigatory Powers Act 2000; Criminal Justice and Police Act 2001 (c.16); Anti-Terrorism Crime and Security Act 2001; Proceeds of Crime Act 2002; Criminal Justice Act 2003 (c.44); Sexual Offences Act 2003; Domestic Violence, Crime and Victims Act 2004; Prevention of Terrorism Act 2005; Terrorism Act 2006; Fraud Act 2006; Serious Crime Act 2007; Corporate Manslaughter and Corporate Homicide Act 2007; Counter-Terrorism Act 2008; Criminal Justice and Immigration Act 2008 (c.4); Crime and Security Act 2010; Police Reform and Social Responsibility Act 2011; Domestic Order, Crime and Victims Amendment Act 2012; Legal Aid, Sentencing and Punishment of Offenders Act 2012; Crime and Courts Act 2013; Anti-Social Behaviour, Crime and Policing Act 2014; Criminal Justice and Courts Act 2015; Serious Crime Act 2015.

[38] See Chapter 1 above; see also James Chalmers and Fiona Leverick, 'Tracking the Creation of Criminal Offences' 2013 *Crim LR* 543–60; James Chalmers and Fiona Leverick, 'Quantifying Criminalization' in R. A. Duff et al. (eds), *Criminalization: The Political Morality of the Criminal Law,* (Oxford: Oxford University Press 2015) Chapter 2; James Chalmers, '"Frenzied Law-Making": Over-Criminalisation by Numbers' [2014] 67 *Current Legal Problems* 483; Jeremy Horder, 'Bureaucratic "Criminal" Law: Too Much of a Bad Thing?', in R.A. Duff et al. (eds), *Criminalisation: The Political Morality of the Criminal Law* (Oxford: Oxford University Press 2014) Ch 4.

The Crown Prosecution Service currently publishes a list of over 300 criminal offences in what are usually seen as the 'core' areas of criminal law such as offences against the person, terrorism, illegal drugs, sexual offences, offences of dishonesty, offences against public order and public justice.[39] But this is the tip of the iceberg. In 1980, a Committee of the organization *Justice* reported that, upon conducting a search, they found over 7,200 offences.[40] David Ormerod has estimated that by March 2011 there were more than 10,000 offences excluding those created by by-laws.[41] And in a consultation paper in 2010,[42] the Law Commission estimated that in the thirteen years from 1997 more than 3,000 criminal offences had come on to the statute book. They also provided a longer-term analysis of the growth of criminal legislation, pointing out that the then current edition of Halsbury's Statutes of England and Wales:

has four volumes devoted to criminal laws that (however old they may be) are still currently in force. Volume 1 covers the offences created in the 637 years between 1351 and 1988, and is 1382 pages long. Volumes 2 to 4 cover the offences created in the 19 years between 1989 and 2008, and are 3746 pages long. So, more than 2 and a half times as many pages were needed to cover offences created in the 19 years between 1989 and 2008 than were needed to cover the offences created in the 637 years prior to that.[43]

Even this isn't the whole story: the Commission estimated that about 3,000 pieces of secondary legislation are passed each year, and many of these too create criminal offences. They give a striking example:

The Department for the Environment, Food and Rural Affairs (DEFRA) in 2008, introduced the Transmissible Spongiform Encephalopathies (No 2) (Amendment) Regulations 2008. These regulations created 103 criminal offences aimed at reducing the risk posed by the spread of bovine

[39] http://www.cps.gov.uk/publications/docs/annex_1b_table_of_offences_scheme_c_class_order.pdf (accessed 18 September 2015).

[40] JUSTICE, *Breaking the Rules* (London: JUSTICE 1980) p. 53.

[41] David Ormerod, *Smith and Hogan's Criminal Law* (13th ed., Oxford: Oxford University Press 2011).

[42] Law Commission of England and Wales, *Criminal Liability in Regulatory Contexts: A Consultation Paper,* No. 195 (London: The Stationery Office 2010).

[43] Ibid. p. 5.

spongiform encephalopathy. The Department for Business, Innovation and Skills (BIS) is likewise a Government department with major and widespread responsibilities. The department regularly plays a role in the creation of criminal offences relating to its core concerns. For instance, in 2008 it introduced 74 offences by way of regulation or order, or in schedules to pieces of primary legislation.[44]

So we can be fairly confident that 'formal criminalization'—the scope of criminal law on the statute book—has increased by a very substantial amount in recent times; and that this change has accelerated since at least 1990. But even this fails to give us the whole picture, because it does not tell us how many of these offences are enforced, or make little difference because they overlap with older offences. Nor does it tell us how many are ineffective because the courts lack the specialist knowledge to enforce them properly.[45] Moreover, it does not tell us how widely they are being interpreted. In other words, we still need to know about what we might call substantive criminalization, or the law in action.[46]

Of course, we know the total numbers prosecuted over this time—and we know that this has not risen in any proportion to the increased scope of criminal law. But the global figure of numbers prosecuted and convicted do not really give us an adequate grasp of the significance of these legal changes, and of the huge discretionary power which they have put into the hands of not only police and prosecutors, but a range of enforcement agencies such as local authorities, housing associations, regulatory agencies, and so on. Evidently, this raises important questions about consequent changes in the quality of criminalization generally and about the implications for practices of responsibility-attribution in particular. Here I want to draw attention to several significant features of recent criminalization.

First, there has been a tendency to push the boundaries of criminalization back in time—pre-inchoate or preventive offences such as preparation in the terrorism legislation, based on an approach to responsibility-attribution founded in a combination of risk and character. A good example of this would be the offence of preparation of terrorist acts under section 5 of the Terrorism Act 2006:

[44] Ibid. p. 6.

[45] Ibid. Appendix A (Julia Black, 'A Review of Enforcement Techniques').

[46] See further, Nicola Lacey, 'Historicising Criminalisation: Conceptual and Empirical Issues' 72 *Modern Law Review* (2009) 936–61 and Chapter 1 above, p.15 ff.

(1) A person commits an offence if, with the intention of—
    (a) committing acts of terrorism, or
    (b) assisting another to commit such acts,

    he engages in any conduct in preparation for giving effect to his intention.

(2) It is irrelevant for the purposes of subsection (1) whether the intention and preparations relate to one or more particular acts of terrorism, acts of terrorism of a particular description or acts of terrorism generally.

(3) A person guilty of an offence under this section shall be liable, on conviction on indictment, to imprisonment for life.

A second significant development has been towards creating hybrid forms of criminalization: civil orders like the Anti-Social Behaviour Order (ASBO) which then have criminal sanctions attached to them. And a third, closely related, trend has been to engage in de facto criminalization beyond the formal criminal law in areas such as immigration detention.[47] Arguably, this amounts to an extension of status or group-membership based criminalization which in areas like terrorism looks more and more like a revival of the idea of criminalizing people for manifestations of bad character, with scant attention paid to proof of engaged capacity, but with a notable emphasis on the risk of harmful outcomes. In other words, we are seeing a realignment of risk and character-based patterns of criminal responsibility attribution.

Take, for example, civil preventive hybrid orders aimed at preventing risk or at preventing harm (ASBO's and their successors, discussed in Chapter 5 below; travel restriction orders, football spectator banning orders, drinking banning orders, risk of sexual harm or violent crime orders); civil preventive orders such as anti-social behaviour injunctions; pre-trial orders such as remands in custody; licence conditions on release from a sentence of imprisonment; or criminal court orders aimed at preventing harm or risk of harm, such as disqualification from driving or from being a company director. A criminal conviction resulting from the breach of any of these orders is a form of criminalization, which applies specifically to a group identified in terms of its subjection to the relevant order. In each case, what we see is the extension of patterns of responsibility-attribution based on newly institutionalized forms of bad character, combining with an

[47] See Andrew Ashworth and Lucia Zedner, *Preventive Justice*, for a comprehensive discussion of these developments, and, in particular, a discussion of their application in the immigration context: pp. 224–49.

accentuated focus on harmful outcomes and/or risk.[48] These features of criminal law are genuinely new in their scope and scale, and it is incontrovertible that they have changed the balance of power both as between state and prosecuting authorities and ordinary citizens; and, potentially, between different groups and kinds of citizens, entailing a redistribution as well as a curtailment of power.

The Anti-Social Behaviour, Crime and Policing Act 2014 is a good example of many of these themes. This piece of legislation covers 246 pages and boasts 186 sections and 11 Schedules, the first 122 of which are centrally in the area of criminal law, including provisions on, for example, dangerous dogs, firearms, and forced marriage. But the really striking feature of the Act is that it also significantly pushes outwards the terrain of hybrid and de facto criminalization, with not only the reworking of the ASBO but also the creation of a panoply of new preventive orders backed up by sanctions on breach. These include criminal behaviour orders, remedial orders, fixed penalty notices, public spaces protection orders, consumption of alcohol in breach of prohibition in orders, orders restricting the public right of way over the highway, sexual harm prevention orders and sexual risk orders, violent offender orders, forced marriage protection orders, and community protection notices. All of these, it should be noted, speak to the perceived interests of the decisive median voter—and, of course, of the politicians who depend on their support for election.

Apart from the criminal/civil law hybridity of these provisions, we should also note their distinctive remedies. For example, remedial orders and fixed penalty notices, confiscation of property and repossession of dwelling houses, or exclusion from a dwelling seem likely to raise difficulties of enforcement, as well giving rise to serious social effects, for example on homelessness. These remedies are, in addition, in the hands of a distinctive range of enforcement bodies: both local authorities and bodies other than local authorities with statutory functions in relation to land. Hence, they extend discretionary power well beyond criminal justice agencies, in a decentralizing move which is remarkably reminiscent of some of the features of the *ancien régime* system which was swept away in the late eighteenth century. Also relevant here is the legislation's attempt to stimulate 'active citizenship' by providing in s 101 for the creation by the police/local authority of a 'community remedy document', entailing the involvement of 'community representatives'

[48] See further below, Chapter 5.

in consultation, defined in s 101 (9) as basically whoever the police think represent the community. If not quite amounting to the reinvention of eighteenth century prosecution associations, there is nonetheless a distinct decentralizing 'Big Society' or 'localism' theme here (also reflected in the prominent role envisaged in the enforcement picture for 'community support officers'). Giving more power to localities appears democratic. But the fact is that the turnout in local elections tends to be low, and is likely to be demographically biased towards the more privileged. That may help to explain why evidence from US, which has far more local control of criminal justice than as yet prevails in England and Wales, shows that these sorts of locally specific regulations are used disproportionately against the poor, while the powers which they give are used disproportionately by the privileged. Moreover, their structure—moving people on, excluding them from certain areas, and so on—contributes to special segregation, concentrations of poverty and violence, and social exclusion.[49] Hence these developments speak powerfully to the accretion of both political and economic inequality, with further implications for the development of the practice of responsibility-attribution.

If we accept that these have been significant changes, how does the distribution of political interests explain their genesis? We have to accept that our politicians believe that this increasing strategy of 'governing through crime' is both sensible and electorally attractive. But what broader or deeper factors might be at play? As I shall argue in greater detail in Chapter 5, the following interpretations merit consideration. First, we have to consider, as Garland has argued,[50] government's sense of the pressure on it to represent itself as effective in response to social problems in a world in which economic management has become harder to do nationally: criminalization is symbolically decisive and does not require the creation of new institutional infrastructure. Second, we might argue, as Peter Ramsay

[49] Nicola Lacey and David Soskice, 'Why are the Truly Disadvantaged American, when the UK is Bad Enough? A Political Economy Analysis of Local Autonomy in Criminal Justice, Education, Residential Zoning' (2013) *Law Society Economy Working Papers* no. 11, http://ssrn.com/abstract=2264749> and 'Crime, Punishment and Segregation in the United States: The Paradox of Local Democracy', (2015) *Punishment and Society* Vol. 17(4) 454–481.

[50] David Garland, 'The Limits of the Sovereign State: Strategies of Crime Control in Contemporary Society' 36 *British Journal of Criminology* (1996) 445–71; and *The Culture of Control* (Oxford: Oxford University Press 2001).

has done,[51] that the New Labour ideology which contributed decisively to the acceleration of formal criminalization was premised on the need to address, politically, citizens' vulnerability as an index of their freedom—what Ramsay calls their 'vulnerable autonomy'—and to do so by framing criminal laws in such a way as to encompass not only harmful conduct but, more broadly, conduct which fails adequately to reassure fellow citizens in a world in which fear of crime and a more general sense of insecurity is widespread.

Third, and not necessarily inconsistent with Ramsay's explanation, but with a somewhat different emphasis, we might focus on links between these developments and their implications for what I have called the redistribution of power, and growing inequality. In other words, we might explain both the scope of insecurity and the popularity, particularly among key swing voters, of policies such as the ASBO, draconian terrorism legislation, curtailment of migrants' rights and their de facto criminalization, as a reaction to growing social and economic inequality. Particularly in relation to certain stigmatized groups—migrants and young black socially disadvantaged men are key examples in a number of societies—this inequality is eroding the degree to which we all see ourselves as sharing a common fate. It increases a kind of individualism in which people focus on protecting, as it were, their own patch and, as we might say, worry more about their own security than about the implications of criminal legislation for the freedom, rights, or security of troublesome others. In other words, increasing criminalization—and the increasing temptation to think of criminal responsibility as founded in some combination of bad character and risk—might be a symptom, as well as a cause, of growing social polarization in a world in which a significant minority of people are being defined as outsiders to the scope of full civil rights and freedoms. To the extent that such an argument is convincing—a matter to which we will return in Chapter 5—the implication is that patterns of criminal responsibility attribution are rooted in the deep political and social power dynamics which shape prevailing interests. Any effort to intervene in these dynamics, and hence with the mechanisms of criminal responsibility-attribution, will need to be tackled in relation to social and economic policy, and not simply criminal justice policy.

[51] Peter Ramsay, *The Insecurity State*. Note that Ramsay argues this political logic to be self-defeating; the very strategies aimed at protecting vulnerable autonomy tending in fact to create further insecurity, not least by undermining the civic trust which makes civil society possible.

4

Institutions

In the previous chapter, I reviewed the categories of power and interest which might be thought to shape the development of patterns of responsibility-attribution in criminal law, and provided some case studies to illustrate the ways in which criminal responsibility has been shaped by power. But, as those case studies make abundantly clear, vectors of power and interest do not exist in the abstract but rather work through institutional frameworks. The institutional structures available for the realization of the legitimation and coordination roles of criminal responsibility have changed over time and, hence, have differently conditioned the ways in which those roles can proceed, both constraining and providing opportunities.

A vast range of institutions has been directly or indirectly involved in the development of criminal responsibility. Many of these, of course, have to do with the **criminal justice system.** During the period under consideration, the **pretrial process** shifted from a system dominated by lay voices in the form of grand juries and justices, sometimes operating from their own homes, to a system dominated by lawyers and police officers operating in police stations and magistrates' courts. **The trial** shifted from trial by altercation—an institutional structure that, despite this description, involved an active role for the judge reminiscent of the inquisitorial system on the continent of Europe—to trial by lawyers, in which jury and judge became passive decision-makers rather than active participants and defendants were increasingly silenced,[1] while the expansion of the summary jurisdiction entailed a significant increase in

[1] John H. Langbein, *The Origins of Adversary Criminal Trial* (Oxford: Oxford University Press 2003).

the capacity of the criminal courts to process cases.[2] As the twentieth century passed, the rapid growth of **plea bargaining** ushered in a significant (if not always acknowledged) change in criminal procedure, implying as it did a decisive growth in prosecutorial power and a more bureaucratized system, legitimized by the defendant's consent, yet facilitating the influence of covert assessments of character.

These obvious changes in the criminal justice system are themselves related, however, to a much more general shift in the nature of professions, and of professional bureaucracies, from the late eighteenth century through to the mid-twentieth century. One of the most consequential institutions for substantive criminalization—**the police**—was invented as a professional bureaucracy in the late eighteenth and early nineteenth centuries. The police shifted from village constables to a professional force whose relationship to political power itself changes over time. While **the legal profession** was, of course, of long standing, its structure, too, changed materially, particularly in the twentieth century. Legal training shifted from an oral tradition and social gatekeeping to formal gatekeeping through an increasingly organized and increasingly regulated set of professional structures. As mentioned in our review of **professional power structures** in the previous chapter, whole entirely new professions were invented on the back of new knowledges and new disciplinary and governmental ambitions. Notable examples include criminologists, psychologists, psychiatrists, statisticians, social workers, and their specialist cousins, probation officers, psychotherapists, youth justice professionals and, more recently, restorative justice coordinators. The structure and influence of this **professional bureaucracy,** not only criminal justice professionals but also welfare professionals and a range of civil servants whose advice is part of the policy process, have decisively shaped the trajectory of ideas of criminal responsibility. These developments in professional bureaucracies have had implications, moreover, for the structure of lay participation in the criminal process. Juries have gradually been squeezed out of the vast majority of criminal trials by institutional pressures conducing to high levels of plea bargaining. Lay magistrates, while still key to the disposition of the vast majority of criminal cases, are embedded within an institutional structure much more firmly geared to the

[2] Lindsay Farmer, *Criminal Law, Tradition and Legal Order: Crime and the Genius of Scots Law, 1747 to the Present* (Cambridge: Cambridge University Press 1997).

application of formal legal norms than was that of their eighteenth- or early nineteenth-century predecessors.

Each of the professions, with its distinctive institutional framework, were products of the changing needs and capacities of **the overarching political system**. The developing institutional form of the political system—the structure and power of the legislature, its relationship with the executive and the judiciary, the scope of the franchise, and the mechanisms for registering votes and allowing votes to shape the development of the law—changed fundamentally over the course of the nineteenth and early twentieth centuries. To paint with broad brushstrokes, even at the beginning of the nineteenth century, a highly decentralized system prevailed. Indeed it scarcely made sense to think in terms of 'a' criminal justice system, so great was the measure of decentralized governance, in criminal justice and beyond, with significant power residing in the hands of local landowners. This system gradually gave way, through the nineteenth century, to a centralized state apparatus, with the criminal justice system as one of its core tools of governance. This, as we saw in the first case study of the previous chapter, was particularly evident in the rapid expansion of summary jurisdiction at mid-century, as the tools of criminal responsibility-attribution based on harmful outcomes were marshalled in the service of producing stability and order in the teeming urban environments which were so crucial to the success of industrial capitalism. This centralizing project, realized through legislation, was based on a mix of outcome- and capacity-based responsibility-attribution geared to the production of social order, with character-based attribution zoned into particular 'exceptional' areas, generally outside the core of criminal law doctrine. Something like this balance persisted through the period of penal welfarism, as the democratic governmental project was rolled out across ever greater portions of the population (albeit, as we shall see in the next chapter, with various fluctuations. But it was decisively disrupted by the huge economic and social restructuring of the 1970s, generating a recalibration of political and, most recently, legal institutions through developments such as the growth of plea bargaining and, most recently, decisive reductions in funding for legal aid, the effects of which are still being felt. In the wake of this restructuring, patterns of responsibility-attribution are undergoing a realignment. The balance between capacity and outcome patterns, which had gradually displaced character responsibility during the late eighteenth and nineteenth centuries, persisted throughout much of the twentieth century. But it is now being complicated by the revival of a newly configured practice of character responsibility, often combined with a focus on risk.

CASE STUDIES

The Institutional Logic of Character Responsibility in the Mid-Eighteenth Century Criminal Process

Notwithstanding contemporary criminal law scholars' justified respect for the great treatise writers of the seventeenth and eighteenth centuries, the fact is that criminal law formalized and professionalized in England significantly later and less completely than did much of the civil law. In particular, the structure of the felony trial and of the criminal process meant both that comprehensive criminal law doctrines were slower to develop and had less complete reach over actual practice in the courts; and that representation by legal professionals was not a regular feature of the trial process.[3] Other than in exceptional cases such as treason, the relatively few misdemeanour cases tried at Westminster, and very serious cases such as homicide, the criminal trial up to the early nineteenth century was a lay-dominated rather than a lawyer-dominated affair,[4] and one trained for the most part on facts rather than on law.[5] Until 1836,

[3] Though cf. the argument put forward by Cathrine O. Franks in relation to the law of succession: *Law, Literature and the Transmission of Culture in England, 1837–1925* (Farnham: Ashgate 2010).

[4] Of course the persistence and empirical dominance of magistrates' courts today demonstrates that this tradition of lay justice remains central to the operation of English criminal law. However, from the early nineteenth century, lay decision-making began to be more structured, through the mechanisms of treatises, manuals for magistrates' guidance, and, finally, the appointment of legally qualified clerks.

[5] See Nicola Lacey, 'In Search of the Responsible Subject: History, Philosophy and Criminal Law Theory' 64 *Modern Law Review* (2001) 350–71, 'Responsibility and Modernity in Criminal Law' 9 *Journal of Political Philosophy* (2001) 249–77, 'Character, Capacity, Outcome: Towards a Framework for Assessing the Shifting Pattern of Criminal Responsibility in Modern English Law', in Markus D. Dubber and Lindsay Farmer (eds), *Modern Histories of Crime and Punishment* (Stanford: Stanford University Press 2007), and *Women, Crime and Character: From Moll Flanders to Tess of the d'Urbervilles* (Oxford: Oxford University Press 2008); cf. Arlie Loughnan's analogous argument about the insanity defence: 'Manifest Madness: Towards a New Understanding of the Insanity Defence' 70 *Modern Law Review* (2007) 379–401, and *Manifest Madness: Mental Incapacity in the Criminal Law* (Oxford: Oxford University Press 2012).

felony defendants had no right to be fully represented by counsel, and while no such bar affected those charged with misdemeanours, by no means all of them would have had the resources to pay a lawyer.[6] Although of distinctive social and legal importance, the misdemeanour cases initiated on the Crown side of King's Bench at Westminster seem likely to have constituted a tiny fraction of the overall number of criminal cases.[7] The vast majority of criminal trials were heard in localities, and of these the large majority were heard not by judges at the Assizes but by magistrates whose grasp of (indeed whose access to) legal authorities was patchy. As Peter King has emphasized, this implied a highly decentralized system, featuring much local variation and an approach geared to pragmatic dispute resolution rather than formal rules.[8]

In this context, it would scarcely be an exaggeration to say that, even in late eighteenth-century England, criminal law was not fully

[6] Thomas P. Gallanis, 'Making Sense of Blackstone's Puzzle: Why Forbid Defense Counsel?' 53 *Studies in Law, Politics, and Society* (2010) 35–57.

[7] Douglas Hay (ed.), *Criminal Cases on the Crown Side of King's Bench: Staffordshire, 1740–1800* (Staffordshire Record Society 2010). In the Staffordshire cases from 1740 to 1800 analysed by Hay, only 2 per cent of all cases at Quarter Sessions, Assizes, and King's Bench fell into this category (p. 2). Given that misdemeanour cases have so far been the object of much less historical investigation than felony cases, my claim that they made up a 'tiny fraction' in general is a tentative one. (Henry Mares' ongoing research on misdemeanours in the late sixteenth to the late seventeenth century, for example, suggests that they may have been considerably more common than in Hay's Staffordshire sample. Mares concludes, persuasively, that 'a focus on felonies on the Crown side at Assizes has served to distract us from the interest that these cases have'. Mares, 'Criminal Informations of the Attorneys-General in the King's Bench from Egerton to North', in Matthew Dyson and David Ibbetson (eds), *Law and Legal Process: Substantive Law and Procedure in English Legal History* (Cambridge: Cambridge University Press 2013).) Whatever their number, the distinctive importance of these cases came from the subject matter of misdemeanours, which encompassed an array of offences stretching from poaching and attempted rape to the political offences of riot and seditions libel (Hay, *Criminal Cases: Staffordshire* p.10). The more serious of these cases typically involved representation by leading barristers, significant expense, relatively high status defendants, and, therefore, substantial interest in the press and in county society (ibid. pp. 9, 17–18). Yet although a far higher proportion of these cases than of Assize or Quarter Sessions cases involved points of law requiring technically sophisticated professional analysis, only four of Hay's group of 129 cases featured points of law of sufficient importance to be reported in the law reports (ibid. p. 21). These distinctive features of misdemeanour cases render them a fascinating object of study in their own right, but perhaps justify the primary focus in recent historiography, as in this book, on the history of felony cases, very few of which were tried at King's Bench (ibid. p. 10). See also Allyson N. May, *The Bar and the Old Bailey, 1750–1850* (Chapel Hill: University of North Carolina Press 2006) p. 130.

[8] Peter King, *Crime, Justice and Discretion, 1740–1820* (Oxford: Oxford University Press 2000); and *Crime and Law in England 1750–1840: Remaking Justice from the Margins* (Cambridge: Cambridge University Press 2006) Chapter 1.

legalized. In other words, findings of criminal liability turned on moral, conventional, and pragmatic considerations as much as on legal standards. The institutional conditions favourable to a gradual development, refinement, *and* systematic application of general doctrines—legal representation, rules of evidence, systematic reporting of criminal cases, legal education and, finally, at the end of the nineteenth century, a system of appeals—were gradually constructed over a period of almost 200 years. Legal education, based in the Inns of Court, of course has a long history, but for the purposes of the argument of this chapter, it is crucial to note that its origins lay in teaching not so much legal doctrine as the application of rhetorical skills to cases and statutes.[9] A regular appellate system was not implemented until 1908, although alternative mechanisms for testing and challenging decisions did exist, notably by writ of certiorari to the King's Bench.[10] As late as 1840, there was still no authoritative written statement of the rules of the court of King's Bench—a situation which must have accorded the Court Clerks, with their 'monopoly of practical knowledge', huge power.[11] As for law reporting, the accuracy of reports was notoriously unreliable, and the coverage of cases uneven, until the establishment of the Council of Law Reporting in 1865—another instance of professionalization.[12]

Most contemporary criminal law scholarship proceeds on the assumption that capacity responsibility has dominated practices of responsibility-attribution throughout the modern period. But, in fact, a number of institutional features of the English criminal process up to the late eighteenth century lent themselves to the attribution of responsibility on the basis of an assumption of bad character rather than a finding of criminal conduct accompanied by the engagement of capacity in the relevant sense. First we must consider *the decentralized criminal process and the selection of cases for trial.* Even in the late eighteenth century, the governmental insfrastructure of England and Wales was highly decentralized. As one scholar puts it, England was 'not so much a state as a federation of semi-autonomous units'.[13]

[9] See Paul Raffield, 'The Elizabethan Rhetoric of Signs: Representations of *Res Publica* at the Early Modern Inns of Court' 7 *Law, Culture and the Humanities* (2010) 244–63, at 248. On early legal education at the Inns of Court, see also A. W. B. Simpson, 'The Circulation of Yearbooks in the Fifteenth Century' 73 *Law Quarterly Review* (1957) 492–505.

[10] Hay (ed.), *Criminal Cases on the Crown Side of King's Bench: Staffordshire, 1740-1780* p. 8.

[11] Ibid. pp. 28–9.

[12] C. K. Allen, *Law in the Making* (Oxford: Clarendon Press 1964) pp. 220ff.

[13] David Philips, 'A New Engine of Power and Authority: The Institutionalization of Law Enforcement in England, 1780–1830', in V. A. C. Gatrell, Bruce Lenman, and

This decentralization had a number of important implications for the operation of the criminal process. For example, though precise estimates are difficult to make, detailed research suggests strongly that the proportion of crimes actually brought to trial was smaller than it is today. This was a system in which prosecutions had to be initiated by the victim and financial support from either the state or private prosecution associations was patchy; in which much depended on the local discretion of parish constables and Justices of the Peace; in which there was an elaborate system of compensatory payments and settlements; and in which indictments were filtered by hearings before Grand Juries before coming to trial. From such facts it can be inferred that a large proportion of 'crimes' were being managed by informal local processes of social control.[14] The relative lack of geographical mobility and the consequent degree of social interdependence at the local level, in the context of the relatively high degree of consensus underpinning the content of the most regularly enforced property crimes[15] (if not the penalties which attached to them) would have been conducive to a highly selective process geared to the formal criminalization of those who lacked the recognized marks of good character.

Another important factor to be taken into consideration in assessing how practices of responsibility-attribution worked was *the nature of the evidence received in court*. Research on Assize records and other eighteenth century papers such as Judges' notes[16] shows that evidence of character

Geoffrey Parker (eds), *Crime and the Law: The Social History of Crime in Western Europe since 1500* (London: Europa 1980) p. 156, at p. 159.

[14] J. M. Beattie, *Crime and the Courts in England, 1660–1800* (Princeton, Princeton University Press, 1986) Part I (see on character especially pp. 8–10), and 'Scales of Justice: Defence Counsel and the English Criminal Trial in the Eighteenth and Nineteenth Centuries' 9 *Law and History Review* (1991) 221–67.

[15] See Beattie, *Crime and the Courts in England, 1660–1800* and Beattie, 'Scales of Justice'; Peter King, 'Decisions and Decision-Makers in English Criminal Law, 1750–1800' 27 *Historical Journal* (1984) 25–58; Peter King, 'Illiterate Plebeians, Easily Misled: Jury Composition, Experience and Behaviour in Essex, 1735–1815' and Thomas A. Green, 'A Retrospective on the Criminal Trial Jury, 1200–1800', both in J. S. Cockburn and T. A. Green (eds), *Twelve Good Men and True: The Criminal Trial Jury in England, 1200–1800* (Princeton: Princeton University Press 1988).

[16] John H. Langbein, in 'Shaping the Eighteenth Century Criminal Trial: A View from the Ryder Sources' 50 *University of Chicago Law Review* (1983) 1–136, argues that the Ryder sources show that few trials were contested and operated in effect on the basis of a presumption of guilt; pretrial confessions gradually became the dominant mode of proof, with witness testimony as to the confession displacing depositions as the basis for the trial (pp. 82ff.).

was an overwhelmingly important feature of trials on indictment. In the absence of an elaborated law of evidence (which emerges gradually from the second half of the eighteenth century but which is not fully established until the late nineteenth century),[17] the jury's knowledge, not only about previous convictions but also more generally about the defendant's social reputation, was central to trial decision-making.[18] Furthermore, since it has been established that the criminal trial on indictment at this time lasted an average of thirty minutes,[19] it can safely be assumed that the facts as set out in the depositions collected by magistrates were generally accepted by the court. In this context, it seems likely that the defendant's testimony was generally brief, its reception itself shaped by the jury's view of his or her character.

Also important to understanding how practices of responsibility-attribution were shaped by institutions in the eighteenth century was *the nature of the (petty) jury and its relationship with the judge, along with the relatively infrequent appearance of lawyers* on behalf of prosecution and (particularly) defence. Relative to criminal trials today, the jury was a less passive member of the tribunal. It was able to ask questions and offer information and, particularly towards the end of the eighteenth century, was often composed of experienced jurors.[20] The judge played an inquisitorial role, questioning the parties, and the process was relatively unprofessionalized. These features would have

[17] See John. H. Langbein, 'Historical Foundations of the Law of Evidence' 96 *Columbia Law Review* (1996) 1168–90.

[18] Peter King, 'Illiterate Plebeians, Easily Misled: Jury Composition, Experience and Behaviour in Essex, 1735–1815' and Thomas A. Green, 'A Retrospective on the Criminal Trial Jury, 1200–1800'; see also Douglas Hay, 'The Class Composition of the Palladium of Liberty: Trial Jurors in the Eighteenth Century', in J. S. Cockburn and T. A. Green (eds), *Twelve Good Men and True: The Criminal Trial Jury in England, 1200–1800* (Princeton: Princeton University Press 1988).

[19] Beattie, 'Scales of Justice'; cf. Langbein, 'Shaping the Eighteenth Century Criminal Trial' p. 115 (the Ryder sources refer to 16 trials conducted over three days); see also Langbein's 'The Criminal Trial before the Lawyers' 45 *University of Chicago Law Review* (1978) 263–316 and Peter King, 'Punishing Assault: The Transformation of Attitudes in the English Courts' 27 *Journal of Interdisciplinary History* (1996) 43–74, at 50–1; King also notes the low level of not guilty verdicts and the emphasis on informal settlement in the late eighteenth century.

[20] See Peter King, 'Illiterate Plebeians, Easily Misled' pp. 285ff.; Douglas Hay, 'The Class Composition of the Palladium of Liberty' pp. 344–5; Thomas A. Green, 'A Retrospective on the Criminal Trial Jury, 1200–1800' p. 392. Both the degree of experience and the social class of jurors varied between the different kinds of jury, with the Assize Grand Jury at the top of the hierarchy and the Quarter Sessions Petty Jury at the bottom.

facilitated the application of broad community standards of responsibility and guilt[21] and made the detailed elaboration of legal criteria of liability unnecessary for the practical conduct of the trial process. Such criteria would in any event have been difficult to handle given low levels of professional legal representation.[22]

Finally, a review of the institutional factors underpinning character responsibility attribution in the eighteenth century would not be complete without mention of *the structure of the penal process*. Even at the end of the eighteenth century, the death penalty applied to a vast range of offences, including, most significantly, larceny. The implementation of transportation at mid-century had somewhat expanded the range of penalties. But in a large proportion of criminal trials, the main question at issue was simply whether or not the draconian penalty of death was to be applied to the defendant, or whether they were to be spared this fate by the exercise of the jury's 'pious perjury' that the larceny was of a low value and hence susceptible of benefit of clergy (thereby escaping liability to the capital sentence), or by its recommendation of mercy, which might or might not be taken up by the judge and the executive.[23]

[21] On the influence of local knowledge (and hence the existence of local variation), see Bruce Lenman and Geoffrey Parker, 'The State, The Community and Criminal Law in Early Modern Europe', in V. A. C. Gatrell, Bruce Lenman, and Geoffrey Parker (eds), *Crime and the Law: The Social History of Crime in Western Europe since 1500* (London: Europa 1980) at pp. 22, 26.

[22] On the trial process, see David J. A. Cairns, *Advocacy and the Making of the Adversarial Criminal Trial, 1800–1865* (Oxford: Clarendon Press 1998), which argues that the conditions for a fully adversarial trial were not fully in place until the enactment of the Prisoners Counsel Act 1836; and Beattie, 'Scales of Justice' pp. 223ff., which notes the earlier introduction, in the Treason Act 1696, of a right to counsel for defendants in treason trials. This development appears to be attributable not simply to the class status and social influence of the typical treason defendant but rather to a perceived injustice given the legal complexity of treason trials—an explanation which resonates with the argument about professionalization set out in Case Study 2 below: see Langbein, 'The Criminal Trial before the Lawyers' p. 310 and *The Origins of Adversary Criminal Trial*. Langbein traces the growing role of defence counsel from their early eighteenth-century restriction to arguing points of law through to the early nineteenth-century right of cross-examination and, finally, in 1836, the right to address the jury. It is interesting to note that legal representation came earlier in civil than in criminal law, suggesting that the process of individualization, modernization, and professionalization infused that field more quickly than the criminal law, which was able to rely on community resources of legitimation for a longer period. See also Martin J. Wiener, 'Judges and Jurors: Courtroom Tensions in Murder Trials and the Law of Criminal Responsibility in Nineteenth Century England' 17 *Law and History Review* (1999) 467–506.

[23] See J. M. Beattie, 'Scales of Justice' pp. 231–2; Peter King, 'Decision-Makers and Decision-Making in the English Criminal Law, 1750–1800' pp. 43ff., which argues that the pardoning process was influenced above all by evidence of previous good character. The phrase 'pious perjury' is drawn from William Blackstone, *Commentaries on the Laws of England* Vol. IV (1765–9: Chicago and London: University of Chicago Press 1979).

In effect, therefore, the typical mid-eighteenth-century[24] trial was a relatively cursory investigation of the facts reflected in the depositions collected by magistrates, and a decision about whether these facts, afforced by evidence of the defendant's character and reputation supplied by the jury and inferred from the defendant's closing speech to the jury, justified severe punishment.[25] This was a trial process which neither needed, nor had the conceptual or institutional resources to investigate, individual responsibility in the early twenty-first-century sense of *mens rea*. Unless the defendant was manifestly insane,[26] or under-age (a condition set at a lower threshold than today[27]), or a limited number of exculpating factors in relation to homicide, such as provocation or self-defence, were at issue (factors which themselves resonated with prevailing understandings of honour and good character[28]), it was assumed that the conditions of liability were met.

As Langbein[29] has argued, the trial was at this stage essentially a chance for the defendant to explain himself or herself: the process was based not on a presumption of innocence, but rather on the assumption that the defendant was guilty. The questions of moral grading in criminal justice had to do with the decision to prosecute and the penalty to be applied. Here—in line with George Fletcher's assertion of a conception of 'manifest criminality' in the early modern common

[24] It is interesting to speculate whether political trials, and particularly those involving defendants of relatively high social status, followed a similar logic. Though this question is beyond the scope of this chapter, it is worth noting that provision was made for legal representation of treason defendants in 1696, and hence over a century earlier than in felony trials.

[25] On the importance of character at this stage of the process, see J. M. Beattie, 'London Juries in the 1690s', in J. S. Cockburn and T. A. Green (eds), *Twelve Good Men and True: The Criminal Trial Jury in England, 1200–1800* (Princeton: Princeton University Press 1988), at p. 250.

[26] See Joel Peter Eigen, 'Lesion of the Will: Medical Resolve and Criminal Responsibility in Victorian Insanity Trials' 33 *Law and Society Review* (1999) 425–59. Eigen shows that up to the mid-eighteenth century, judgments of insanity were based on the lay evidence of friends and neighbours. Medical evidence does not begin to be received until 1760, and is not fully established until the creation of the special verdict in 1800. In the eighteenth century, therefore, insanity is seen as visible and manifest to the ordinary community. See also Roger Smith, *Trial by Medicine: Insanity and Responsibility in Victorian Trials* (Edinburgh: Edinburgh University Press 1981) Chapter 4. For further discussion, see Chapter 2 above, p. 64 ff.

[27] Leon Radzinowicz and Roger Hood, *The Emergence of Penal Policy in Victorian and Edwardian England* (Oxford: Clarendon Press 1990) Chapter 6: children only completely escaped criminal liability until the age of 7. From 7–13 they were assumed to be *doli incapax* unless malice was proven, and from the age of 14 they were treated as full adults.

[28] See Jeremy Horder, *Provocation and Responsibility* (Oxford: Clarendon Press 1982).

[29] Langbein, 'Shaping the Eighteenth Century Criminal Trial' p. 123.

law of crime[30]—the key question was the defendant's reputation as a member of the law-abiding community. Hence, at an interpretive level, it seems plausible to think that character responsibility in mid-eighteenth-century criminal law was playing a structural role rather similar to the role played by individual, capacity-based responsibility today. In other words, like ideas of responsibility, in the sense of fair opportunity to act otherwise and to understand the nature of one's acts, which had established itself by the early twentieth century, notions of character responsibility played a key role in both coordinating the factual basis on which judgments of criminal liability were made and in legitimating the ultimate exercise of the state's power to punish. Through a decentralized system of courts and a jury system, the mid-eighteenth-century criminal process could call upon local knowledge which mapped onto widely accepted judgments of criminality as founded in the failure to establish one's character in the local community.[31] Both its resources and its needs in the areas of coordination and legitimation were, in short, vastly different from today.

The Professionalization and Systematization of Criminal Justice in the Nineteenth Century: Democracy and the Rise of Capacity and Outcome Responsibility

In considering the institutional preconditions for the reshaping of practices of criminal responsibility after the eighteenth century, it is worth focusing on perhaps the most obviously relevant institutional factor: the *professionalization, expansion, and autonomization of criminal law and the legal profession*, followed by the criminal justice system's increasing association with welfarist aspirations in the twentieth century and its ultimate blending with risk-based modes of governance in the late twentieth and early twenty-first centuries.[32]

[30] George P. Fletcher *Rethinking Criminal Law* (Boston and Toronto: Little, Brown 1978) Chapters 2 and 3; see discussion in Chapters 1 and 3 above.

[31] Cf. Peter Ramsay's analysis of the recent emergence of liability based on a failure to assure—and hence protect the vulnerable autonomy of—others: *The Insecurity State: Vulnerable Autonomy and the Right to Security in the Criminal Law* (Oxford: Oxford University Press 2012); for further discussion, see below Chapter 5.

[32] Nicola Lacey, 'What Constitutes Criminal Law?', in R. A Duff, Lindsay Farmer, S. E. Marshall, Massimo Renzo, and Victor Tadros (eds), *The Constitution of the Criminal*

Most histories of criminal law in the nineteenth century are dominated by discussions of the long struggle to rationalize criminal law through codification, represented by the reports of the various criminal law commissions that had been established since 1833.[33] None of these attempts was successful, and, notwithstanding several substantial efforts of legislative consolidation, the substantive criminal law of the 1900s, though containing vast amounts of new legislation, was hardly more coherent (according to the Commissioners' criteria) than that of the 1800s. The work of the Commissioners did, however, represent the first systematic governmental attempt to give coherent form to the criminal law and to explicate it as a body of doctrine in relation to certain general principles. The rule of law ideals of rationality, coherence, and predictability that informed these unsuccessful attempts and the Benthamite view of the rational, deterrable subject of criminal law that underpinned them continue to resonate in English criminal law nearly two centuries later. The Benthamite model also implied a distinction between the deterrability of those who committed offences advertently and that of those who committed them inadvertently—hence arguably providing the foundations for a gradual elaboration of what we now understand as the distinction between the subjective and objective forms of *mens rea* in criminal law.[34]

This impulse to systematize criminal law—to reconstruct it as a coherent body of doctrine capable of being applied in an even-handed and impersonal way[35]—is closely related to the developing project of modern governance, along with a distinctively modern idea(l) of legality.[36] Furthermore, two other contemporaneous and more fully realized reform projects were also of significance to the development of criminal law in this period. These were the centralization and

Law (Oxford: Oxford University Press 2012); see also David Garland, *Punishment and Welfare: A History of Penal Strategies* (Brookfield: Gower 1985).

[33] See, for example, K. J. M. Smith, *Lawyers, Legislators and Theorists: Developments in English Criminal Jurisprudence 1800–1957* (Oxford: Clarendon Press 1998).

[34] Ibid. at pp. 67–123. In contemporary criminal law doctrine, a subjective principle of fault is one that judges the defendant in terms of his or her own beliefs, capacities, intentions, and so on, while an objective principle judges the defendant in terms of the beliefs, capacities, or intentions that a reasonable person would have had in the circumstances. See Celia Wells and Oliver Quick, *Lacey, Wells and Quick, Reconstructing Criminal Law: Critical Perspectives on Crime and the Criminal Process* (4th ed., Cambridge: Cambridge University Press 2010) 104–19.

[35] See Randall McGowen, 'The Image of Justice and Reform of the Criminal Law in Early Nineteenth-Century England' 32 *Buffalo Law Review* (1983) 89–125.

[36] Lindsay Farmer, *Making the Modern Criminal Law: Criminalization and Civil Order* (Oxford: Oxford University Press 2016) Chapter 5.

professionalization of enforcement[37] and penal processes[38] and the articulation of rules of criminal evidence. Each of these changes expressed a need to autonomize criminal justice by specifying distinctive personnel, institutions, processes, responses, and special kinds of knowledge that came within its purview. For example, the specification of distinctive rules for assessing and filtering evidence received from the social world implies a very basic change in conceptions of knowledge and proof. The move towards an adversarial trial as the best process for the discovery of truth marked a gradual move away from a system in which jury perceptions *via* common sense, local knowledge, the testimony of witnesses, and the statement of the defendant were the best source of proof.[39] Furthermore, the development of legal representation in the criminal courts, accelerated by the Prisoners' Counsel Act 1836, which, for the first time, entitled all defendants to be represented by lawyers at every stage of the trial, including the address to the jury, led to a significant professionalization of criminal legal practice.[40] Finally, the gradual development of systematic law reporting and, significantly later, a system of criminal appeals, provided further foundations for the development of a rationalized system of criminal law doctrine.[41] Each of these forces can reasonably be inferred to have militated in favour of the gradual development of technical conceptions of responsibility articulated in terms that did not rely on shared, lay evaluations.

The institutions that affected the course of criminal responsibility were not confined to those that were part of the criminal process or even the political process, however. For example, *industrialization and urbanization*[42] fundamentally altered the resources available for the criminal justice system to coordinate and legitimate judgments of responsibility. Greater social mobility—in both

[37] See, for example, David Philips, *Crime and Authority in Victorian England: The Black Country, 1835–1860* (London: Rowman and Littlefield 1977).

[38] See Radzinowicz and Hood, *The Emergence of Penal Policy in Victorian and Edwardian England*.

[39] See J. M. Beattie, 'Scales of Justice' and *Crime and the Courts in England, 1660–1800* p. 634 (tracing the emergence of the criminal standard of proof, the presumption of innocence, and the law of evidence in the eighteenth and early nineteenth centuries); David J. A. Cairns, *Advocacy and the Making of the Adversarial Criminal Trial, 1800–1865*.

[40] Ibid. pp. 126–76.

[41] See K. J. M. Smith, *Lawyers, Legislators and Theorists* at 42–54, 361–68.

[42] See J. M. Beattie, *Crime and the Courts in England, 1660–1800* at 637; Bruce Lenman and Geoffrey Parker, 'The State, the Community and the Criminal Law in Early Modern Europe' pp. 11, 38; J. J. Tobias, *Crime and Industrial Society in the Nineteenth Century* (London: Ratsford 1967).

the geographical and socioeconomic senses—weakened the local basis for judgments of character and reputation and complicated the shared evaluation of serious wrongs that had arguably underpinned the (relatively restricted) criminal justice system in the seventeenth and eighteenth centuries.[43] As we have seen in the previous chapter, during the nineteenth century the regulatory ambitions of the state increased, prompting the expansion of summary jurisdiction and the explosion of regulatory offences based on outcome responsibility from the mid-century on. These developments facilitated the pursuit of those regulatory ambitions through the criminal justice system,[44] but they also rendered problems of legitimation and coordination of criminal law ever more intense. As confidence in substantive evaluations of character diminished, demands for legitimation increased. Therefore, the criminal process was in search of a conception of criminal responsibility that could be explicated in legal, technical terms and, hence, legitimated as a form of specialist knowledge underpinning an impersonal mode of judgment.[45] The full articulation of such a system depended, however, on a number of other institutional features that developed gradually from the late eighteenth century on: an adversarial trial dominated by lawyers; a sophisticated law of evidence; and a further professionalization of legal practice. In short, interests and ideas shaped these institutional changes, along with many others, yet the institutional changes also shaped the way in which those ideas could be expressed and those interests pursued.

In the context of this gradual evolution of the institutional arrangements which enabled the trial to function as an effective form for the investigation and proof of capacity-responsibility, the continuing vitality in late nineteenth century criminal law of the presumption that a defendant has intended the natural and probable

[43] Thomas A. Green, *Verdict According to Conscience: Perspectives on the English Criminal Trial Jury, 1200–1800* (Chicago and London: University of Chicago Press 1985) (arguing that under the 'communitarian view' the jury's operation in the later modern period was grounded in a high level of consensus about the central norms governing offences against the person and against property—a consensus that did not always extend to political cases, such as treason—and about the indices of character and reputation that rendered the application of the capital sentence unjust).

[44] See Lindsay Farmer, *Criminal Law, Tradition and Legal Order* pp. 57–99, 119 (discussing summary jurisdiction and character evidence at the start of the nineteenth century).

[45] See Randall McGowen, 'The Image of Justice and Reform of the Criminal Law in Early Nineteenth-Century England' p. 89.

consequence of her actions is highly significant.[46] For it provides a crucial bridge between the later, subjective, psychologized conception of *mens rea* with its paradigm of intention[47] and the earlier confidence in 'recognizing crime when one saw it'. It is also a legal mechanism, which effaces the conceptual distinction between subjective and objective principles of *mens rea.* Its gradual transformation from a legal to an evidential presumption,[48] and its—often unnoticed—survival well into the twentieth century is one of the most eloquent pieces of evidence in favour of the proposition that responsibility as based on the investigation (as opposed to assumption) of individual subjective capacity had not yet become the settled conception deployed by criminal courts at the end of the nineteenth or even in the early years of the twentieth century. Arguably, not until the the mid 1930s was the presumption fully laid to rest.[49] Rather, the courts saw it as normatively appropriate to assume that the defendant's responsibility could simply be 'read off' his or her conduct in much the way that the eighteenth-century jury was expected to recognize criminality, without the aid of technical legal definitions, when they saw it. The fact that, at the end of the nineteenth century, the process of criminal judgment remained significantly decentralized, and significantly subject to the influence of local norms and customs,[50] further helps to explain the fact that, contrary to

[46] See K. J. M. Smith, *Lawyers, Legislators and Theorists* p. 262. James Fitzjames Stephen, *A General View of the Criminal Law of England* (London: Macmillan 1863), provides an interesting example of a view intermediate between the emerging subjectivism and the older conception of criminal malice as 'wickedness'. While arguing that malice, will, and intention were distinct from one another, he asserted that all were presumed to exist unless rebutted by special evidence such as evidence of insanity or self-defence.

[47] On the links between the emerging paradigm of intention and the doctrinal focus on homicide, see Lindsay Farmer, *Criminal Law, Tradition and Legal Order* Chapter 5; on the contemporary significance of intention see, from different perspectives, Alan Norrie, *Crime Reason and History: A Critical Introduction to the Criminal Law* (2nd ed., Cambridge: Cambridge University Press 2001) Chapter 3 and R. A. Duff, *Intention, Agency and Criminal Liability* (Oxford: Basil Blackwell 1990) Part I.

[48] See James Fitzjames Stephen, *A History of the Criminal Law of England* (London: Macmillan 1883) Vol. II, p. 111; C. S. Kenny, *Outlines of Criminal Law* (Cambridge: Cambridge University Press 1902) p. 333.

[49] *DPP v Woolmington* [1935] *UKHL* 1 famously instituted the doctrine of the presumption of innocence. On the history of the presumption of innocence, and the demise of the presumption that natural consequences are intended, see Lindsay Farmer, *Making the Modern Criminal Law* Chapter 6.

[50] See Carolyn A. Conley, *The Unwritten Law: Criminal Justice in Victorian Kent* (Oxford: Oxford University Press 1991), tracing the persistence of 'community' law into even the late nineteenth century, and arguing that, even once established, the presumption of innocence continued to operate in favour of the respectable (pp. 57ff.); David Philips, *Crime and Authority in Victorian England* and 'A New Engine of Power and

the assumption of many commentators, the *legal* elaboration of 'general principles of criminal law' such as those we take for granted today was, like the Benthamite project of codification, scarcely further advanced at the end of the nineteenth century than at its start.[51]

Nonetheless, the *structure of the criminal trial* changed decisively in the course of the nineteenth century, and one institutional development of particular significance for changing patterns of responsibility-attribution is the defence lawyers' gradual infiltration—persuasively charted by Langbein[52] and Beattie[53]—of the criminal trial, and public reactions to this infiltration. A vigorous and long-lasting debate about legal representation, particularly in relation to felony defendants, began in the early nineteenth century and haunted not merely Parliament but also, for a further three decades after reform in 1836, the press, periodicals, and the realist novel. And, as I shall argue in the remainder of this section, an analysis of this debate discloses a continuing resistance to the idea of criminal law as an object of professional definition, interpretation, and control—a resistance which produced a further legitimation problem which had to be addressed by institutional means.[54]

Authority', especially p. 159. See also A. W. Brian Simpson's fascinating *Cannibalism and the Common Law* (Chicago: Chicago University Press 1984), which shows how the case of *R v Dudley and Stephens* (1884) 14 QBD 273, which rejected the application of a defence of necessity to murder, was consciously used by the legal authorities in order to delegitimize maritime customs allowing cannibalism under certain circumstances. Both the fact that these customs were still widely influential in the late nineteenth century and the fact that the legal establishment saw it as important to assert the exclusive authority of state criminal law are significant for my argument.

[51] Martha Merrill Umphrey, 'The Dialogics of Legal Meaning' 33 *Law and Society Review* (1999) 393–423 provides an interesting insight into the coexistence of different (and competing) principles of responsibility (resembling the character and capacity models) in US criminal law of the early twentieth century.

[52] John H. Langbein, 'The Criminal Trial before the Lawyers', 'Shaping the Eighteenth Century Criminal Trial: A View from the Ryder Sources', and *The Origins of Adversary Criminal Trial.*

[53] J. M. Beattie, *Crime and the Courts in England, 1660–1800*, 'Scales of Justice', and *Policing and Punishment in London, 1660–1750: Urban Crime and the Limits of Terror* (Oxford: Oxford University Press 2001).

[54] For detailed and meticulous discussions of this history, see David J. A. Cairns, *Advocacy and the Making of the English Criminal Trial, 1800–1865*; Jan-Melissa Schramm, *Testimony and Advocacy in Victorian Law, Literature and Theology* (Cambridge and New York: Cambridge University Press 2000); Allyson N. May, 'Advocates and Truth-Seeking in the Old Bailey Courtroom' 26 *The Journal of Legal History* (2005) 83–90; and *The Bar and the Old Bailey, 1750–1850.* Thomas Gallanis has argued that the puzzle about why defence counsel should have been excluded for felony and treason but not misdemeanour is to be explained by the fact that prosecutions for the first two, but not the last, had been understood as an *ex officio* exercise of the King's authority since at

Of course, *the establishment of professional autonomy and legitimacy* was a huge issue across many sectors in the nineteenth century.[55] The legal profession, as compared with its counterparts, was already relatively organized, but its traditional forms of organization were inadequate in the context of the expansion of personnel and diversification of functions.[56] Hence the various branches of the legal profession were slowly reorganizing themselves so as to put their credentials on a more secure footing, through more systematic provision of training, the imposition of training requirements, and better organized professional bodies and disciplinary proceedings. As analyses of the phenomenon of professionalization have shown, a key requirement for the effective legitimation of professional autonomy is the construction of credible markers of expertise sufficient to justify an exclusive right to perform the relevant tasks.[57] This proved especially difficult for criminal lawyers to demonstrate, for two

least the time of Edward I. Defence counsel would, on this view, have been committing something akin to treason. It is doubtful, however, how many defendants charged with serious misdemeanours had the resources to employ counsel. In felony cases, even once the courts had begun to allow counsel to cross examine, by the end of the eighteenth century, only about a quarter of defendants were in fact represented: Gallanis, 'Making Sense of Blackstone's Puzzle' p. 36.

55 Sir Llewellyn Woodward, *The Age of Reform, 1815–1870* (2nd ed., Oxford: Oxford University Press 1962) pp. 17–18. On the place of this debate in the contemporary novel, see Nicola Lacey, 'The Way We Lived Then: The Legal Profession and the Nineteenth Century Novel' 33 *Sydney Law Review* (2011) 599–621; Jan-Melissa Schramm, *Testimony and Advocacy*; and 'Is Literature More Ethical than Law? Fitzjames Stephen and Literary Responses to the Advent of Full Legal Representation of Felons', in Michael Freeman and Andrew Lewis (eds), *Current Legal Issues Volume 2: Law and Literature* (Oxford: Oxford University Press 1999).

56 There is a lively debate about whether this era was one of continuity or of change in the structure of the legal profession: see, for example, Daniel Duman, 'Pathway to Professionalism: The Legal Profession in the Nineteenth Century' 13 *Journal of Social History* (1980) 615–28; Raymond Cocks, *Foundations of the Modern Bar* (London: Sweet & Maxwell 1983); Wesley Pue, 'Exorcising Professional Demons: Charles Rann Kennedy and the Transition to the Modern Bar' 5 *Law and History Review* (1987) 135–74; Patrick Polden, *A History of the County Court*, 1846–1971 (Cambridge: Cambridge University Press 1999); W. Prest (ed.), *The Professions in Early Modern England* (London: Croom Helm 1987). On the longer term history of the legal profession, see Paul A. Brand, *The Origins of the English Legal Profession* (Oxford: Blackwell 1992); Patrick Polden, 'The Legal Professions', in William Cornish, J. Stuart Anderson, Raymond Cocks, Michael Lobban, Patrick Polden, and Keith Smith (eds), *The Oxford History of the Laws of England* Vol. XI (Oxford: Oxford University Press 2010) Part IV. On the contemporary profession, see Richard L. Abel, *The Legal Profession in England and Wales* (Oxford: Basil Blackwell 1988).

57 Magali Sarfatti Larson, *The Rise of Professionalism: A Sociological Analysis* (Berkeley: University of California Press 1977); Harold Perkin, *The Rise of Professional Society: England Since 1880* (London: Routledge 2002); W. Prest (ed.), *The Professions in Early Modern England*; W. J. Reader, *Professional Men: The Rise of the Professional Classes in*

reasons. First, there persisted a deep-rooted feeling that the definition of crime and of criminal guilt—particularly in key areas such as theft and personal violence—is a matter of common sense or morality, not to be corrupted by technicalities and professional obfuscation.[58] Second, criminal barristers' most evident skill was that of advocacy in their clients' interest. This made them vulnerable to the dual charge that they manipulated rhetoric to defend the guilty for mercenary reasons; and that their rhetoric displaced the defendant's own voice, which gave better access to the truth of guilt or innocence. Why would anyone need a lawyer if they were innocent? And if they were guilty, would it not be immoral to try to escape conviction through deployment of professional assistance?[59] Such scepticism about the role of lawyers had an important bearing on the debate about reform of the criminal trial. Hence we see essayists and novelists, as well as opponents of reform in Parliament, questioning the propriety of lawyers' speaking for the defendant,[60] developing a critique of legal representation as the triumph of power, money and rhetoric exploiting specious technicalities over common sense and morality;[61] and articulating a persistent idea that true innocence needs no legal representation.

Nineteenth-Century England (London: Weidenfeld 1966); Daniel Duman, 'The Creation and Diffusion of a Professional Ideology in Nineteenth Century England' 27 *Sociological Review* (1979) 113–38; Penelope J. Corfield, *Power and the Professions in Britain, 1700–1850* (London and New York: Routledge 1995).

[58] See James Q. Whitman, *The Origins of Reasonable Doubt: Theological Origins of the Criminal Trial* (New Haven: Yale University Press 2008) Chapters 6 and 7; Loughnan, 'Manifest Madness' and *Manifest Madness: Mental Incapacity in the Criminal Law*; Lacey, *Women, Crime, and Character.*

[59] As Paul Raffield has shown, this sort of scepticism about lawyers reaches back in England at least to the time of Shakespeare, though it undoubtedly had a marked intensity in relation to criminal defence lawyers in the nineteenth century ('The Elizabethan Rhetoric of Signs'; see in particular pp. 246, 253, and 258–60). As Raffield puts it, from the sixteenth century, in the wake of the secularization of the legal profession, commentators saw lawyers as 'operating in an ethical vacuum' (ibid. p. 246). On the ways in which modernizing law accordingly continued to deploy images and strategies of legitimation associated with an older symbolic order, see also Lacey, 'The Way We Lived Then: The Legal Profession and the Nineteenth Century Novel'.

[60] Key examples would include the polemical commentary on Brougham's defence of Queen Caroline and, in the 1840s, of Charles Phillips' defence of Courvoisier, in periodicals such as *Punch* and *The Examiner.* See Jan-Melissa Schramm, *Testimony and Advocacy* pp. 114–20; David J. A. Cairns, *Advocacy and the Making of the Adversarial Criminal Trial, 1800–1865* pp. 131–42; Allyson N. May, *The Bar and the Old Bailey, 1750–1850* pp. 209–36; Elizabeth Gaskell, *Mary Barton: A Tale of Manchester Life* (1848: New York: Penguin 1996); George Eliot, *Felix Holt: The Radical* (1866: London: Penguin 1995).

[61] Jan-Melissa Schramm, '"The Anatomy of a Barrister's Tongue": Rhetoric, Satire and the Victorian Bar in England' 32 *Victorian Literature and Culture* (2004) 285–303 and

But the argument about legal representation for felony defendants also had a bearing on the legitimation of criminal law itself, and the rich literature about the ethics of criminal defence sheds light on the historical development of criminal law.[62] For, underlying these debates, it is clear that there are two competing conceptions of crime and guilt in social circulation. The resistance to lawyers' developing dominance in the criminal trial represents, as we have seen, a deep-rooted popular sentiment that the definition of criminal guilt and innocence—and hence, at some level, of crime itself—is a matter of common sense and morality, which cannot entirely be captured in law or interpreted by lawyers. In the pre-reform era, the fact that felony trials featured an 'altercation'[63] between defendant and prosecution, mediated by the judge—a figure who represents not merely the law but also both common sense and standards of fair play—provided a framework of legitimation and coordination which spoke to that sense of the popular ownership of crime as public wrong, itself emerging slowly from an older order in which serious crime was understood primarily as a wrong against the monarch.[64] The public nature of trials, and the location of many criminal hearings in local venues such as inns, in a world in which court buildings were still relatively few, constituted the interpretation of criminal law as an issue in which the community could play a role.[65] But as the lawyers gradually infiltrated the felony trial through the course of the eighteenth century—first on the prosecution side, then, by degrees, on the defence side—this fostered a further professionalization of lawyering, which gave a new impetus to the refinement of distinctive criminal law doctrines, notably in the areas of evidence and procedure. As the rules of both substantive law and procedure formalized, the older equilibrium between lay and judicial conceptions of crime came under

'Is Literature More Ethical than Law?' For contemporary concerns expressed in fiction, see Anthony Trollope, *Orley Farm* (1861–2: Oxford: Oxford World's Classics 2000).

[62] See also David J. A. Cairns, *Advocacy and the Making of the Adversarial Criminal Trial, 1800–1865*; Jan-Melissa Schramm, *Testimony and Advocacy*.

[63] See John Langbein, *The Origins of Adversary Criminal Trial*.

[64] See Gallanis, 'Making Sense of Blackstone's Puzzle: Why Forbid Defense Counsel?' On crime as public wrong, see also Jeremy Horder, *Ashworth's Principles of Criminal Law* (2016) Chapter 3.

[65] See Jonathan H. Grossman, *The Art of Alibi: English Law Courts and the Novel* (Baltimore: Johns Hopkins University Press 2002); Linda Mulcahy, *Legal Architecture: Justice, Due Process and the Place of Law* (London: Routledge 2011).

strain.[66] The most obvious sign of this strain related to the structure of the criminal trial. But the tension between technical and lay conceptions of criminal law also bore on the legitimation of law itself, with both the (ultimately unrealized) possibility of codification and the vast expansion of the criminal jurisdiction disrupting the mechanisms whereby the common law of crime celebrated by Blackstone had connected up common sense and legal judgment. And with the expansion of criminal legislation into new regulatory areas in the middle of the nineteenth century,[67] the link between common moral sense and crime was further weakened, resulting in a persistent legitimation problem for criminal law, which the emerging conception of capacity responsibility helped to address.

The extension and refinement of a doctrine of capacity-responsibility, enabled by the professionalization and systematization of the trial process, was however not the only innovation geared to addressing the emerging legitimation problem faced by nineteenth century criminal law. Indeed, as the problem gradually presented itself, the British political system was inventing, by fits and starts between about 1820 and 1860, a new set of institutional arrangements, which, potentially, solved or at least mitigated it. If the definition of crime no longer rested with traditional values, a shared sense of public wrong, and a set of practices (notably, the non-lawyer-dominated jury trial) geared to tracking those shared sentiments, the era of reform offered a new framework for legitimation. The most vivid instance of reform—and the most urgent—was the abolition of two-thirds of the existing capital statutes in 1832, addressing the problem of cultural legitimation posed by the 'Bloody Code' in a world in which civilized sentiments were turning against displays of public violence. This radical reduction in the applicability of the death penalty also served to develop new forms of political legitimation *via* procedure and system, taking as it did a decisive step towards the rationalizing modernization initiated by Romilly's reforms of 1808 by turning away from the *ancien régime* mode of threatened death tempered by a

[66] See Keith Smith, 'Criminal Law', in William Cornish, J. Stuart Anderson, Raymond Cocks, Michael Lobban, Patrick Polden, and Keith Smith (eds), *The Oxford History of the Laws of England* Vol. XIII (Oxford: Oxford University Press 2010) Part 1.

[67] Raymond Cocks, 'Statutes, Social Reform, and Control', in William Cornish, J. Stuart Anderson, Raymond Cocks, Michael Lobban, Patrick Polden, and Keith Smith (eds), *The Oxford History of the Laws of England* Vol. XIII (Oxford: Oxford University Press 2010) Part 2.

widespread but unaccountable discretionary prerogative of mercy. In 1820, there were well over 200 capital offences; by 1841, only murder and treason remained.[68] Also important was the comprehensive—and decades-long—reform and rationalization of criminal procedure and the foundation of a professional police force with the establishment in 1829 of the Metropolitan Police. But also key here, I would argue, was *the founding of the definition of crime (as indeed of procedural arrangements and many instance of penal reform) in legislation which had the imprimatur of (albeit radically imperfect) representative democracy* and—had the grand ambition of codification ever been realized—of association with self-consciously modern values such as rationality, clarity and publicity.

Though full codification never came in England and Wales, legislative domination of criminal law most certainly did.[69] The substantial consolidating legislation steered through by Robert Peel in 1827–30 and further revised in 1861 made a significant gesture towards the rationalized common source which codification would have offered. Lindsay Farmer has shown that, notwithstanding the failure of the codification project, not to mention the very slow movement towards a universal jurisdiction (which was not achieved until the late twentieth century) a gradual rationalization of criminal law during the nineteenth century is powerfully reflected in a flourishing genre of treatises, primarily written for practitioners and magistrates. This, itself, was to be supplemented and even superseded in the late nineteenth and twentieth centuries by the student-oriented textbook, a product of the development of university education in law from the late nineteenth century.[70] While not

[68] See Clive Emsley, 'The History of Crime and Crime Control Institutions', in Mike Maguire, Rod Morgan, and Robert Reiner (eds), *The Oxford Handbook of Criminology* (3rd ed., Oxford: Oxford University Press 2002). On changing attitudes to violence, see also David Garland, *Punishment and Modern Society* (Oxford: Oxford University Press 1990) Chapter 10; these changes had ramifications not only for penal regimes but for the criminal law: Martin J. Wiener, *Men of Blood: Violence, Manliness and Criminal Justice in Victorian England* (Cambridge: Cambridge University Press 2006).

[69] See David Lieberman, *The Province of Legislation Determined* (New York: Cambridge University Press, 1989); Jerry Postema, *Bentham and the Common Law Tradition* (Oxford: Clarendon Press 1986); Lindsay Farmer, *Making the Modern Criminal Law: Criminalization and Civil Order* Chapter 3.

[70] See Lindsay Farmer, 'Of Treatises and Textbooks: The Literature of Criminal Law in Nineteenth Century Britain', in Angela Fernandez and Markus D. Dubber (eds), *Law Books in Action: Essays on the Anglo-American Legal Treatises* (Oxford: Hart Publishing 2012); see also Michael Lobban,'The English Legal Treatise and English Law in the

necessarily presenting criminal law as a principled, coherent body of doctrine, nor looking very deeply into the rationale for or distinctiveness of criminal law as form of legal regulation, these treatises, as Brian Simpson has argued, all in some sense presented criminal law as a unity—and hence as a discrete object of professional interpretation and deployment.[71] This, certainly, would have fostered coordination of criminal law as an integrated body of doctrine; but I would argue that it would also, in the context of modernizing sensibilities, have helped to legitimate criminal law as an object of professional interpretation. The necessity of such treatises, particularly for lower courts, was stimulated by the burgeoning of criminal legislation in new areas of regulatory concern, prompted by economic and social developments such as industrialization and urbanization. But that legislative origin of much criminal law itself provided an increasingly strong source of legitimation. Until at least the 1860s, the professional credentials of defence lawyers remained suspect.[72] But in the context of the increasing franchise, the parliamentary origins of a greater part of criminal law, along with the authority of a judiciary and court system itself being reorganized on more modern, systematic lines, with greater capacity for testing points of law,[73] helped to glue together the formal and the popular definition of crime–villainy and felony, as Leo Katz has put it[74]–recreating the nexus between lay and legal constitutions of crime to a level adequate for legitimation.

But how effectively has this underlying tension about who has the power and authority to define crime—the lawyer or the lay person—been resolved? In fact, the tension continues to haunt English criminal law today. As leading comparativist Mirjan Damaska has noted, the English legal process presents an instance of what may fairly be described as a system of coordinate authority.[75] While the jury's role has been restricted in scope and attenuated in substance over the centuries, the role of lay decision-making in

Eighteenth-Century' 13 *Iuris Scripta Historica* (1997) 69–88; on jurisdiction, see Lindsay Farmer, *Making the Modern Criminal Law: Criminalization and Civil Order* Chapter 4.

[71] A. W. B. Simpson, 'The Rise and Fall of the Legal Treatise: Legal Principles and the Forms of Legal Literature' 48 *University of Chicago Law Review* (1981) 632–79.

[72] As is reflected in James Fitzjames Stephen's essay on 'The Morality of Advocacy' 3 *Cornhill Magazine* (1861) 447–59; see further, Schramm, *Testimony and Advocacy*.

[73] See Lacey, 'In Search of the Responsible Subject'.

[74] See Leo Katz, 'Villainy and Felony: A Problem Concerning Criminalization' 6(1) *Buffalo Criminal Law Review* (April 2002) 451–82.

[75] *The Faces of Justice and State Authority* (New Haven: Yale University Press 1991).

both jury trials and magistrates' courts is a striking exemplification of the implicit recognition that the definition of criminality is not purely a matter of law. Of course, magistrates are advised by a legally qualified clerk and juries are meant to be restricted to questions of fact. But when questions of fact include findings on 'reasonableness', 'dishonesty', 'immoral purposes', and so on[76]—open-textured and incompletely specified concepts which are key to the definition of specific crimes—the line between fact and law is fine to vanishing point. Moreover criminal courts' decision-making goes forward in a context in which lay persons outside the court will often have views about innocence and guilt, and on occasion make their voices heard on the matter, potentially producing significant social conflict about who has the better view.[77] Hence the tension between lay and professional definitions of crime, which underpinned the nineteenth century argument about criminal defence continues to echo in contemporary English criminal law.

The same is true of difficulties entailed by the specific way in which English criminal law developed democratic forms of legitimation through parliamentary democracy in the course of constitutional development between the seventeenth and the nineteenth centuries. The particular structure of English parliamentary sovereignty, finally completed with the full extension of the adult franchise in 1928, is potentially very responsive and electorally sensitive to popular opinion, and is largely unconstrained by substantive constitutional standards. This means that, in the English system, the direct democratic legitimation of the legal definition of crime came at a price. This was not so evident during the early part of the twentieth century, in

[76] As, for example, in the case of theft as defined by the Theft Act 1968 s. 1; involuntary manslaughter as defined by the common law; and soliciting for immoral purposes as defined by the Sexual Offences Act 1956 s. 32.

[77] This is, of course, particularly striking in notorious cases such as the spectacular miscarriage of justice cases which haunted the English criminal process in the 1990s, and which Nobles and Schiff have analysed persuasively: Richard Nobles and David Schiff, *Understanding Miscarriages of Justice* (Oxford: Oxford University Press 2000). Nobles and Schiff draw on systems theory to argue that there is an inherent instability in any social process in which different groups claim a right of definition, those definitions being informed by irreconcilable assumptions. In this case, the media's conception of guilt and innocence was different from that implied by the law. The self-referential nature of the legal and media subsystems hence caused a significant legitimation problem for criminal law, and one which the law had to try to resolve while being inherently incapable of doing so. This is, of course, a very particular example but the same logic underpins the much more common complaint about defendants 'getting off on a technicality'.

which the standard and scope of education across the populace was relatively low, and elite leadership more or less taken for granted. But it began to be a real issue from the 1970s on. As education has become better and more widespread, and as deference to established elites has diminished, a more generally populist critique of formalized definitions of crime is of increasing importance.[78] As scholars writing on criminal law in England and Wales today are only too aware, the very responsiveness of the political system to perceived swings in popular opinion means that, under certain environmental conditions, the definition of crime is liable to become highly politicized. In the absence of effective processes for a more deliberative form of popular participation, this makes for highly volatile criminal policy, and increasing incoherence in the concept of crime.

From this point of view, legitimation through a system of democratic parliamentary sovereignty, which provides a direct link between electoral pressures and criminal policy, is problematic. As we saw in the previous chapter, our adversarial political system has led to a law and order 'arms race' and to rampant criminalization. And when criminalization is used indiscriminately and pragmatically for political ends—as, arguably, has been in the case in Britain over the last fifteen years—the legal definition of crime is liable to become both ever more detached from the core popular conception, and ever harder to conceptualize or rationalize within a unitary account of its distinctive features. Hence, what Husak dubs 'overcriminalization' is very much a double-edged sword as far as legitimation is concerned, as well as being a clear problem from the point of view of legitimacy in a normative sense.[79] For all the obvious differences—the move to universal suffrage in 1928, the establishment of a national police force, a rationalized sentencing system—contemporary debates about the difficulty of bringing the chaotic panoply of criminal legislation within any coherent rationalizing frame are strongly reminiscent of debates in late eighteenth-century England when Parliament indulged in similarly pragmatic deployments of criminalization.[80]

[78] See Mick Ryan, *Penal Policy and Political Culture in England and Wales* (Winchester: Waterside Press 2003).

[79] Douglas Husak, *Overcriminalization* (New York: Oxford University Press 2007); see also Nicola Lacey, 'Principles, Policies and Politics of Criminal Law', in Julian Roberts and Lucia Zedner (eds) *Principled Approaches to Criminal Law and Criminal Justice: Essays in Honour of Andrew Ashworth* (Oxford: Oxford University Press 2012).

[80] See Peter King, *Crime, Justice and Discretion, 1740–1820.*

(Parallel problems arise for law enforcement under conditions of low legitimacy, as the police discovered at the time of the urban disorders of the early 1980s and indeed of August 2011.[81]) Note the very different situation in countries like Germany or the Nordic group, where a consensus still prevails around the authority of a core criminal code and around constitutional restrictions on criminalization which were part of an initial settlement of the powers of the modern state.[82]

Much of the literature on criminalization acknowledges the central part which politics plays in the process. One the one hand, the normative literature on criminalization is firmly located within political philosophy, with the role of the state and its criminal justice branch a key feature of many of the most famous political theories of the post-Enlightenment era. The vision of criminalization to be derived from Mill's (notoriously indeterminate, yet intuitively commanding) harm principle[83] is the most obvious example, but Hobbes, Hume, Locke, Kant, and Hegel are equally concerned with the role of criminal punishment in the modern state.[84] On the other hand, the explanatory literature—most of it located in criminology rather than criminal law theory—is preoccupied with the role of electorally driven political pressure in widening the boundaries of criminalization,[85] while, in relation to decriminalization, the way in which changing social mores are filtered through political processes has also drawn attention.[86] In

[81] See Richard Kinsey, John Lea, and Jock Young, *Losing the Fight Against Crime* (London: Blackwell 1986).

[82] See Nicola Lacey, *The Prisoners' Dilemma: Political Economy and Punishment in Contemporary Democracies* (Cambridge: Cambridge University Press 2008) Chapter 3; John Pratt, 'Scandinavian Exceptionalism in an Era of Penal Excess', Parts I ('The Nature and Roots of Scandinavian Exceptionalism') and II ('Does Scandinavian Exceptionalism Have a Future?') 48 *British Journal of Criminology* (2008) 119–37 and 275–92; Tapio Lappi-Seppälä, 'Penal Policy in Scandinavia', in Michael Tonry (ed.), *Crime and Justice* Vol. 36: *Crime, Punishment, and Politics in Comparative Perspective* (Chicago: University of Chicago Press 2007) and 'Trust, Welfare, and Political Culture: Explaining Difference in National Penal Policies', in Michael Tonry (ed.), *Crime and Justice* Vol. 37: *A Review of Research* (Chicago: Chicago University Press 2008); Nicola Lacey and Hanna Pickard, 'The Chimera of Proportionality: Institutionalising Limits on Punishment in Contemporary Social and Political Systems' 78(2) *Modern Law Review* (2015) 216–40.

[83] John Stuart Mill, *On Liberty* (1859: London: Penguin 1974).

[84] See Alan Norrie, *Law, Ideology and Punishment: Retrieval and Critique of the Liberal Idea of Criminal Justice* (Dordrecht: Kluwer 1991); Alan Brudner, *Punishment and Freedom: A Liberal Theory of Penal Justice* (Oxford: Oxford University Press 2009).

[85] Katherine Beckett, *Making Crime Pay: Law and Order in Contemporary American Politics* (New York: Oxford University Press 1997); Nicola Lacey, *The Prisoners' Dilemma*.

[86] Troy Duster, *The Legislation of Morality: Law, Drugs, and Moral Judgment* (New York: Free Press 1970).

relation to Britain, electoral pressures are widely credited with (or rather blamed for) an explosion of criminalization during the last two decades[87] (there exist parallel, extensive literatures on other countries, notably the United States[88]).

In both explanatory and normative cases, the history of the institutions under scrutiny makes a real difference to the intellectual task of analysis or prescription. The nature of the state, of government, and of the political system has changed—and expanded—over time, encompassing functions not anticipated in the great modern political theories, and necessitating some imaginative extension of the principles which have informed liberal and democratic thought over the last centuries. And the empirical pressures and constraints upon criminalization have also changed markedly over time. Hence, large social changes such as the professionalization and formalization of criminal law and the emergence of newly democratic foundations for criminal legislation are of key relevance to the development of criminal law.

Hence the history of not merely the professionalization of criminal law practice and the formalization of criminal law doctrine, but also of constitutional reform and democratization presents itself as a key resource in our understanding of criminalization. Yet relatively little has been written about the impact of the transition to representative democracy in Britain or in other countries on these pressures and constraints, or about how they are filtered through political institutions and expressed in the legislative process. There is a vast literature on the lengthy parliamentary effort to achieve codification and

[87] David Downes and Rod Morgan, 'No Turning Back: The Politics of Law and Order into the Millennium', in Mike Maguire, Rod Morgan, and Robert Reiner (eds), *The Oxford Handbook of Criminology* (4th ed., Oxford: Oxford University Press 2007); Tim Newburn, '"Tough on Crime": Penal Policy in England and Wales', in Michael Tonry (ed.), *Crime and Justice* Vol. 36: *Crime, Punishment, and Politics in Comparative Perspective* (Chicago: University of Chicago Press 2007); Tim Newburn and Robert Reiner, 'Crime and Penal Policy', in Anthony Seldon (ed.), *Blair's Britain, 1997–2007* (Cambridge: Cambridge University Press 2007); Robert Reiner, *Law and Order: An Honest Citizen's Guide to Crime and Control* (Oxford: Polity Press 2007); Nicola Lacey, *The Prisoners' Dilemma* Chapters 2 and 4.

[88] See, for example, Husak, *Overcriminalization*. Chapter 1; David Garland, *The Culture of Control: Crime and Social Order in Contemporary Society* (Oxford: Oxford University Press 2001); David Garland (ed.), *Mass Imprisonment: Social Causes and Consequences* (London: Sage 2001); Jonathan Simon, *Governing Through Crime: How the War on Crime Transformed American Democracy and Created a Culture of Fear* (New York: Oxford University Press 2007).

criminal law reform in the nineteenth century on which to draw in constructing such an account,[89] but much less on the significance of the larger dynamics of electoral reform for criminal law. Since the comparative literature on criminalization and punishment suggests that the structure of electoral democracy is an important factor in explaining country differences today,[90] the path to democracy, and the specific form of the constitutional settlement which (re)formed itself in the nineteenth and early twentieth centuries in Britain, seem obvious objects of concern.

Unlike in the countries of continental Europe where, for all their important differences, there was a key moment of modernization and state-building, which was accompanied by a formal codification of criminal law which has proved to be remarkably durable, Britain followed a more incremental path to legal modernization and (partial) rationalization, as well as an earlier path to (partial) democracy.[91] Rooted in the history of a power struggle between the monarchy and the landed aristocracy, the seventeenth century achievement of a sovereign parliament with virtually unrestricted legislative powers survived the nineteenth century extension of the franchise, potentially allowing a wide range of interests a say in the legislative definition of crime. Accordingly, it offered a potential solution to the legitimation problem described in the previous section: the perceived gap between popular and official definitions of crime.

Of course, this solution was barely plausible in the era immediately following the Reform Act 1832. But it began to have rather more plausibility after 1867 (around the date, incidentally, at which the debate about criminal defence representation appears to have lost steam, presumably as a result of progress in both professional organization and the rationalization of legal doctrine through consolidating

89 Notably Leon Radzinowicz's monumental five volume, *A History of English Criminal Law Since 1750* (Oxford: Oxford University Press 1948–1986). See also Coleman Phillipson, *Three Criminal Law Reformers: Beccaria, Bentham, Romilly* (London and Toronto: J. K. Dent and Sons 1923); K. J. M. Smith, *Lawyers, Legislators and Theorists*; Richard R. Follett, *Evangelicalism, Penal Theory and the Politics of Criminal Law: Reform in England, 1808–30* (Basingstoke: Palgrave 2001).

90 See Lisa L. Miller, *The Perils of Federalism: Race, Poverty, and the Politics of Crime Control* (New York: Oxford University Press 2008); Vanessa Barker, *The Politics of Punishment: How the Democratic Process Shapes the Way America Punishes Offenders* (New York: Oxford University Press 2009); Nicola Lacey, *The Prisoners' Dilemma* Chapters 2 and 4.

91 James Q. Whitman, *Harsh Justice: Criminal Punishment and the Widening Divide Between America and Europe* (Oxford: Oxford University Press 2003).

legislation). In short, once those who decried the power of the lawyers started to have more political power through the ballot box, the criminal law's legitimation problem reduced as a result of the possibility of according technical definitions of crime the imprimatur of democratic origins. At the same time, the increasing professionalization of law—reflected in both the organization of the profession itself and in phenomena like practitioner treatises—stabilized the legitimacy of judicial interpretation. Note, however, that the shape of criminal law's legitimation problem is historically specific: it presents itself in different ways at different times. The outcry in the run-up to and in the wake of the Prisoners' Counsel Act of 1836 was driven by an emerging bourgeois elite who, in the context of rapid and poorly organized urbanization, were both much concerned about crime, in particular in relation to the protection of interests in property, and rather suspicious of a *parvenu* group—the new breed of defence barristers—whom they saw as lacking proper professional credentials, with patchy provision for training, and a system of discipline which was both incomplete and poorly suited to the needs of a rapidly expanding profession.[92] This bourgeois elite was the very group whose electoral power was on the rise—a fact which enhanced the capacity of democratization to deliver greater legitimacy for criminal law, squaring the circle by combining increasing technical control over the interpretation of crime with (in principle) lay control over its legislative definition.

[92] See Lacey, 'The Way We Lived Then: The Legal Profession and the Nineteenth Century Novel'.

5

Explaining the Shifting Alignment of Ideas of Responsibility in the Vortex of Interests and Institutions

Towards a Political Economy of Responsibility in English Criminal Law

I have argued so far that, while the apparently competing ideas of criminal responsibility as founded in character, capacity, outcome, and risk reviewed earlier can and do coexist in criminal law, their alignment and relative influence changes over time. Moreover, we should see those shifting alignments as a reflection not only of the history of ideas but also of systematic changes in interests and institutional dynamics, fundamentally affecting the nature and scope of criminal law as a system producing social meaning and social governance. If this broad approach is right, approaches to legal scholarship that place emphasis on the autonomy of law are fundamentally misconceived. Legal doctrines and ideas may have a certain independent force, with the closure of legal reasoning providing some insulation for legal ideas, but the larger intellectual, institutional, and interest-based environment has a decisive bearing on the changing shape of legal concepts over time. In the next and final chapter, I will take up these methodological questions. In this chapter, drawing on both the analytic framework and the case studies presented in previous chapters, I will offer an interpretation of the trajectory of criminal responsibility in modern English criminal law. I will argue that, while multiple conceptions of criminal responsibility have coexisted throughout modern English legal history, there has been a broad move through four configurations of responsibility[1] from the early eighteenth to the early twenty-first century.

The Era of Character

Character Responsibility, a Presumption of Capacity, and Outcome Responsibility at the Margins

In the eighteenth century, the terrain of responsibility was dominated by the pattern of attribution based on evidence or assumptions about bad character (in particular, the malice principle in the common law). Capacity in its subjective sense was shaping the slow development of defences (notably the emergence of emotional distress defences) and the attribution of responsibility in some of the most serious offences, notably murder and treason. And outcome responsibility was on the margins, often manifesting itself in local regulation of particular activities through by-laws and specific legislation, such as the memorably named 'Bumboat' Acts which sanctioned the carrying of stolen property by shipping on the Thames.[2] This configuration reflects both opportunities for, and limits on, legitimation and coordination within a non-democratic political system, a society structured by status hierarchy, and a decentralized social order whose institutions of both informal and formal social control were situated importantly at the local level and in lay hands.[3]

[1] My four 'eras' very broadly correspond with Lindsay Farmer's historical periodization between eighteenth century conceptions of responsibility, nineteenth century legislative conceptions, early twentieth century subjectivist conceptions, and later twentieth century punishable subjecthood (*Making the Modern Criminal Law: Criminalization and Civil Order* (Oxford University Press 2016) Chapter 6, though I attach more importance to the thematic emergence of what I see as a new version of a character/risk hybrid in the late twentieth century.

[2] Bruce P. Smith, 'The Presumption of Guilt and the English Law of Theft, 1750–1850' 23 Law and History Review (2005) 133–71; see also Jeremy Horder, *Ashworth's Principles of Criminal Law* (Oxford University Press 2016) Chapter 2: Horder's reminder that the legislative origins of such offences as far back as the fifteenth century suggests that the centralizing and regulatory tendencies of the criminal law which have played such a central role in its modernization have roots in earlier legal and political history.

[3] Nicola Lacey, *Women, Crime, and Character: From Moll Flanders to Tess of the d'Urbervilles* (Oxford: Oxford University Press 2008); and 'The Resurgence of Character: Responsibility in the Context of Criminalization', in Anthony Duff and Stuart Green (eds), *Philosophical Foundations of Criminal Law* (Oxford: Oxford University Press 2011).

The eighteenth-century criminal process appears accordingly to have operated quite effectively without the doctrines of responsibility-attribution, which now form the backbone of criminal law. Today, the state's responsibility to prove not only conduct but individual responsibility lies at the heart of criminal law's legitimation as a system of justice rather than one of sheer force: the fairness of criminalization is fundamentally premised on the idea that an offender's capacities of understanding and self-control were properly engaged at the time of the alleged offence. In the eighteenth century, by contrast, the legitimation of criminal justice was provided by rather different institutional processes. Culpability requirements such as having acted 'maliciously', 'wickedly', or 'feloniously' were far from equating to the psychological and capacity-based requirements of *mens rea*—literally, a guilty mind—with which we are now familiar. Many modern commentators have assumed that *mens rea*, as we broadly understand it today, was already a feature of English criminal law by the eighteenth century. But, as we have seen, there are practical and conceptual reasons to doubt this assumption. First, in the light of institutional features such as speed of trial, lack of legal argumentation, and predominance of lay justice, it seems unlikely that the usual eighteenth century trial process could have managed evidence of *mens rea* in the modern, psychological sense as a formal object of proof. Rather, the trial was an opportunity for exculpation, and proceeded on a broad presumption of the defendant's guilt. Second, and more fundamentally, as Jeremy Horder has argued,[4] concepts such as 'malice' in early modern criminal law operated in significantly different ways from modern notions of *mens rea*, and invited not the finding of a 'state of mind' or even attitude but rather a holistic evaluation of conduct.

So how did responsibility-attribution work? Beyond an assumption of capacity (which could be displaced by evidence of manifest insanity), the trial was focused not on *internal* questions about the defendant's state of mind but rather on *external* facts of conduct. Where evidence about conduct was questionable, the patterns of attribution based on knowledge about character and reputation, which dominated the pre-trial process, also informed the trial itself. In effect, then, a judgment of criminal responsibility was a judgment of bad character.

[4] Jeremy Horder, 'Two Histories and Four Hidden Principles of *Mens Rea*' 113 *Law Quarterly Review* (1997) 95–119.

This pattern of character-based responsibility-attribution, which I maintain dominated the eighteenth-century criminal trial, and persisted in some areas long into the nineteenth century, shares some obvious features with George Fletcher's deservedly influential notion of 'manifest criminality'.[5] I seek, however, to account for the emergence and influence of this distinctive pattern of responsibility-attribution in terms of a more encompassing historical and institutional explanation than Fletcher is willing to give. The pattern of 'manifest criminality' rests on the assumption that crime is readily recognizable by members of the community. It is therefore underpinned by a belief in a widely shared ability to make confident evaluations on the basis of appearances. As we saw in Chapter 3, in Fletcher's account this pattern of manifest criminality is gradually displaced in the nineteenth century by a 'subjective pattern' which locates criminality in the intention of the defendant, alongside a 'harm—or risk-based pattern' which focuses on outcomes or potential outcomes. Why should this have been the case? My argument is that the institutional mechanisms needed to render subjective responsibility an object of proof in a criminal trial were not yet in place in the eighteenth century. Nor was the lack of them yet felt to be a pressing practical or ethical problem in a world which had yet to make Maine's famous move from 'status to contract', and in which the institutional mechanisms supporting findings of 'manifest criminality' remained, conversely, relatively robust. But this world was beginning to change and the 'long eighteenth century' saw the gradual assembly of many of the doctrines and institutional arrangements that we take for granted as features of criminal law today.

The Era of Transition

The Partial Eclipse of Character and the Gradual Realization of Capacity Responsibility, with Outcome Responsibility Expanding its Terrain through the Domination of Legislation Yet Remaining on the Ideological Periphery

From at least the middle of the nineteenth century through to the latter part of the twentieth century, character responsibility in its more extreme forms was on the wane. Certainly, traces of older notions of character responsibility could be found in judicial

[5] Fletcher, *Rethinking Criminal Law* (Boston and Toronto: Little, Brown 1978); see discussion in Chapters 1 and 3 above.

condemnations of offenders' evildoing, particularly at the sentencing stage; in the survival of pre-modern *mens rea* terms such as 'malice' and 'wickedness' and the continued (indeed, in some areas, increasing) moralization of criminalization;[6] in the persistence of the presumption that a defendant has intended the natural consequence of his or her actions, discussed in Chapter 4; and in the persisting relevance of motive to responsibility-attribution.[7] The notion of the offender as wrongdoer remained central to the practice of criminal condemnation, albeit mediated through increasingly elaborated legal doctrines. We could also cite the nature of certain stigmatizing penalties as reflecting the view of criminal conviction as expressing a judgment of bad character. But, particularly in treatises and in the reports of the various Criminal Law Commissions—strongly influenced by Bentham's focus on advertence—the development of doctrinal conceptions of *mens rea* was becoming markedly psychological. The question of wrongdoing was, accordingly, increasingly separated from attribution of responsibility, which was premised on the finding of 'intention', knowledge, or foresight. Such an attribution was, certainly, regarded as a *sine qua non* for culpability and hence—absent any defence—wrongdoing. But the finding of responsibility itself—or at least the view of the paradigm states of responsibility, such as intention, knowledge, or foresight—was increasingly elaborated in factual, psychological terms, even though it did not become a full object of proof in the trial until the 1930s.

Other things being equal, it seems clear that this would have made legal doctrine less hospitable to character responsibility. Whereas it is natural to think in terms of a 'malicious' or 'wicked' person, to think in terms of an 'intentional' person makes no sense whatsoever. So once intentionality becomes the key marker of agency and responsibility, an inference from responsibility to character becomes less straightforward. Moreover, the move to a psychological paradigm of intentionality engendered a dualistic approach in legal doctrine. Did the defendant commit the alleged criminal conduct? Was he or she responsible for doing so?[8] The evaluative weight of criminal judgment was projected, in other words, onto the definition of criminal conduct—a

[6] For example, the sexual offences in the latter part of the century: see Lindsay Farmer, *Making the Modern Criminal Law* Chapter 9.

[7] On the persisting importance of motive, see Alan Norrie, *Crime, Reason, and History* (3rd ed., Cambridge: Cambridge University Press 2014) Chapter 3.

[8] R. A. Duff, 'Codifying Criminal Fault', in I. H. Dennis (ed.), *Criminal Law and Criminal Justice* (London: Sweet and Maxwell, 1987).

tendency which, given the dearth (until recently[9]) of normative scholarship on criminalization, left a gap at the heart of criminal law theory. Hence, it was not only a question of evaluation no longer being projected onto character as opposed to conduct: the discipline of criminal law scholarship—perhaps even the practice of criminal law—evinced something akin to a discomfort with the evaluative aspect of criminal law more generally. Older ideas of crime as public wrong were gradually undermined by a more extensive criminal law and a more heterogeneous society. At the same time, the problem of political legitimation was being accentuated by the spread of egalitarian sentiments, which coincided with the inegalitarian impact of criminalization. As a result, the burden of legitimating criminal culpability was borne to an ever greater extent by the general part, in which increasingly elaborate psychological doctrines of *men rea* and defence came to occupy a significantly larger proportion during the course of the late nineteenth and the twentieth centuries.[10] To put this in Farmer's terms, the project of securing civil order was itself premised on a very particular, modern construction of criminal law's subjects as responsible agents.[11]

Past bad character as evidence tending to the proof of criminal responsibility had also experienced a decisive change in fortunes. Throughout the eighteenth century, as we have seen, trials were dominated by evidence about the accused's (and witnesses') standing and reputation. But as rules of evidence began to be formalized, doubts arose about the reliability and legitimacy of evidence of bad character, and those doubts themselves added to the impetus for reform. The relatively static, predictable world in which reputation or known qualities of status were regarded as reliable indicators of credibility—either of witness testimony, or of a 'not guilty' plea—was being displaced by an increasingly individualistic world in

[9] Joel Feinberg, *The Moral Limits of Criminal Law*, Vol. 1: *Harm to Others*, Vol. 2: *Offense to Others*, Vol. 3: *Harm to Self*, Vol. 4: *Harmless Wrongdoing* (New York: Oxford University Press 1987–1990); Douglas Husak, *Overcriminalization* (New York: Oxford University Press 2007); Jonathan Schonsheck, *On Criminalization* (New York: Springer Verlag 1994); Leo Katz, 'Villainy and Felony: A Problem Concerning Criminalization' 6 *Buffalo Criminal Law Review* (2002) 451–82; R. A. Duff, Lindsay Farmer, S. E. Marshall, Massimo Renzo, and Victor Tadros (eds), *The Boundaries of the Criminal Law* (Oxford: Oxford University Press 2010).

[10] See Lindsay Farmer, *Criminal Law, Tradition and Legal Order* (Cambridge: Cambridge University Press 1996) Chapter 1; Nicola Lacey, 'Contingency and Conceptualism: Reflections on an Encounter between Critique and Philosophical Analysis of Criminal Law', in R. A. Duff (ed.), *Philosophy and the Criminal Law* (Cambridge: Cambridge University Press 1998).

[11] Lindsay Farmer, *Making the Modern Criminal Law: Criminalization and Civil Order* Chapter 6.

which, particularly in the cities, the old distinctions between insiders and outsiders, on which English mechanisms of social control had long relied, made little sense. Moreover, a freely choosing, responsible citizen stood centre stage in the contemporary social imaginary, posing new legitimation problems as well as new challenges of coordination. In terms of legitimation, the proposition that the proof of a subject's guilt should be facilitated by mechanisms based on the assumption that his or her previous behaviour manifested a criminal character suggestive of a propensity to commit a crime was at odds with the vision of freedom implicit in the emerging social imaginary, and might moreover be seen as introducing information which was irrelevant to the charge at issue. The seeds, in other words, of what we today think of as objections to character evidence based on moral autonomy and double jeopardy were sown.[12] The emerging conception of individual agency was reflected in the provisions of the Criminal Evidence Act 1898, which re-established the accused's opportunity to give testimony in their own defence, thus producing in the late nineteenth century context a new form of knowledge available to courts.[13] This, in turn, provided resources for putting into operation a notion of criminal responsibility as residing in psychological states of mind—an evidentiary matter to which, as we saw in Chapter 2, the emerging forensic sciences and sciences of mind and brain were also able to make a contribution. Presaging these developments, character evidence was rendered inadmissible other than in some special cases from the early nineteenth century.[14]

[12] See Paul Roberts and Adrian Zuckerman, *Criminal Evidence* (2nd ed., New York: Oxford University Press 2010) Chapter 14.

[13] On the background to the Act, which, while according the defendant a right to silence, rendered the exercise of that right liable to the interpretation that the defendant had something to hide, see David Bentley, *English Criminal Justice in the 19th Century* (London: Hambledon Press 1998) 171–86.

[14] There is some doubt about the timing and causes of the demise of character evidence. John Langbein attests to doubts about its reliability from the mid-seventeenth century: John H. Langbein, *The Origins of Adversary Criminal Trial* (Oxford: Oxford University Press 2003) pp. 190–202, in particular p. 191, citing John W. Strong et al. (eds), *McCormick on Evidence* (5th ed., St. Paul: West Group 1999) p. 649 para 186. David Leonard, who traces a rule of limited admissibility subject to (inadequately rationalized) exceptions to the early nineteenth century, explores doubts about character evidence's relevance and its fairness, given its capacity to surprise (often unrepresented) defendants and present problems of rebuttal. David Leonard, *The New Wigmore: A Treatise on Evidence: Evidence of Other Misconduct and Similar Events* (Austin: Wolters Kluwer, Aspen Publishers 2009) Chapters 1–3. See further T. P. Gallanis, 'The Rise of Modern Evidence Law' 84 *Iowa Law Review* (1999) 499–560; C. J. W. Allen, *The Law of Evidence in Victorian England* (Cambridge: Cambridge University Press 1997); Mike Redmayne, *Character in*

Given the case that can undoubtedly be made for the relevance and legitimacy of reliance on character evidence,[15] this policy of exclusion is of real significance. The reasons appear to have been anxiety about the reliability of such evidence; anxiety about surprising the defendant with a very difficult task of rebuttal; and about its capacity to have undue sway with juries, with the result that its prejudicial effect might outweigh its probative force. But it is important to see that this anxiety (which, it should be remembered, was never decisive in the civilian systems, where official scrutiny of evidence in the inquisitorial process is regarded as a sufficient safeguard, and the contextualization of a defendant's actions within a broader narrative of his or her life was normal[16]) was itself shaped, and its intensity increased, by broader social changes. These changes disrupted the dense networks of local knowledge which, centuries after the demise of the self-informing jury, continued to allow evaluation of character to play a robust and central role in the criminal trial. Amid an ever more individualistic society, confidence about evaluations of character—or jurors' ability to 'read' character from conduct, reputation, or appearance—declined sharply, and long-standing doubts about the unduly prejudicial effect of airing the defendant's 'dirty linen' prevailed.[17] Just as doctrinal standards of responsibility shifted from external, evaluative to internal, psychological modes, so favoured forms of evidence shifted from a concern with external appearances or status to a focus on direct reports of experience, opinion, and observation.[18]

the Criminal Trial (Oxford: Oxford University Press 2015). As Lindsay Farmer has pointed out to me, with the emergence and spread of professional policing in the nineteenth century, the exclusion of character evidence further served to reduce the incentives for the police to rely on 'rounding up the usual suspects'.

[15] See Mike Redmayne, 'The Relevance of Bad Character' 61 *Cambridge Law Journal* (2002) 684–714; and 'The Ethics of Character Evidence' 61 *Current Legal Problems* (2008) 371–99.

[16] S. A. Field, 'State, Citizen and Character in French Criminal Process' 33 *Journal of Legal Studies* (2006) 522–46; cf. Mirjan R. Damaška's distinction between systems of 'coordinate' and 'hierarchical' authority: *The Faces of Justice and State Authority: A Comparative Approach to the Legal Process* (New Haven: Yale University Press 1991).

[17] See Julius Stone, 'The Rule of Exclusion of Similar Fact Evidence: England' 46 *Harvard Law Review* (1933) 954–85, at 983–4; David P. Leonard, 'Character and Motive in Evidence Law' 34 *Loyola of Los Angeles Law Review* (2001) 439–537, at 450; Nicola Lacey, *Women, Crime and Character* pp. 34–40.

[18] On changing conceptions of what counted as the most persuasive form of evidence in the process of modernization, see T. P. Gallanis, 'The Rise of Modern Evidence Law'; Alexander Welsh, *Strong Representations: Narrative and Circumstantial Evidence in England* (Baltimore: The John Hopkins University Press 1992).

With ever greater centralization, professionalization, and systematization during the nineteenth century and with the diffusion of democratic ideas about individual agency and more psychological views of human subjectivity, the patterns and principles of attribution based on capacity were accordingly strengthened and refined. Additionally, the patterns and principles based on character declined as autonomous forces, though they did continue to shape decision-making at the prosecution and sentencing stages. They also became intertwined in interesting ways with notions of capacity. New regulatory institutions of governmental control, including but not restricted to criminal justice, assumed an ability to incentivize the formation of habits of good citizenship and, hence, in some sense to shape character, temporarily effecting a particular reconciliation of character and capacity as bases for criminal responsibility.[19] Yet, as we saw in Chapter 2, new challenges for the criminal process were implicit in this emerging democratic culture as it moved gradually towards an ideal of full citizenship for all. The resultant idea of individuals as citizens rather than subjects brought with it a more pressing burden on the government to legitimate its expanding resort to criminalizing and penal power.[20] At the same time—indeed, hence—patterns and principles based on outcome began to occupy a larger terrain as a result of the growing regulatory ambitions of the nation state, notably in the expansion of summary jurisdiction, facilitating the implementation of criminal law in areas such as factory legislation and licensing.[21]

In the context of my hypothesized trajectory from primarily 'character-based' attributions of responsibility to those trained rather on the defendant's mental state or engaged capacities, the late nineteenth century presents itself as an interesting focus. By this time, most of the institutional changes which distinguish the modern criminal justice system—legal representation by defence lawyers, systematic law reporting, an organized legal profession, a developed law of evidence, a professional police—were in place. And the growth

[19] See John Bender, *Imagining the Penitentiary: Fiction and the Architecture of Mind in* Eighteenth-*Century England* (Chicago and London: University of Chicago Press 1987) (discussing the notion of character informing the penitentiary movement); Leon Radzinowicz and Roger Hood, *The Emergence of Penal Policy in Victorian and Edwardian England* (Oxford: Clarendon Press 1990) at 35–6 (addressing the role of character in the shaping of social policy); Martin Wiener, *Reconstructing the Criminal* (Cambridge: Cambridge University Press 1990) at 14–158.

[20] J. S. Mill, *On Liberty* (1859: Harmondsworth: Penguin 1974).

[21] See Lindsay Farmer, *Criminal Law, Tradition and Legal Order* 57–99.

of what we would now call the medical and psychological sciences had rendered plausible and, presumptively, practicable a trial process which set up the state of a defendant's mind as an object of proof. Moreover, these legal and procedural changes arguably mapped on to a deeper set of changes in ideas of human identity or selfhood. While social institutions in the still stratified and relatively stable world of eighteenth century England exhibited a confidence about reading character, credit, and even conduct from status[22] and surface, the more mobile, urbanized world of the nineteenth century was generating a new set of coordination problems by undermining the practical basis for these individual assessments. At the same time, it was experiencing an acute legitimation need, as emerging democratization posed a demand for more individualized assessments of credibility, while the emergence of the romantic movement had consolidated a developing trend to see the essence of human identity as residing not in the external markers of conduct but rather in the inner recesses of the mind or soul.[23]

Furthermore, this was a rapidly changing world, and one in which conflict about even core values informing an (itself expanded) criminal law was on the increase. In this context, and that of the rapidly expanding regulatory tasks to which criminal law was being put, as Lindsay Farmer has argued,[24] the notion of crime as reflecting a widely shared notion of 'public wrong', articulated with some confidence by Blackstone, became elusive. The result was that, as confidence in consensus and in the recognizability of criminal conduct declined, even among elites, the weight of criminal law's legitimation was projected onto the proof of individual responsibility, further conducing to a decline of evaluative notions of responsibility such as acting 'maliciously' or exhibiting 'bad character', and to a rise of 'factualized' notions of responsibility such as 'intention'.[25] In each

[22] Much the same was true in the areas of finance and science: see, respectively, Margot C. Finn, *The Character of Credit: Personal Debt in English Culture, 1740–1914* (Cambridge: Cambridge University Press 2003); Stephen Shapin, *A Social History of Truth: Civility and Science in Seventeenth-Century England* (Chicago: University of Chicago Press 1983).

[23] Dror Warhman, *The Making of the Modern Self* (New Haven: Yale University Press 2004).

[24] *Criminal Law, Tradition and Legal Order* Chapters 1 and 4, *Making the Modern Criminal Law* Chapters 3 and 6.

[25] Alan Norrie, *Crime, Reason and History*; Nicola Lacey, 'In Search of the Responsible Subject: History, Philosophy and Criminal Law Theory' 64 *Modern Law Review* (2001) 350–71.

of these contexts, the promise of scientific insight into the workings of the human mind was seductive indeed. But had 'character' disappeared? Or had it merely been realigned in relation to the newer discourses of responsibility-attribution? Even in London, evidence about character and reputation remained important to social control. The Old Bailey insanity cases for the 1880s feature copious character evidence, while Conley's study of late Victorian Kent shows that 'local knowledge' and informal mechanisms of judgment remained central to criminal justice control.[26] But the 'economy of character'[27] could no longer be relied upon as a social mechanism for distinguishing criminality. Indeed both the surface signals of human character and the psychological depths of engaged human capacity presented problems of legibilty in the late Victorian criminal courts.

The Dual Track Era

Criminal Law as Divided between Capacity and Outcome Responsibility, with Character Mainly Displaced from the Substantive Law to the Prosecution and Sentencing Processes

The gradual construction of a welfare state from the early twentieth century on, bringing with it new, ameliorative ideologies and bureaucratic institutions for the criminal process,[28] had important consequences for criminal responsibility. The upshot of these developments was a realignment of patterns of responsibility-attribution in criminal law towards a reinforced emphasis on the practical and ideological importance of capacity—itself crucial to the penal welfarist ambition—across the terrain of the 'real crime' which preoccupied text book writers,[29] combined with a reliance on outcome responsibility in an intellectually siloed (yet empirically growing) area of 'regulatory crime'. For reasons which I will canvass below, character principles and patterns in fact experienced a limited but

[26] Carolyn A. Conley, *The Unwritten Law: Criminal Justice in Victorian Kent* (Oxford University Press 1991).

[27] See Deidre Shauna Lynch, *The Economy of Character: Novels, Market Culture, and the Business of Inner Meaning* (Chicago: University of Chicago Press 1998).

[28] As described in detail in David Garland, *Punishment and Welfare: A History of Penal Strategies* (Aldershot: Gower Publishing 1985).

[29] See Celia Wells and Oliver Quick, *Lacey, Wells and Quick's Reconstructing Criminal Law* (4th ed., Cambridge: Cambridge University Press) Chapter 1.

important revival with the emergence of ideas of social and psychological pathology in the latter part of the nineteenth century and first part of the twentieth century, notably in the form of criminal classification statutes enacting special regulatory regimes for the feeble-minded, the inebriate, the vagrant, and the fallen woman.[30] Indeed, coinciding as they did with the emergence and consolidation of criminology as a discipline, we could see these statues as early manifestations of the character/risk hybrid pattern of responsibility-attribution which, as we shall see below, has emerged in the late twentieth century. But they were gradually modified by their association with welfare principles: criminal justice assumed a capable, responsible subject whose agency was susceptible to being deployed in the service of ameliorative projects premised on reform, rehabilitation, and culturally legitimated within a 'civilized' scientific discourse, as well as efforts at social inclusion, albeit within a still relatively hierarchical system of social ordering. As Farmer has noted, the twentieth century has accordingly been an era of growing dominance for the *mens rea* principle, and not, *pace* Barbara Wootton, of its decline.[31] With the growth of organized legal education, including universities, and the consequent diffusion of systematic texts and treatises, the idea of capacity responsibility assumed dominance in the first half of the twentieth century, alongside a continuing edifice of outcome-based practices grounded in a parallel, and very different, set of legitimating principles and coordinating practices.[32] Moreover, the line between the objects of regulation encompassed by capacity and outcome practices has never been stable: both drug and traffic offences are good examples of areas in which no clear line between regulatory and core

[30] Lucia Zedner, *Women, Crime, and Custody in Victorian England* (Oxford and New York: Oxford University Press 1991) pp. 219–96.

[31] Lindsay Farmer, *Making the Modern Criminal Law* Chapter 6; Barbara Wootton, *Crime and the Criminal Law* (London: Stevens and Sons 1964). As Farmer notes, the increasing emphasis on subjective *mens rea* as legitimating criminalization has moreover provided a rationale for expanding the boundaries of the criminal law: Farmer, *Making the Modern Criminal Law* Chapters 8 and 9.

[32] Lindsay Farmer, 'Of Treatises and Textbooks: The Literature of the Criminal Law in Nineteenth Century Britain', in Markus D. Dubber and Angela Fernandez (eds), *Essays on the Anglo-American Legal Treatise* (Oxford: Hart Publishing 2012) and *Making the Modern Criminal Law* Chapter 5; see, more generally, A. W. B. Simpson, 'The Rise and Fall of the Legal Treatise: Legal Principles and the Forms of Legal Literature' (1981) 48 *University of Chicago Law Review* 632–79.

terrains can be drawn.[33] The two ideational and practical worlds were, however, related *via* the fair opportunity version of the capacity principle, in the form of both negligence offences (such as involuntary manslaughter) in the 'core' of criminal law and due diligence offences (such as health and safety offences, either premised on proof of lack of due diligence or subject to a due diligence defence) on the periphery of regulatory offences based on harmful outcomes. The existence of both groups of offences has moreover implied a struggle between objective and subjective forms of capacity-based *mens rea*, finding significant expression in appellate cases in the last third of the twentieth century.

The Resurgence of Character and the (Re-)Emergence of Risk

A Further Pluralization of Patterns of Responsibility-Attribution in the Late Twentieth and Early Twenty-First Centuries

This dual system began to be disrupted in the latter part of the twentieth century with the increasing politicization of criminal justice and an intensified focus on insecurity. This period accordingly saw the emergence of a new alignment of principles. Capacity responsibility still occupied a secure role among core criminal offences (and a legitimating effect radiating more widely), but there emerged a new discourse of responsibility founded in the presentation of risk. This promoted a hybrid pattern and practice of responsibility based on a combination of putative outcome and a new sense of bad character, not as religiously inflected sinfulness but rather as the status of presenting risk or being 'dangerous'. Arguably driven not only by the feelings of insecurity associated with life in late modern societies,[34] but also by rapidly developing technologies of risk assessment in medicine, psychiatry, geography, and demography, this pattern has been particularly evident in the areas of both terrorism and drug regulation, in the de facto revival of status offences, and in the construction

[33] The radical instability of the distinction between 'real' and 'regulatory' crime has been brought into sharp relief in the late twentieth and early twenty-first centuries by persistent moral panics about serious offences in the areas of fraud, tax evasion, and insider trading.

[34] Anthony Giddens, *Modernity and Self-Identity: Self and Society in the Late Modern Age* (Palo Alto, CA: Stanford University Press 1991).

of a vast area of preventive justice through the expansion of inchoate, and the creation of 'pre-inchoate', offences.[35] Moreover, these developments have been facilitated by the dramatic rise in the discretionary power of police and prosecutors, which was accorded by the emergence of plea bargaining as a fundamental coordinating mechanism in criminal justice. Indeed plea bargaining might justly stand as the key symbol of contemporary criminal justice: at once bureaucratized, dominated by professionals, and subject to the formal consent of individual, 'responsible' offenders, yet simultaneously embracing discretionary practices founded on unstated assumptions of dangerousness or bad character. It renders an extensive system of regulatory criminalization affordable while, at the same time, preserving an aura of constitutional propriety and respect for individual responsibility.

There is therefore reason to think that in substance, if not always in form, character-based patterns of attribution are enjoying a revival in contemporary English (and American) criminal responsibility-attribution. Emerging from their subterranean position in prosecution and sentencing practice, they are enjoying an explicit revival not only in mandatory sentencing laws applying to particular categories of 'dangerous' offender, and in phenomena such as sex offender notification requirements or probation orders based on risk factors, but also in the substantive law, particularly that dealing with terrorism, and in the operation of evidential presumptions, detention rules, practices of offender profiling, and the renewed admissibility of evidence of bad character. In the remainder of this chapter, I further describe and analyse this development, offering an interpretation of its origins, its significance, and the normative questions which it raises.

The Subterranean Survival of Character

Before considering the reasons for this apparent renewal of practices of responsibility-attribution based on evaluations of or assumptions about bad character, it is worth considering how far and in what ways character-based patterns persisted in often covert ways even in the

[35] See Andrew Ashworth and Lucia Zedner, 'Defending the Criminal Law: Reflections on the Changing Character of Crime, Procedure, and Sanctions' 2 *Criminal Law and Philosophy* (2008) 21–51; for further discussion, see Chapter 3 above, pp. 91–106.

twentieth century—the period in which the dual system of capacity- and outcome-based criminalization was most fully realized.

Character Responsibility in Substantive Criminal Law

Even amid the supposed triumph of subjective, capacity-based criminal responsibility, we see a somewhat mixed picture in terms of patterns of responsibility-attribution. Though reliable evidence is hard to find,[36] offences of strict liability have increased in number, particularly in the mid-twentieth century.[37] Human rights or other constitutional standards—fast becoming the standard resort of criminal law theorists in search of something hopeful to say about how rampant criminalization might be restrained[38]—hold out no cause for optimism here, at least in England and Wales, given that strict liability has been held to be compatible with the European Convention.[39] Moreover, notwithstanding the House of Lords' resounding defence of 'subjectivism'—*mens rea* as founded in subjective mental states such as intention or foresight—in *B v DPP*,[40] and the demise of 'objective recklessness'—failure to attend to a risk which would have been obvious to a reasonable person—in *R v Graham*,[41] the terrain over which subjectivism holds sway consists in a relatively restricted range

[36] See Nicola Lacey, 'Historicising Criminalization' 72 *Modern Law Review* (2009) 936–61; Andrew Ashworth, 'Is the Criminal Law a Lost Cause?' 116 *Law Quarterly Review* (2000) 225; James Chalmers and Fiona Leverick, 'Tracking the Creation of Criminal Offences' 2013 *Crim LR* 543–60; James Chalmers and Fiona Leverick, 'Quantifying Criminalization', in R. A. Duff et al. (eds), *Criminalization: The Political Morality of the Criminal Law,* (Oxford: Oxford University Press 2015) Chapter 2; James Chalmers, '"Frenzied Law-Making": Over-Criminalization by Numbers' [2014] 67 *Current Legal Problems* 483; Jeremy Horder, 'Bureaucratic "Criminal" Law: Too Much of a Bad Thing?', in R. A. Duff et al. (eds), *Criminalization: The Political Morality of the Criminal Law* (Oxford: Oxford University Press, 2014) Chapter 4.

[37] Ashworth and Zedner, 'Defending the Criminal Law' p. 32, quoting an unpublished paper by Ashworth, 'Criminalization: What do 2005's New Crimes Tell us about the Law?' at note 39.

[38] See, for example, Ashworth and Zedner, 'Defending the Criminal Law'; Douglas Husak, *Overcriminalization.* For a provocative argument that formalization via constitutional challenges can have counter-productive effects, see William J. Stuntz, 'The Political Constitution of Criminal Justice' 119 *Harvard Law Review* (2006) 781–851.

[39] *R v G* [2008] UKHL 37: as Paul Roberts has noted, Art. 6(2) of the European Convention was not designed, and is ill adapted, to deliver a constitutionalization of the *mens rea* principle: 'Strict Liability and the Presumption of Innocence: An Exposé of Functionalist Assumptions', in A. P. Simester (ed.), *Appraising Strict Liability* (Oxford: Oxford University Press 2005) p. 193.

[40] *B v DPP* [2000] 2 AC 428; cf. *R v G* [2008] ibid.

[41] *R v G* [2003] UKHL 50.

of criminal offences. Admittedly many of them, such as murder, assaults, and theft, lie in what is perceived as the core of criminal law. But, even leaving aside the impact of plea bargaining, they hardly constitute the overwhelming majority of criminal laws actually enforced. As Victor Tadros has emphasized,[42] the widespread operation of reasonableness standards—not only in offences of negligence, including manslaughter and, in effect, rape and sexual penetration, but also in defences such as self-defence and duress—may assume the meaning of an imposition of character liability through an *inference* from conduct to character. For there is nothing in the doctrinal standard itself which argues one way or another on the question of whether, in effect, such standards imply that *the person* who behaved in a particular way was unreasonable, or that they have *done* what was unreasonable. (Note that this ambiguity exists whether or not they allow for investigation of the individual defendant's capacity to reach the reasonable standard of conduct or care.) It is contextual factors, external to legal doctrine, which shape this aspect of the social meaning of the standard.

Perhaps more surprisingly, a similar story can be told when we move from 'objective' and reasonableness-based *mens rea* mechanisms to 'subjective' and psychological ones. Motive, though technically irrelevant to psychological notions of *mens rea* such as intention, has always entered into the 'interpretive construction' of *mens rea*, through mechanisms such as shifts in time frame,[43] and is arguably enjoying a new prominence, notably in the form of aggravated liability attendant on racial or religious motivation.[44] Where liability turns on motive, assumptions about good and bad character are invited into jury deliberations. And at the very heart of the doctrinal marker of criminal law's modern formalization of *mens rea*, subjective *mens rea* concepts such as intention or knowledge are susceptible to interpretation as bearing on character as much as—or rather than— on conduct. As George Fletcher has noted in relation to the American Law Institute's Modern Penal Code, even subjective liability for unsuccessful (including impossible) attempts—the prime terrain of the modern liberal doctrine of

[42] Victor Tadros, *Criminal Responsibility* (Oxford: Oxford University Press 2005).

[43] See Alan Norrie, *Crime, Reason and History* pp. 365–73; Mark Kelman, 'Interpretive Construction in the Substantive Criminal Law' 33 *Stanford Law Review* (1981) 591–673.

[44] Crime and Disorder Act 1998, ss 28–32 (amended to include religion by the Anti-Terrorism, Crime and Security Act 2001).

autonomy-respecting principles of criminal responsibility—is susceptible to capture as a mechanism for criminalizing bad character:

> The contemporary justification for focusing on the internal attitude of the actor is that acting on the intention to cause harm to others represents a rejection of the legal order ... The frame of mind that underlies expansive attempt liability resembles, therefore, the us-against-them social policy that has led to the use of life sentences against third-time offenders ...
>
> [T]wo anti-liberal principles convince many jurists that they should punish innocuous attempts ... The first is the principle of gearing the criminal law to an attitude of hostility toward the norms of the legal system. The second is changing the focus of the criminal law from acts to actors. These two are linked by the inference: people who display an attitude of hostility toward the norms of the system show themselves to be dangerous and therefore should be subject to imprisonment to protect the interests of others.[45]

Doctrinal mechanisms in modern criminal law are not, in short, absolutely decisive as between capacity- and character-based approaches to responsibility-attribution, which are driven rather by extra-doctrinal factors to which we shall turn below. This, it should be noted, strengthens the case made in Chapter 1 for the analysis of practices of responsibility-attribution within the context of criminalization overall. However, it should not obscure the fact that recent criminal legislation includes developments which actually invite—rather than merely respond to—a more expansive practice of criminalization on the basis of assumptions about character: nor should it be taken to deny that criminal law doctrines were reconstructed and refined through the nineteenth and twentieth centuries in a way which fundamentally invited, and often required, judgments based on assessments of capacity responsibility. The area in which we see the clearest evidence of a revival of something akin to a character principle of responsibility is that of terrorism.[46] For many years, criminal provisions directed specifically at terrorism in England and Wales were crafted with the specific case of Northern Ireland in mind. They were, formally, emergency powers. Accordingly, the Prevention of Terrorism Act had to be

[45] George P. Fletcher, *Basic Concepts of Criminal Law* (New York: Oxford University Press 1998) pp. 179–80 (with thanks to Peter Ramsay).

[46] This is not to imply that counterterrorism law is the only area in which we see the emergence of forms of character responsibility. For example, hate crime laws also

renewed by Parliament each year. Over the last fifteen years, we have seen a vivid case of the 'normalization of special powers',[47] with no fewer than eight substantial pieces of legislation specifically directed to the criminalization of terrorism, even leaving to one side provisions within other pieces of legislation which were drafted with an eye to terrorism or are susceptible to being used in terrorist cases.[48] The extraordinary events of September 2001 are, of course, an important part of the genesis of this new legislative concern with the criminalization of terrorism. But many of the powers and regulations which have been enacted in the wake of public anxiety about global terrorism may be deployed against suspected offenders who have no link with terrorism whatsoever. As we saw in Chapter 3, the anti-terror reaction has created a wave of criminalization—particularly of what we might call preliminary or pre-inchoate activities—which significantly expands the boundaries of criminal law.[49] In doing so, it adds to police and prosecutorial power, weakens defence lawyers, curtails the scope of judicial discretion, and, in some of its more radical 'adjustments' to normal standards of procedure, arguably deploys some of the methods of terror itself.

Why should we regard anti-terrorism criminalization as a form of character responsibility? The offences require, after all, proof of dangerous or harmful conduct, or at least planning or preparation for such conduct. Are terrorist offences not, therefore, perfectly standard cases of criminalized conduct? This is, up to a point, a valid view. But only up to a point. To see why, consider the fact that the 'acts of

operate by re-criminalizing conduct which is already criminally proscribed, and moreover do so by categorizing those who commit them as being a certain kind of person. I am grateful to Ely Aaronson for this point.

47 Paddy Hillyard, 'The Normalization of Special Powers', in P. Scraton (ed.), *Law, Order and the Authoritarian State* (Philadelphia: Open University Press 1987).

48 Terrorism Acts 2000, and 2006; Anti-Terrorism, Crime and Security Act 2001; Prevention of Terrorism Act 2005; Counter-Terrorism Act 2008; Terrorist Asset-Freezing Etc. Act 2010; Terrorism Prevention and Investigation Measures Act 2011; Counter-Terrorism and Security Act 2015; see also Criminal Justice Act 2003, Coroners and Justice Act 2009. Of the terrorism-specific statutes, only the Prevention of Terrorism Act 2005 is subject to the renewal requirement that characterized the earlier legislation. For discussion, see Victor Tadros, 'Justice and Terrorism' 10 *New Criminal Law Review* (2007) 658–89; Lucia Zedner, *Security* (London: Routledge 2009) pp. 116–42; Tom Bingham, *The Rule of Law* (London: Allen Lane, Penguin Books 2010) Chapter 11; Paddy Hillyard, 'The Normalization of Special Powers', Andrew Ashworth and Lucia Zedner (eds), *Preventive Justice* (Oxford: Oxford University Press 2014) pp. 171–96.

49 Victor Tadros, 'Justice and Terrorism' pp. 670–5; and 'Crimes and Security' 71 *Modern Law Review* (2008) 940–70. See also Chapter 3 above, p. 99 ff.

terrorism' which form the ostensible object of public concern—and, hence, one assumes, of criminalization—are acts which are already proscribed. Leaving aside the expansion of liability into pre-inchoate areas, such as holding information or being a member of a proscribed group, most of what is encompassed by anti-terror legislation could be prosecuted irrespective of its existence. When we seek the rationale for the criminalization of terrorism specifically, we see, certainly, governments seeking to bolster their electoral credibility by 'doing something' about terrorism. But in the meaning of what they create, we see something akin to character responsibility: the idea that, on top of committing or planning acts of violence, there is something additionally and intrinsically wrong about being a certain kind of person, engaged in a certain kind of activity—an aggravation of blameworthiness which justifies a special criminalization regime.

Notwithstanding the House of Lords' finding that section 23 of the 2001 legislation (the application of indefinite detention exclusively to foreign nationals) contravened the Human Rights Act, much of the counterterrorism legislation—notably, as discussed below, the control order, implemented as a result of the House of Lords' decision—is redolent of the criminalization of status.[50] Note, for example, the assertion of Lord Phillips, the Lord Chief Justice, in a key case examining the ECHR-compatibility of control orders under section 3 of the Prevention of Terrorism Act 2005, that 'The PTA seeks to achieve this object [of preventing or restricting a person's further involvement in terrorism-related activity] by empowering the Secretary of State to impose control orders on those suspected of *being terrorists*.'[51]

Another way of putting this would be in terms of motive: normalized terrorism legislation introduces a motive-based differentiating principle into the heart of an allegedly universal criminal law, and does so in terms of an inference about criminality drawn from that particular motivation. A natural (though not a necessary) implication of such an inference is a judgment of bad character. As Tadros puts it, these are 'individualized' offences, targeting members of a particular group.[52] A further whiff of character responsibility lies in the

[50] *A v Secretary of State for the Home Department* [2004] UKHL 56.

[51] *Secretary of State for the Home Department v M.B.* [2006] EWCA 1140 (emphasis added). The case subsequently went to the House of Lords, where Lord Bingham's analysis was more careful in preserving the fragile line between conduct- and character-based liability: [2007] UKHL 46.

[52] Victor Tadros, 'Justice and Terrorism' pp. 683–5.

legislation's extended conception of accomplice liability via membership offences, which enact 'the fallacy of "guilt by association"'.[53] Moreover, the articulated rationale of both the legislation and aspects of foreign policy in relation to international terrorism (notably cooperation with 'extraordinary renditions' and counterterrorism operations in countries such as Afghanistan, Iraq, and Pakistan) participates in a strong form of character essentialism and character determinism: the assumption is that there is a finite number of 'bad people' who are 'terrorists', and if we can simply detain or 'take out' enough of them, the world will be a safer place for those of 'good character', who alone deserve the full protection of the rule of law.

Character as Evidence

Part 11 of the Criminal Justice Act 2003 fundamentally changes the rules on admissibility of evidence of bad character.[54] Departing from a long-established principle of the restricted admissibility of such evidence, section 101(1) of the Act allows evidence of bad character, in the sense not only of previous convictions, but also of previous misconduct or reprehensible behaviour, to be admitted so long as its probative value is not outweighed by its prejudicial effect; and so long as it passes one of seven tests or 'gateways'. These include not only circumstances where the defendant has put his/her own character in question by questioning that of another witness, or where all parties agree to the evidence being admitted, but also—most significantly for our purposes—where it is important explanatory evidence, where it is relevant to an important matter in issue between the defendant and the prosecution, or where it has substantial probative value in relation to an important matter at issue between the defendant and a co-defendant.

A 2009 study of the operation of the new provisions conducted for the Ministry of Justice suggested that by far the most common use

[53] Lucia Zedner, *Security* p. 130. For an example of the power which this mechanism can exert, see Amy E. Lerman and Vesla M. Weaver, *Arresting Citizenship: The Democratic Consequences of Crime Control* (Chicago: University of Chicago Press 2014) pp. 79–81, discussing the use in the US of blanket injunctions curtailing freedom of association for those suspected of gang membership.

[54] For a comprehensive analysis, see Mike Redmayne, *Character in the Criminal Trial*. The Crown Prosecution Service's policy in relation to character evidence is set out at http://www.cps.gov.uk/legal/a_to_c/bad_character_evidence/ (accessed 26 July 2015).

of the provision was through the gateway of 'relevant to an important matter in issue', with 'important explanatory evidence' as the next most cited but far rarer justification, and assault and theft cases the most common context.[55] Among the cases in which character evidence was admitted in relation to a matter at issue, the main use of the evidence was to establish propensity. A vivid sense of the sort of argument enabled by the legislation is given in the report, which cites the Crown Prosecution in one case as stating that 'the defendant is of bad character as he has previous reprehensible behaviour' which was relevant, as it relates to 'an important matter in issue' between the prosecution and defence. 'He has several times been physically and verbally abusive to [the complainant] throughout the course of their sexual relationship when [the complainant] was only 14 or 15 at the time. These matters demonstrate a propensity to commit offences of child abuse. He has admitted the sexual relationship commenced when [the complainant] was 14 years old. She became pregnant with his child when she was 15 years old.'[56] It is hard to think that the prejudicial force of such a sketch would be other than significant.

It is important not to exaggerate the practical significance or broader ramifications of section 101. The research study suggests that the provision is being used primarily to introduce evidence of previous convictions, particularly in relation to similar crimes. Among contested cases, half concerned similar offences, with 29 per cent concerning offences featuring a similar *modus operandi*, and only 13 per cent featuring a claim about propensity to commit crime founded more generally on past reprehensible behaviour.[57] Furthermore, evidence of bad-character-based propensity did already find its way into the courts. For example, in *R v Kingston*,[58] the House of Lords upheld a defendant's conviction for indecent assault on a young boy notwithstanding the defendant's involuntary intoxication, on the basis that the finding of child pornography at his home supported

[55] Morgan Harris Burrows LLP, Ministry of Justice Research Series 5/09, Office for Criminal Justice Reform, March 2009, at pp. 14–23; for a considered review of the operation of the new law, see Roberts and Zuckerman, *Criminal Evidence* Chapter 14; and for cases illustrating the potential breadth of the new provisions, see *R v McMinn* [2007] EWCA 3024, and with specific reference to the relevance of previous reprehensible but non-criminal conduct, see *R v Manister* [2006] 1 WLR 1885.

[56] Morgan Harris Burrows, Ministry of Justice Research Series 5/09 p. 20.

[57] Ibid. pp. 15, 17, 23.

[58] *R v Kingston* [1994] 3 WLR 519.

an inference that he had the relevant *mens rea* notwithstanding his intoxication. Nonetheless, the fact that, with the 2003 Act, a political/legislative decision was made explicitly to enlarge the admissibility of evidence of bad character tells us something important about the politics of criminal justice, about contemporary conceptions of criminality, and about the legitimation of punishment. For the legislative change appears to proceed from a view of criminality as importantly located in stable features of character or personality, which underpin the claim of propensity.[59]

But do these and other possible examples really amount to a belief in criminal character: to what I called in Chapter 2 'character essentialism' and 'character determinism'? Or do they rather amount to a sorting for convenience into types, on an actuarial basis?[60] Might the persistence of such short cuts to proof in the English system proceed from an anxiety about the power to coordinate information adequately for satisfying what criminal law scholars take to be 'normal' standards of proof? And might this anxiety itself proceed from concern about the incentives for law-abiding behaviour among those not fully included in society, polity, or economy, which poses a risk to criminal law's role of social coordination, as well as problems of political legitimation? In tracing the gradual erosion, in practice, of the distinction between bad character as tending to proof of guilt and character as constitutive of guilt, the causation is hard to trace, and seems likely to run in more than one direction. In this context, it is worth noting that another evidential mechanism geared to easing the path to conviction—the reversal of burdens of proof—has itself tended to be deployed in areas, notably that of drug regulation and terrorism, in which the object of criminalization is what is regarded as a dangerous lifestyle, group membership, or set of beliefs as much as an individual criminal act. As we shall see below, these patterns are strongly suggestive of a certain realignment of character responsibility with a notion of risk. In this sense, Farmer's diagnosis of the

[59] As anti-terrorism legislation suggests, the intensity of the character inference in current evidence law is context-dependent: while the case law tends to give weight to how recent a previous conviction is, this criterion will be regarded as of lesser importance in areas such as very serious or sexual crimes: *R v M* [2006] EWCA Crim 3408; *R v Cox* [2007] EWCA Crim 3365.

[60] Bernard Harcourt, 'From the Ne'er-Do-Well to the Criminal History Category: The Refinement of the Actuarial Model in Criminal Law' 66 *Law and Contemporary Problems* (2003) 99–152.

contemporary era as dominated by neoclassicism[61] seems to give a partial picture. The neoclassical claim to a just attribution of responsibility *via* a finding of blameworthiness undoubtedly plays a legitimating role, which radiates beyond the offences to which it plausibly applies, just as, in penal policy and practice, desert principles soon gave way to hybrids combining desert with incapacitation and deterrence. But, at the same time, in attributions of responsibility, notions of bad character have increasingly become associated with diagnoses of risk.

Character as Status: A Hybrid Character/Risk Model?

A further aspect of this revival of character-based practices of responsibility-attribution, reaching far beyond the area of counterterrorism, is a renewed emphasis on practices of responsibility-attribution based on character in the sense of status. It is, of course, a truism of contemporary scholarship that modern criminal law eschews the criminalization of status: defendants are punished not for who or what they are, but simply for what they have done (or for what they have attempted, encouraged others, or conspired with others to do). Survivals of status offences or semi-status offences, such as the famous example of prostitution,[62] are, of course, noted and regretted. But it is assumed that it is a fundamental of criminal law in a liberal democracy that criminal responsibility pertains only to voluntary acts (or, more rarely, omissions), and that this is inconsistent with the criminalization of status.

Notwithstanding this theoretical consensus, the history of status criminalization in the English system cannot be told simply as a story of decline. Examples, such as vagrancy and prostitution, as well as regular recreations of 'dangerousness' categories, show that the impulse to organize responsibility-attribution along status lines is a pervasive one in the history of criminal law. Moreover, status categories have often marked the administration of criminal justice: the most spectacular example being the group of late Victorian statutes instituting particular criminalizing regimes for groups such as inebriates and the feeble-minded.[63] The persistence of status offences

[61] Lindsay Farmer, *Making the Modern Criminal Law: Criminalization and Civil Order* Chapter 6.

[62] Nicola Lacey, Celia Wells, and Oliver Quick, *Reconstructing Criminal Law* (3rd ed., Cambridge: Cambridge University Press 2003) Chapter 5.III.b; see also Lindsay Farmer, *Making the Modern Criminal Law: Criminalization and Civil Order* Chapter 9.

[63] Lucia Zedner, *Women, Crime and Custody in Victorian England*; Leon Radzinowicz and Roger Hood, *The Emergence of Penal Policy in Victorian and Edwardian England* (Oxford: Clarendon Press 1990).

may be regarded as a distinct manifestation of the character dimension of criminal responsibility-attribution. Moving beyond the notion of bad character as evidence of individual criminal propensity, the criminalization of status engages directly with the assumed criminality of a type or a group—and hence imposes, in its pure form, a rather extreme form of character responsibility proper. And while such pure forms are, happily, rare, hybrids which bear in practice a family resemblance to character-based status liability—what we might call de facto instances of status criminalization, particularly in relation to terrorist suspects, migrants, and asylum-seekers—appear to be on the increase.

The phenomenon of criminal responsibility-attribution based on status might be thought to belong firmly to pre-modern criminal law systems. As Lucia Zedner has argued, this is unfortunately not the case:

> The recasting of citizenship as a status that has to be earned ... is also discernible in domestic criminal law. Policies directed first against immigrants and asylum seekers, as well as foreign nationals suspected of involvement in terrorism, have come to be applied equally to those who are cast as 'irregular citizens' within society. These include but are not limited to anti-social youth, persistent offenders, sexual offenders, and suspected terrorists, all of whom occupy liminal spaces at the margins of civil society and are consigned to a probationary or provisional status akin to that imposed upon immigrants and asylum seekers.[64]

The proliferation of such arrangements, which forms the core of my diagnosis of a spike in this form of what we might call doctrinally explicit character shortcuts to responsibility, has come to be associated with so-called 'enemy criminal law'.[65] Preventive in temper, disproportionate in reaction, indifferent to normal procedural protections, 'enemy criminal law' is essentially a police power which treats its objects as dangers to be managed, as distinct from citizen

[64] Lucia Zedner, 'Security, the State, and the Citizen: The Changing Architecture of Crime Control' 13 *New Criminal Law Review* (2010) 379–403, at 389.

[65] For a general discussion of the notion of enemy criminal law, originated by German scholar, Gunther Jakobs, see Carlos Gómez-Jara Díez, 'Enemy Combatants versus Enemy Criminal Law' 11 *New Criminal Law Review* (2008) 529–62, at 531, 556; Daniel Ohana, 'Trust, Distrust and Reassurance: Diversion and Preventive Orders Through the Prism of *Feindstrafrecht*' 73 *Modern Law Review* (2010) 721–51 and 'Günther Jakobs, *Feindstrafrecht:* A Dispassionate Account', in Markus Dubber (ed.) *Foundational Texts in Modern Criminal Law* (Oxford: Oxford University Press 2014) 353–71; cf. Tadros's notion of 'individualized' offences', Victor Tadros, 'Justice and Terrorism' pp. 683–5.

criminal law, which responds to subjects invested with rights.[66] Arguably, the most important source of offences which amount to, or come uncomfortably close to, the criminalization of status is the movement towards ever greater preventive criminalization. Preventive criminalization is, of course, not a new phenomenon. Inchoate offences, offences of possession, and the binding over power attendant on an anticipated breach of the peace are long-standing examples of the preventive impulse in English criminal law.[67] But, as we saw in Chapter 4, this preventive turn appears to have taken on a new intensity in the last two decades. In recent work, Andrew Ashworth and Lucia Zedner have identified no fewer than nine families of preventive measures,[68] many of them combining civil and criminal modes of enforcement in what have been widely regarded as troubling ways.[69]

It has been less widely noted that several of these new forms of preventive order impose what is in effect a form of (highly targeted) status liability. Take, for example, civil preventive hybrid orders aimed at preventing risk or at preventing harm (the former Anti-Social Behaviour Orders or 'ASBOs',[70] travel restriction orders, football spectator banning orders, drinking banning orders, risk of sexual harm or violent crime orders); civil preventive orders such as

[66] Gómez-Jara Díez, 'Enemy Combatants' p. 542; on the distinction between police and legal power, see Markus D. Dubber, *The Police Power: Patriarchy and the Foundations of American Government* (New York: Columbia University Press 2005).

[67] On the long English history of preventive justice, see Lucia Zedner, *Security* pp. 30–1; Ashworth and Zedner, *Preventive Justice* Chapter 2.

[68] Lucia Zedner and Andrew Ashworth, 'Preventive Orders: A Case of Under-criminalization?' in Duff et al. (eds), *The Boundaries of the Criminal Law*. See also Ashworth and Zedner, 'Defending the Criminal Law'; Zedner, 'Security, the State, and the Citizen'; Ashworth and Zedner, *Preventive Justice*.

[69] Peter Ramsay, 'What is Anti-Social Behaviour?' *Criminal Law Review* (November 2004) 908–25 and 'The Theory of Vulnerable Autonomy and the Legitimacy of the Civil Preventative Order', in Bernadette McSherry, Alan Norrie, and Simon Bronitt (eds), *Regulating Deviance: The Redirection of Criminalization and the Futures of Criminal Law* (Oxford: Hart Publishing 2009); Andrew Ashworth, 'Social Control and "Anti-Social Behaviour": The Subversion of Human Rights?' 120 *Law Quarterly Review* (2004) 263–91; A. P. Simester and Andrew von Hirsch, 'Regulating Offensive Conduct through Two-Step Prohibitions', in A. P. Simester and Andrew von Hirsch (eds), *Incivilities: Regulating Offensive Behaviour* (Oxford: Hart Publishing 2006); Jeremy Horder, *Ashworth's Principles of Criminal Law* Chapter 2.

[70] On the ASBO as a form of character responsibility, see Peter Ramsay, *The Insecurity State: Vulnerable Autonomy and the Right to Security in the Criminal Law* (Oxford: Oxford University Press 2012) Chapter 2. The ASBO was replaced in 2014 by the Criminal Behaviour Order and by injunctions against anti-social behaviour: see Chapter 4 above.

anti-social behaviour injunctions; pre-trial orders such as remands in custody; licence conditions on release from a sentence of imprisonment; or criminal court orders aimed at preventing harm or risk of harm, such as disqualification from driving or from being a company director. A criminal conviction resulting from the breach of any of these orders is a form of criminalization which applies specifically to a group identified in terms of its subjection to the relevant order. As Ashworth and Zedner have noted, the implications are considerable. They include stigma, the imposition of (often long-lasting) restrictive conditions, and, on breach, possible imprisonment.[71] Hence severe measures associated with the quasi-moral terrain of 'real crime' are finding their way, insidiously, into the terrain of regulatory or police offences. Moreover, in the area of serious crime, the indefinite sentence of 'imprisonment for public protection' (IPP)—a variant of the intermittent attempt to identify 'dangerous' offenders—was more draconian and far-reaching than any previous such provision. It was, moreover, widely used by sentencers, producing a very substantial minority of the prison population serving indeterminate sentences.[72] Following the decision of the European Court of Human Rights in *James, Wells and Lee v UK* that the IPP was in breach of Article 5 of the European Convention of Human Rights, with the Secretary of State being in breach of his public law duty for making proper provision for those subject to the IPP to make progress towards parole, the IPP has been abandoned.[73] The abolition of the IPP has resulted, however, in a dilution rather than a resolution of the problems which it created. Its replacement under the Legal Aid, Sentencing and Punishment of Offenders Act 2012 section 124 by an Extended Determinate Sentence for dangerous offenders convicted of specified violent or sexual offences, and by Mandatory Life Sentences under section 122 for the most serious repeat violent or sexual offenders, might be regarded as an improvement, given that at least the former operates within a broadly determinate framework. But the fact remains that the criteria for risk assessment which proved so malleable under the IPP regime will still have a considerable influence.

[71] Ashworth and Zedner, 'Defending the Criminal Law' p. 36.

[72] Ashworth and Zedner, *Preventive Justice* pp. 140–42, 158–63; see also, on the history and politics of the IPP, Harry Annison, *Dangerous Politics: Risk, Political Vulnerability, and Penal Policy* (Oxford: Oxford University Press, 2015).

[73] *James, Wells and Lee v United Kingdom* (2013) 56 EHRR 399.

Perhaps the most spectacular examples of the latest generation of preventive measures are the notification orders which replaced sex offender registration under the Sexual Offences Act 2003 and the Control Orders applied to those suspected of terrorism from the enactment of the Prevention of Terrorism Act 2005 until their replacement by the Terrorism Prevention and Investigation Measures Act 2011 (see below).[74] Under the former provisions, certain sex offenders must render themselves visible to the police by providing details such as their address, virtually ensuring that they will be investigated should any sexual (or perhaps other) offence be committed in the area. This amounts to a quasi-criminal status—indeed to a *prima facie* judgment of criminal propensity.[75] Reminiscent of ancient sanctions such as maiming and branding, this provision sits unhappily with the idea of punishment as commensurate to crime. It must be set alongside other contemporary initiatives—such as the Control Order and the more general effort to extend the legal period of detention without trial—in assessing how far the criminal law is moving towards a system of de facto status criminalization on the basis of inferences about criminal character. The new 'TPIM' orders introduced by the Terrorism Prevention and Investigation Measures Act 2011 are unlikely to effect anything more than a marginal improvement to this situation. They are based on a slightly more stringent threshold and otherwise feature slightly less restrictive controls on those subject to them, but they retain the troubling mechanism of deploying a criminal sanction to back up a civil order, and share the Control Order's drawback of reducing the chances of invoking a normal prosecution process by complicating the process of gathering evidence.[76]

Explaining the Resurgence of Character

Developing and Testing Hypotheses about what Drives Patterns of Criminal Responsibility-Attribution

The development of responsibility-attribution is, therefore, not a linear trajectory from status to contract, from manifest to subjective criminality, from 'external' to 'internal' practices, from principles based on character to ones based on choice and capacity.

[74] Lucia Zedner, *Security* pp. 132–4; Victor Tadros, 'Justice and Terrorism' pp. 666–70.

[75] Lucia Zedner, *Women, Crime and Custody in Victorian England* p. 74.

[76] Andrew Ashworth and Lucia Zedner, *Preventive Justice* (Oxford: Oxford University Press 2014) Chapters 7 and 8, particularly pp. 186–9.

While a broad trajectory is, as I have argued in this chapter, discernible, that trajectory reveals not so much linear development as a complex and shifting alignment of apparently competing principles, which coalesce, more or less successfully, to legitimate and coordinate criminal judgment under specific social conditions. Only when we understand the conditions which underpin the relative influence of these principles will we be in a position to address the further challenge of how to resist the resurgence of character-based mechanisms which foster the most dangerous aspects of criminalization and punishment as forms of social power. In light of the account given so far of how character, capacity, outcome, and risk have shaped patterns of responsibility-attribution—through the substantive law, through rules of evidence, through pre-trial discretionary decision-making—over the last 250 years, it is now time to advance a thesis about how these shifting patterns may be explained.

Consider the following model—simplified but perhaps suggestive. A pattern of responsibility-attribution based on character made a great deal of practical and cultural sense in an environment that was stable, relatively homogeneous, non-democratic, and based on status hierarchy. Moreover, the impulse to invoke criminalizing power on the basis of character responsibility was not, in that context, inhibited to anything like the same extent as it later became by the diffusion of liberal sentiments about individual freedom or of norms of civility inhospitable to violence. In that eighteenth-century environment, the state had limited ambitions and capacities, but was able to draw on considerable local resources of knowledge, norm enforcement, and regulation. Local knowledge provided evidence of character in relation to insiders. The wandering mobility of the poor had long been regarded as a significant social problem to be curtailed by the town watch and the structure of the poor law:[77] the simple fact of being an outsider carried with it a stigma of presumptive criminality. Character evidence was key to the conduct of the

[77] A telling example is the fourteenth century policy on 'sturdy beggars': 'the royal council ... alerted local officials not only to the excessive demands of wage labourers but to the accompanying prevalence of "sturdy beggars", who refused work and took to crime. Following the biblical injunction that "he who will not work neither shall he eat", it forbade giving them alms or charity. In the last quarter of the century, petitions and legislation against vagrants and "vagabonds" attempted to curb mobility, requiring all beggars to stay in their own vill and all vagabonds to return there': Gerald Harriss, *Shaping the Nation: England 1360–1461* (Oxford: Oxford University Press 2005) 244.

trial, criminality was readily associated with status (an association also reflected in stigmatizing physical punishments that left marks on the body), criminal prosecution was based on an assumption of bad character, and criminal conviction gave an official imprimatur to that assumption.[78]

With a move to a more individualized, mobile, anonymous, and democratic world, the shape of legitimation and coordination problems changed. The subject of criminal law gradually became a rights-bearing agent, entitled to be judged in terms of his or her own particular capacities, intentions, and knowledge.[79] At the same time, local resources for knowledge coordination diminished, and a formalized system of policing and criminal trials had to be gradually constructed to facilitate gathering the evidence necessary for trial. Furthermore, the gradual domination of the trial by lawyers allowed the refinement of technical doctrines of culpability, as the prevailing legal and political culture, influenced by Enlightenment conceptions of agency and utilitarian theories of human psychology, attached special importance to individual mental states.[80] In relation to cultural legitimation, the increasingly systematic procedural regulation of the trial provided a counterpart in criminal law to the 'civilization' of punishment with the move from corporal to carceral penalties. And the emerging psychological and essentially factual view of responsibility diverted attention from any contested issues of values in an environment that urbanization, social mobility, and democratization were already rendering less morally homogeneous, hence reducing problems of political legitimation.

This trajectory—at least across the terrain of 'serious' criminal law—towards an advertence-based standard of responsibility proceeded relatively smoothly due to the creation of many strict liability regulatory offences, which allowed the emerging state to pursue its instrumental goals cheaply and efficiently, and to the extraordinary success of the early Victorian state's creation of a modern criminal justice system featuring, in particular, a regular police force and an extensive prison system.[81] Crime, especially in the rapidly expanding

[78] Nicola Lacey, *Women, Crime, and Character* pp. 34–40.

[79] Ibid. pp. 51–97.

[80] Bruce P. Smith, 'The Presumption of Guilt and the English Law of Theft, 1750–1850'.

[81] Leon Radzinwicz and Roger Hood, *The Emergence of Penal Policy in Victorian and Edwardian England.*

cities, became a serious social concern. But this spurred further institutional innovation. In a fascinating amalgam of character and capacity cosmologies, the penal system of the first two-thirds of the nineteenth century organized itself to shape convicts' own capacities to work on ameliorating their own characters as declining crime rates fostered the perceived legitimacy and effectiveness of the gradually modernizing system.[82]

But, as the case of the outcome-based regulatory offences reveals, this move towards the investigation of individual capacity responsibility was never complete, not least because the costs of fully realizing the ideal of capacity responsibility proven beyond a reasonable doubt would have been prohibitive, even had the newly created criminal justice infrastructure been extensive enough to deliver it. Shortcuts to proof, such as the presumption that a defendant has intended the natural consequences of his or her actions, and indeed more radical reversals of the purportedly inviolate presumption of innocence expressed in the usual burden of proof remained important, even in relatively peaceful and optimistic times. In more difficult periods, when the costs of determining individual capacity responsibility were particularly high (for example, because of the scale of perceived crime problems), the shortcuts seemed particularly tempting. And such shortcuts tended to be nested, explicitly or implicitly, within a legitimating framework of criminal character shaped by scientific or religious doctrines. Hence, the historical trajectory towards proof of individualized capacity responsibility was not unbroken.

A world which purports to give priority to capacity-based practices of responsibility-attribution—one which claims to take individuals and their engaged capacities rather than their social status or appearance seriously—is a world in which there is a strongly felt sense of the legitimation requirements posed by individual freedom, and one which enjoys some confidence in its institutional capacity to deliver such individualized judgments while maintaining adequate levels of social control. Such a world has arguably never existed. But that individualizing impulse has most certainly had a significant impact on the form of (significant parts of) criminal law over the course of its 'modernization', particularly during the first two-thirds of the twentieth century. Indeed, the marked insistence on individual responsibility, even in the face of the facts about the

[82] See Martin Wiener, *Reconstructing the Criminal* (Cambridge University Press 1990).

impact of structural disadvantage on the opportunity to conform one's behaviour to the precepts of criminal law—hence, arguably, affecting the 'fairness' of that opportunity—is testimony to its continuing centrality as a diffuse legitimation device even amid a world in which patterns of responsibility-attribution based on character, risk, and outcome are gaining ground.[83] It therefore seems likely that, at times when the sentiments underpinning norms towards equal liberties are fragile, perhaps because of fears about crime, or terrorism, or order more generally, explicitly character-based patterns of attribution tend to enjoy a revival. And, as a number of social theorists have argued, thanks to a welter of political, social, and economic conditions, this is precisely the situation we find ourselves in the UK, the USA, and indeed several other liberal market economies today.[84] Moreover, as worsening conditions in our overcrowded prison systems attest, as new forms of status differentiation and conceptions of essentialized bad character emerge, the 'civilized' norms of humane treatment may themselves become diluted, weakening the constraints posed by the demands of cultural and political legitimation in relation to the criminalization and punishment of certain groups.

As I have suggested, an interesting precursor of the current revival of a character-based pattern of responsibility-attribution can be found in the criminal classification statutes of the late nineteenth and early twentieth centuries. And, significantly, the late nineteenth century British context bears some striking analogies with our world today. Democracy had extended in 1884 to male householders, and covered about 60 per cent of the adult male population, yet social stratification remained the order of the day, and the 'degenerate' classes were widely seen by the 'respectable' as posing a threat to social order. But it was not only the 'degenerate classes' which threatened traditional ideas of authority and social order. There were also factors such as an economic recession which spanned the 1870s and 1880s, early

[83] As Lerman and Weaver (*Arresting Citizenship: The Democratic Consequences of American Crime Control*, Chapter 7) have shown through ethnographic and survey analysis, the ideology of individual responsibility equally pervades the consciousness of those subject to structural disadvantage.

[84] See, for example, David Garland, *The Culture of Control* (Chicago: Chicago University Press 2001); Jock Young, *The Exclusive Society* (London: Sage 1999); Nicola Lacey, *The Prisoners' Dilemma: Political Economy and Punishment in Contemporary Democracies* (Cambridge: Cambridge University Press 2008).

intimations of the collapse of empire, and incipient troubles in Ireland in the form of Fenian activities and the struggle for Home Rule. These went alongside the perceived loosening of traditional structures of inheritance and family in an era of individual choice and the challenges to religion and tradition represented by increasingly secularized political authority and increasingly professionalized scientific practice.

Science and medicine were, as they are today, ambivalent developments. On the one hand, they seemed to promise a new technology of proof and legitimation; on the other, the currency of evolutionary theory and early medical science was perceived as threatening individual responsibility.[85] Science at once threatened the established order, and promised resources for recreating a new form of 'manifest criminality' through the methods designed to identify criminal character—a development which would of course echo through the criminology of the early twentieth century, giving a new spin to the construction of 'external' patterns of responsibility-attribution. In the end, the capacity principle gained a serious foothold in the law governing the more serious criminal offences, displacing explicit character attribution onto the less visible areas of the prosecution and sentencing processes. Meanwhile, technologies geared to the identification of criminals—from professional detective work and policing through Lombrosian criminology and statistics, to contemporary offender profiling—multiplied, in a succession of developments which have walked a curiously separate track from the criminal law's professed commitment to establishing responsibility by investigating whether a defendant's psychological capacities were properly engaged at the time of her offence. Over time, these developments gradually laid down the foundations for the emergence of a pattern of responsibility-attribution founded in bad character understood as the presentation of risk—or even others' apprehension of risk.

With the resolution of the economic and social crisis in the 1890s, positivist criminology was, at least in England, gradually consigned

[85] This prompted one reviewer of Robert Louis Stevenson's hugely popular *Jekyll and Hyde*—a novella much taken up with these issues—to complain that Stevenson's story added to this culture by 'reducing individual freedom to zero, weakening the sense of responsibility'. John Addington Symonds, quoted in Robert Mighall, 'Diagnosing Jekyll: The Scientific Context to Dr Jekyll's Experiment and Mr Hyde's Embodiment', in Robert Louis Stevenson, *The Strange Case of Dr Jekyll and Mr Hyde and Other Tales of Terror*, edited by Robert Mighall (London: Penguin 2002) p. 145.

to the academy rather than the prison or reformatory. Criminal types legislation gradually fell into disuse and, at the turn of the century, political, institutional, and procedural bases were gradually assembled for the 'penal welfarist' settlement which endured until the 1970s, sustained by a relatively stable social culture that had perhaps been fostered by the First and Second World Wars.[86] And just as the penal system was being reconstructed on more reformist and inclusionary lines, so were capacity-based and subjective principles of responsibility continuing their steady progress in the courts and the legislature during the major part of the twentieth century. They found their intellectual acme in Glanville Williams's *Criminal Law: The General Part*[87] and their fullest legislative support in section 8 of the Criminal Justice Act 1967, which, by effectively reversing *Director of Public Prosecutions v Smith*,[88] finally and decisively abandoned the presumption that natural consequences are intended.

As many commentators have argued,[89] this penal welfarist settlement began to break down in the early 1970s, under pressure from increased crime and a welter of economic, demographic, and cultural changes that were fundamentally altering the structure of criminal justice politics in the UK and in many other countries, including the United States. This is not the place to rehearse the familiar story of how, amid a 'culture of control', penal welfarism gave way to increasing punitiveness—to 'penal populism'—creating a 'prisoners' dilemma' for politicians and a tendency to 'govern through crime'.[90] The power of the narrative is, sadly, attested to in the soaring imprisonment rates in the liberal market economies that have seen this trend. I suggest that these factors, charted so persuasively

[86] David Garland, *Punishment and Welfare: A History of Penal Strategies.*

[87] Glanville Williams, *Criminal Law: The General Part* (2nd ed., London: Stevens and Sons 1961). At the turn of the century, one of the most influential texts was still conflating objective and subjective *mens rea* standards, blurring the boundary between the two. C. S. Kenny, *Outlines of Criminal Law* (1st ed., Cambridge: Cambridge University Press 1902).

[88] [1961] A.C. 290 (H. L.)

[89] See, e.g., David Garland, *The Culture of Control.* John Pratt, *Penal Populism* (London: Routledge 2006); Robert Reiner, *Law and Order: An Honest Citizen's Guide to Crime and Control* (London: Polity Press 2007); Jock Young, *The Exclusive Society* (London: Sage 1999).

[90] Lacey, *The Prisoners' Dilemma*; Jonathan Simon, *Governing Through Crime: How the War on Crime Transformed American Democracy and Created a Culture of Fear* (Oxford: Oxford University Press 2007); Alessandro di Giorgi, *Rethinking the Political Economy of Punishment: Perspectives on Post-Fordism and Penal Politics* (Aldershot: Ashgate 2006).

by criminologists in relation to criminal justice arrangements, such as policing and punishment, also explain the changing patterns and principles of criminal responsibility charted in this book, in particular the reemergence of patterns of attribution based on a version of character aligned with a new conception of risk. The revival of 'character' in contemporary criminal justice might be seen as the criminal law manifestation, in short, of what David Garland has called 'the culture of control': a reverberation of anxiety in a world marked by renewed economic and social insecurity, and one in which some countries have manifested an impulse to ever greater criminalization and penal harshness: 'governing through crime', and 'overcriminalization', in the words of Jonathan Simon's and Douglas Husak's recent contributions to the analysis of these worrying social developments.[91] In our world, as in the late nineteenth century, the burgeoning of theory and practice in the sciences—notably in the fields of psychiatry, psychology, psychoanalysis, neuroscience, statistics—has done little to address the resultant moral and political uncertainties.

To chart the analogies between just one of these broad criminal justice hypotheses and the trajectory of criminal responsibility-attribution, let us focus on Garland's influential thesis about the emergence of a 'culture of control'. Garland argues that the dynamics of criminal justice policy in the United States and, to a significant extent, the United Kingdom, have since the 1970s been importantly shaped by factors such as changes in the structure of social and family life, accentuated structural inequalities, and a sense of diminished governmental capacity in a range of other (notably economic) policy areas. In this context, criminal justice is becoming an increasingly politically salient yet also an increasingly bifurcated field. For, while a range of crimes are 'normalized' and dealt with, as far as consistent with legitimation imperatives, by relatively de-moralized managerial strategies, a narrower, but still highly significant, range of serious crimes are dealt with in increasingly punitive terms, through strategies which further accentuate the already strong dynamics of social polarization. This apparently unstable yet practically powerful combination of 'denial' of much 'ordinary' crime and 'acting out' in terms of the vilification and increasingly intense punishment of the most serious offenders has been argued to be most representative of the United States, with England

[91] Jonathan Simon, *Governing Through Crime*; Douglas Husak, *Overcriminalization*.

(thankfully) lagging some way behind, though still displaying tendencies recognizable in terms of the American model.

But if we were to look to countries elsewhere in Europe and Scandinavia—to Germany or Sweden for example—the picture would be markedly different. This suggests the need for a careful comparative development of our hypotheses.[92] For one way of interpreting the 'culture of control' charted by Garland, and arguably reflected in the resurgence of character-based mechanisms of responsibility–attribution, would be that the particular form of capitalism structuring the political economy of the USA (and, to a lesser extent, the UK), may be characterized by disparities of wealth so large that they are underpinning the creation of something akin to a new form of status society. And it was a status-based society, of course, which viewed as legitimate, and which sustained the coordinating capability of, the character-based principles of responsibility-attribution, as well as the bloody, unevenly enforced penal regime, in England up to the late eighteenth century.[93] Furthermore, there would be reason to think that the late twentieth century impulse to stigmatize as 'other' members of certain groups *via* assessments of 'risky character' might be rendered yet more intense by the lesser acceptance of explicit appeals to traditional status. In other words, in a more horizontal society, with an avowedly democratic and formally egalitarian mentality, markers of status differentiation may, paradoxically, need to be demonizing, hence creating newly intractable forms of social abjection, in part stabilized by criminal law. This tendency, moreover, is considerably stronger in the more individualistic, less coordinated, and less solidaristic social systems of liberal market countries, such as the UK and the USA, as compared with the countries of Western Europe and the Nordic area. And finally, beyond these economic dynamics, a willingness to attribute responsibility on the basis of character may be encouraged by new technologies, notably the emerging genetic revolution, which may have the capacity utterly to disrupt the perceived robustness of the mechanisms of responsibility-attribution which have dominated in the Western world over the last 250 years.

[92] For further argument, see Nicola Lacey, 'Historicising Contrasts in Tolerance', in Tim Newburn and Paul Rock (eds), *The Politics of Crime Control* (Oxford: Oxford University Press 2006).

[93] See further James Q. Whitman, *Harsh Justice* (New York: Oxford University Press 2003).

Hence, both the conditions of existence of practices of character responsibility-attribution in the eighteenth century and the late-Victorian criminal types legislation already discussed provide real clues to the explanation for waxing and waning patterns of character responsibility. Amid a crisis of security analogous to that experienced at the end of the nineteenth century, legislators today are reaching for definitions and mechanisms that can reassure an anxious public that their concerns are being taken seriously and that 'the criminal threat' can be contained. The construction of criminal classifications is a tempting mechanism, and just as the late nineteenth century and early twentieth century classifications reflected prevailing anxieties, scientific theories, and technologies, so today's categories—the anti-social youth, the sex offender, the migrant, and, above all, the terrorist—are appropriate symbols of 'otherness' relative to contemporary anxieties and technologies.

These anxieties and the technologies available to meet them have of course changed. The collapse of Fordism, the partly associated attenuation of social solidarity, the dilution of the welfare state, and an economic crisis that further intensified concerns about insecurity have underpinned developments such as the readmissibility of character evidence and the invention of what amounts to a new generation of criminal status offences. There is reason to fear that those who form easily identifiable objects of anger, fear, or resentment will find themselves increasingly the target for what we might call character-facilitated criminal responsibility-attribution. Non-citizens in general, and recent immigrants and asylum seekers more specifically, are obvious potential targets, particularly where their origins may be associated in popular or police consciousness with either terrorism or drug production.[94] More speculatively, and potentially more nightmarishly, new technologies in fields such as neuroscience and genetics, and computer programs that identify crime 'hot spots' that might be taken to indicate 'postcode presumptive criminality', have potential implications for criminal responsibility. They will offer, or perhaps threaten, yet more sophisticated mechanisms of responsibility-attribution based on notions of

[94] Lucia Zedner, 'Security, the State, and the Citizen'; see also Alessandro de Giorgi, *Re-Thinking the Political Economy of Punishment: Perspectives on Post-Fordism and Penal Politics* (Aldershot: Ashgate 2006).

Loïc Wacquant, '"Suitable Enemies": Foreigners and Immigrants in the Prisons of Europe' 1 *Punishment and Society* (1999) 215–22.

character essentialism combined with assessments of character-based risk, just as the emerging sciences of the mind, the brain, and statistics did in the late nineteenth century. Moreover, several of these new scientific classifications exhibit more extreme forms of character essentialism than did their nineteenth century forbears. The upshot for the conditions of punishment is a further cause for concern.

The resurgence of character-based practices of attribution could be a product, additionally, of diminished confidence in the ability of courts to manage capacity-based judgments. In the context of increasingly complex, sophisticated, and technical developments in the natural and human sciences, it may be that the pragmatic compatibilism of criminal law judgments about capacity or opportunity is being increasingly unsettled by the suspicion that incontrovertible proof of the causally determined nature of much criminal conduct is not far in the future. Ironically, this sense of diminishing confidence in attributions of capacity-responsibility may go hand in hand with a renewal of confidence in the law's authority to make quasi-moral, evaluative judgments, combined with a willingness to be 'up front' about these rather than disguising them beneath purportedly 'factual' findings of intention or knowledge.[95] In a scientifically knowing world in which we cannot be sure if defendants truly had the capacity to do otherwise than they did, it may be tempting to renew our hold on older ideas of right and wrong, of good and evil, hence reconstructing a criminal process which is more explicitly oriented to the moral evaluation of character. We can see, perhaps, echoes of this instinct in 'Left Realist' criminology[96] and in the emergence of an emphasis on victims' interests,[97] both of which emphasize the reality (and socially inegalitarian distribution) of criminal victimization, with a consequently diminished emphasis on the finer points of an offender's responsibility for the pain or harm caused. The insistent New Labour emphasis on the development of victim-oriented policy—including, for example, the Anti-Social

[95] For a persuasive analysis of the dangers of disguising the inevitably evaluative dimension of responsibility attributions, see V. F. Nourse, 'Hearts and Minds: Understanding the New Culpability' 6 *Buffalo Criminal Law Review* (2002) 361–88.

[96] See, for example, Richard Kinsey, John Lea, and Jock Young, *Losing the Fight against Crime* (Oxford: Blackwell 1986).

[97] See Lucia Zedner, 'Victims', in Press 1997 Mike Maguire, Rod Morgan, and Robert Reiner (eds), *The Oxford Handbook of Criminology* (2nd ed., Oxford: Oxford University); Carolyn Hoyle, 'Victims, the Criminal Process and Restorative Justice', in Mike Maguire, Rod Morgan, and Robert Reiner (eds), *The Oxford Handbook of Criminology* (5th ed., Oxford: Oxford University Press 2012).

Behaviour Order—was no less indicative of this kind of trend than a previous Conservative Prime Minister's suggestion that 'we should condemn a little more and understand a little less'.[98] In this context, it is hardly surprising that Prime Minister David Cameron's expressed advice, as leader of the Opposition in 2006, to 'hug a hoodie' has had zero impact on his government's criminal justice policy.[99] While we think of ourselves as a society of equal opportunities and social inclusion, our criminal justice system serves to legitimize the impact of structural inequalities based on social cleavages, such as race, by labelling manifestations of allegedly dangerous difference as criminal.

Conclusion

In this chapter, I hope to have done enough to convince the reader that certain significant recent developments in criminal law and procedure may be justly described as a 'resurgence of character'—as an underlying mechanism facilitating proof of guilt, certainly but also, to some extent, as an organizing principle of, and a message emanating from, responsibility-attribution. I have also offered some explanations, based on the reading of the interests, institutional arrangements, and ideas that have shaped the modern concept of responsibility presented in earlier chapters. This is not, of course, to say that recent developments amount to a reversion to eighteenth-century-type arrangements, nor to claim that the relevant developments are evenly distributed across the three forms of character that I have distinguished. I have already noted that the criminalization of status, albeit in shifting forms, has enjoyed prominence in English criminal law at various points since the eighteenth century. A concern with the prevention of harm most certainly dates back at least to the creation of an expansive administrative state in the first half of the nineteenth century. The specific form taken by today's move to 'preventive justice' is shaped by the particular capacities, dynamics, and aspirations of nation states in a world of advanced technologies of communication, physical mobility, and interdependence; and these

[98] John Major, in a speech delivered in 1993. See Donal MacIntyre, 'Major on Crime: "Condemn More, Understand Less"', *The Independent*, 21 February 1993.

[99] http://www.theguardian.com/politics/2006/jul/09/conservatives.ukcrime accessed 26 July 2015.

have produced a hybrid of responsibility-attribution based on character and risk.[100] Moreover, particularly in the liberal market countries, criminal policy is formed by governments accountable to an electorate within an adversarial system that fosters the politicization of criminal justice, creating a volatile policy-making environment.[101] In stark contrast to the mid-nineteenth century, that electorate is broadly drawn. It is informed by a scientific culture which has made it optimistic about the power to control risk and it is, hence, rather intolerant of it, and rather insistent on government efforts to control it—particularly in the wake of insecurity attendant on economic restructuring and cultural disembedding.[102] And this, as I have suggested, creates a fertile terrain for an expansive criminalization that exceeds or ignores the capacity principle, and increasingly draws on ideas of risk assessment as equating to bad character.

100 Bernard Harcourt, 'From the Ne'er-Do-Well to the Criminal History Category'.
101 Nicola Lacey, *The Prisoners' Dilemma* pp. 62–77.
102 Lucia Zedner, *Security* pp. 91–100.

6

Implications for Legal Theory and Legal Scholarship

It might be objected that the diagnosis of a resurgence of 'character' and the emergence of a new configuration of risk in criminal law presented in the last chapter is an exaggeration. Surely, a sceptical reader might say, most of the recent developments outlined in the previous chapter have to do more with the criminal process, with evidence, and with sentencing than with criminal law proper. They tell us something, and perhaps something worrying, about the failures both of criminal enforcement and of patterns of criminalization to respect the values enshrined in the legal doctrines of individual capacity responsibility, which are the jewel in the crown of the 'general part' of criminal law. But, it might be argued, they do not touch the integrity of those principles, nor do they undermine the claim about the practical triumph of capacity-responsibility, nor its normative recommendations, as set out at the start of this book.

In this chapter, I tackle this argument, considering the broader implications of the argument presented in this book for method in legal theory and indeed in legal scholarship more generally, and in particular developing the argument that the conceptual structure of criminal law must be contextualized within broad practices and functions of criminalization, with 'the law in the books' understood in relation to 'law in action'. I examine first the implications of this book's argument for projects of so-called 'special jurisprudence' which analyse the foundations of key legal concepts, before moving on to examine its implications for 'general jurisprudence'—the project of theorizing law itself—and for the relationship between the analytic, explanatory, and normative tasks of legal scholarship.

Historicizing and Institutionalizing Responsibility: Implications for Special Jurisprudence

Significantly, and not surprisingly, the division of labour between analytic/conceptual and socio-legal/historical approaches in the field of criminal law scholarship is mirrored in the history of legal theory. While conceptual analyses of criminal responsibility belong to the tradition of special jurisprudence in analytical, philosophical mode, the analysis of criminal responsibility as an institutionalized social practice resonates with the traditions of historical and sociological jurisprudence, the sociology of law, and, indeed, the Process School, which was influential in the United States after the Second World War.[1] And the idea that criminal responsibility is shaped by interests resonates with the diverse traditions of Marxist legal theory, some versions of legal realism, and law and economics. As in criminal law theory, so, I shall argue, in jurisprudence: each approach has important insights to deliver; but each taken on its own misses out on key aspects of the social reality of criminal responsibility.

Jurisprudential debates about responsibility have often been focused on the criminal law; but, of course, ideas of responsibility and of responsible agency or legal subjecthood are widely recognized as crucial to the doctrinal structure of civil, public, and international law as well. There is a substantial literature exploring the conceptual or moral contours of legal conceptions of responsibility (and indeed of other legal concepts), or rationally reconstructing legal doctrines so as to accommodate more 'refined' or 'coherent' conceptions along a variety of dimensions. Alongside this literature has grown up a significant critical literature, which unpacks, and subjects to scrutiny, the assumptions in terms of which legal ideas of responsibility have been framed, and the vectors of power which have shaped those assumptions. But given the dominance in recent criminal law theory

[1] Nicola Lacey, 'Jurisprudence, History, and the Institutional Quality of Law', 101 *Virginia Law Review* (2015) 919–45.

of the analytic tradition, it is important to assess its strengths—and weaknesses—by reviewing some of the more influential contemporary theories of criminal responsibility. Because of his influence, I shall use H. L. A. Hart's theory as a suitable exemplar.

Hart's theory of responsibility is grounded in a set of cognitive and volitional capacities, along with an associated theory of the *mens rea* principle in criminal law, a theory of excuses, and a justification of punishment. It is hardly an exaggeration to say that it forms the starting point or a principal object of criticism for virtually all subsequent work in the field. Responsibility in Hart's sense guarantees the justice of criminal punishment by confining that punishment to those who had a fair opportunity to conform their behaviour to the precepts of criminal law. His theory of punishment, with its theoretically disaggregated general justifying aim and principles of distribution, cannot provide any effective normative guidance on when, if ever (as Hart contemplated), the 'compromise' of prima facie unjust 'strict' liability based on pure outcome responsibility (as opposed to a role-based version of outcome–responsibility reconcilable with the fair opportunity principle) would be justified by compensating utilitarian aims.[2] But within the confines of the presumption of a requirement of *mens rea*, his account of responsibility provides both a remarkably accurate fit with certain key aspects of late-twentieth-century criminal law doctrine in both Britain and the USA as well as a persuasive rationalization of the contribution of proof of responsibility to the legitimacy of criminal conviction and sanction.[3]

Yet in relation to his theory of criminal responsibility, Hart's theoretical project encounters at least two forms of methodological complication. First, there is a tension implicit in this genre of middle-order theorizing, which claims to be sensitive to actual practices yet proceeds on the basis of strong assumptions about the possibility of identifying coherent underlying principles with a certain normative validity. This usually means that it is normative

[2] See *Punishment and Responsibility* (Clarendon Press 1968) Chapter 1. For further discussion, see Nicola Lacey, *State Punishment: Political Principles and Community Values* (London: Routledge 1988) pp. 46–56.

[3] This is not to say that Hart's argument has gone unchallenged: see, for example, Victor Tadros, *Criminal Responsibility* (Oxford: Oxford University Press 2005) pp. 54–70; George Sher, *Who Knew? Responsibility Without Awareness* (Oxford and New York: Oxford University Press 2009).

considerations which are in the interpretive driving seat, with aspects of legal reality inconsistent with them driven to the margins of the theoretical picture. Second, there is an ambivalence about the extent to which an account such as Hart's should be grounded in an understanding of the wider practices within which appeals to responsibility are embedded. Unlike his earlier work with Tony Honoré on causation,[4] the work on responsibility draws only sparingly on actual legal materials. But the message is nonetheless clearly that the account of capacity-based responsibility is the best—the most normatively attractive, the most coherent—account of responsibility to be drawn from criminal law. In my terms it is, primarily, if not exclusively, an analysis of responsibility as an *idea*. Hart is not much interested in the institutional features of criminal law which underpin the emergence of this notion of responsibility: once elicited, 'responsibility' is invested implicitly with a sort of objective or even metaphysical status at odds with his professedly linguistic and socially grounded method. Moreover outcome-based strict liability, where it is outside the role-based bounds of the fair opportunity conception of responsibility, floats in a different system, and one which Hart makes no real attempt to integrate within his overall justificatory account.

This argument that phenomena which do not 'fit' with an elegant philosophical conceptualization—such as practices of responsibility-attribution based on outcome, risk, or character, which violate core precepts of the capacity principle—should be evacuated from the range of explanatory theory has a tempting conceptual neatness, and it has long been deployed by criminal-law theorists. Of course, this can be justified in frankly normative terms. One can argue, as Victor Tadros has done, that widespread strict liability, such as that of the so-called 'regulatory offences', simply cannot be rationalized within a morally adequate theory of criminal responsibility, and should be excluded on that basis.[5] But such a strategy calls into question the status of the account as a theory *of* criminal responsibility, understood as a concept which has a real—and changing—social existence. Its effect has been to direct attention away from aspects of criminal law which sit uncomfortably with prevailing normative theories, notably, the widespread existence of strict liability, reverse burdens of proof, reasonableness requirements applied without

[4] *Causation in the Law* (Oxford: Oxford University Press 1959), second edition 1985.

[5] *Criminal Responsibility* pp. 16–17, 73–4.

investigation of individual capacity, and other doctrinal arrangements hospitable to the attribution of responsibility on the basis of character.[6] The unfortunate result is that many criminal law theorists are writing about a small proportion of criminal law. This self-imposed limitation enables them to retain an attachment to the idea(l) of a unitary theory of criminal law—an aesthetically pleasing idea, but one which is seriously at odds with the legal and social reality of both the substance and the source of the supposed object of their analysis. What, we should ask, are the criteria of accountability to actual practices of criminal responsibility which have to be recognized by the criminal law theorist?

This critique implies that there is a further important set of questions underlying legal scholarship: questions, which have received less jurisprudential attention. These concern not so much the conceptual contours of responsibility, as the institutional and other conditions of existence of those conceptions, and the relationship between those actually existing conditions—practices, institutions, attitudes, ideas, or other phenomena—and our conceptual frameworks. To see the intimate links between the development of legal concepts and their institutional basis, we have only to engage in some fairly basic historical or comparative research. For example, the modern, agency-based notion of capacity-responsibility, which Hart articulates, finds strong voice in various forms within Enlightenment political and moral philosophy from the late seventeenth century onwards. Yet, as we saw in Chapter 2, it finds almost no expression in even the most systematic available accounts of the common law of crime until very much later. These substantive questions about the conditions of existence for elegantly theorized concepts are infrequently acknowledged, let alone tackled, by legal theorists. The relationship between these substantive questions and the analytic or conceptual questions more usually addressed in jurisprudence remains, accordingly, murky and contested.

Writing against this rigid division of theoretical labour, I shall argue that the historical and institutional conditions of existence of the concepts which animate legal argumentation—like the historical and institutional conditions of existence of certain forms of law—are

[6] For honourable exceptions, in relation to outcome responsibility, see R. A. Duff, *Answering for Crime* (Oxford: Hart Publishing 2008); Andrew Simester (ed.), *Appraising Strict Liability* (Oxford: Oxford University Press 2005).

of interest not only in their own right, but also because they raise methodological issues for jurisprudence. These include questions about the relationship between philosophical and other forms of legal theory, and about how a jurisprudence largely dominated by philosophical methods may be brought into productive dialogue with other forms of theoretical analysis. Yet, notwithstanding a significant theme within analytical jurisprudence exploring the 'institutional nature of law', featuring scholars of the stature of Joseph Raz, Neil MacCormick and, Ota Weinberger,[7] our grasp of this question about how the institutional conditions of existence of legal systems or particular sets of legal arrangements inflect our theory-building remains, I shall suggest, schematic.

Yet, more fundamentally, there arises here a second issue on which there is a remarkable lack of consensus in contemporary jurisprudence, how we should understand the relationship between a classification, conceptualization, or theory of law or of legal phenomena, and the phenomena, institutions, or practices in question. The very question of what we mean when we claim to present an account or theory 'of' a particular legal or legally related concept, such as responsibility, remains, it seems to me, poorly understood in

[7] See Joseph Raz, *The Authority of Law* (Oxford: Clarendon Press 1979) Chapter 6; Neil MacCormick and Ota Weinberger, *An Institutional Theory of Law: New Approaches to Legal Positivism* (Dordrecht: Kluwer 1986); Neil MacCormick, *Institutions of Law* (Oxford University Press 2007); Ota Weinberger, *Law, Institution and Legal Politics* (Dordrecht: Kluwer 1991); Dick W. P. Ruiter, *Institutional Legal Facts* (Dordrecht: Kluwer 1993); Maksymilian Del Mar, 'Legality as Relative Institutionalization: MacCormick's Diffusionism and Transnational Legal Theory' (2014) 5(2) *Transnational Legal Theory* 177–217. On institutional approaches to criminal law, see Lindsay Farmer, 'Criminal Law as an Institution: Rethinking Theoretical Approaches to Criminalization', in Antony Duff, Lindsay Farmer, Sandra Marshall, Massimo Renzo, and Victor Tadros (eds), *Criminalization: The Political Morality of the Criminal Law* (Oxford: Oxford University Press 2015); Hamish Ross, *Law as a Social Institution* (Oxford: Hart Publishing 2001); Lindsay Farmer, *Making the Modern Criminal Law: Criminalization and Social Order* (Oxford: Oxford University Press 2016) Chapter 2. Close attention to the institutional form of law is also evident in an unpublished paper on discretion by H. L. A. Hart (circulated to the Harvard Legal Philosophy Discussion Group in 1956 and recently discovered by Geoffrey Shaw among the papers of Henry Hart in the Harvard Law School archive (Box 35, Folder 7)), in which the institutional constraints on discretion are argued to be key to explaining its (potential) consistency with the rule of law: see H. L. A. Hart, 'Discretion'; Geoffrey C. Shaw, 'Hart's Lost Essay: *Discretion* and the Legal Process School', and Nicola Lacey 'The Path Not Taken: H. L. A. Hart's Harvard Essay on Discretion', (2013) 127 *Harvard Law Review* at pp. 652, 666 and 636–51 respectively. It remains a fascinating question—and one of some consequence for the subsequent development of legal theory—why Hart's later work was more parsimonious in its analysis of such institutional questions.

the literature. This question—basic as it appears—about the relationship between the concepts whose refinement and analysis has been the primary concern of jurisprudence, which we have already seen arising in relation to Hart's, Moore's, or Tadros's treatment of strict liability, and the phenomena to which they relate, has long preoccupied legal theorists. H. L. A. Hart's inaugural lecture of sixty years ago[8] provides just one example. It nonetheless continues to generate both controversy and confusion.

In thinking about why this should be the case, it is perhaps useful to start out by distinguishing three levels of interpretive analysis in legal theory. At the most concrete level, we have the analysis of concepts that appear on the surface of legal rules, doctrines, or principles: intentional, reckless, or negligent conduct, or the contours of defences such as duress or self-defence, to take some central criminal law examples. At a higher level of abstraction, we have the analysis of concepts that are thought to underlie, explain, or rationalize the normative relationships between the more concrete concepts within legal doctrines: the concept of responsibility would be a prime example. And, finally, we have the ultimate prize for so-called 'general jurisprudence'—the concept of law itself, along with associated concepts such as legality. At all three levels, jurists find themselves dealing with concepts which have both meaning and practical relevance in a number of different fields. But, whereas the question of how legal theorists should distinguish their conception of law from, for example, the laws of gravity, or how responsibility in criminal law relates to moral responsibility, have been key preoccupations, this has been less true in the analysis of 'ground-level' legal concepts.

The reason is not far to seek. While ideas of intentionality, for example, are deployed well beyond the law, their articulation in legal rules or doctrines, in legislation and case law, gives them a mooring, which helps to resolve the question of the relationship between the theoretical account and the object of theorization. In relation to more general jurisprudential questions such as the status of legal rules, the character of law, or the concept of responsibility, however, the (equally important) relationship with broader social ideas and institutions all too often slips out of view. This is not to say that complicated issues do not arise in relation to doctrinal concepts. On

[8] 'Definition and Theory in Jurisprudence' 70 *Law Quarterly Review* 37 (1954).

the contrary, intentionality would be a good example of a concept in relation to which broader cultural, psychological, and philosophical ideas have a potential bearing on how that concept is understood in the law. But since the issues which arise here are raised more starkly and in more intractable form in relation to the more general or abstract concepts, I shall in this chapter concentrate on the second and third forms of analysis.

For any legal system, the delineation of the criteria marking out legal subjects or persons is a key concern. Which human or other entities will enjoy the capacity or power to act legally, making contracts, entering into marriages, or writing effective legal wills, trusts, or other such practical and normative arrangements is both an issue which every legal order has to resolve, and one which raises fundamental jurisprudential questions. The delineation of legal personhood has implications of course not only for the agency and powers of individuals and collective entities within a social order, but also for their obligations and legal liabilities. While perhaps the most obvious normative questions are raised by the substantive content of actual legal rules and principles, the structures of personhood, subjectivity, agency, and responsibility disclosed by particular sets of legal arrangements give rise to questions of a conceptual and normative nature. And these have been the object of extensive jurisprudential analysis, much of it in recent years and flying under the flag of the analysis of 'philosophical foundations' of aspects of the common law. A rich literature has accordingly accumulated.[9] But this literature—like the analytical jurisprudence from which it

[9] See, for example, in Antony Duff and Stuart Green (eds) *Philosophical Foundations of Criminal Law* (Oxford: Oxford University Press 2011); John Gardner, *Offences and Defences* (Oxford: Oxford University Press 2007); Jeremy Horder, *Excusing Crime* (Oxford: Oxford University Press 2004); Victor Tadros, *Criminal Responsibility* (Oxford: Oxford University Press 2005). Much of the inspiration for this flourishing literature lies in H. L. A. Hart's fine *Punishment and Responsibility* (Oxford: Oxford University Press 1968). Although not explicitly preoccupied with the methodological concerns of this essay, it is clear that many of Hart's arguments are consistent with the approach to middle-range theorizing which I defend, since they amount in large part to a thoughtful interpretation of the normative distinctions embedded within a particular set of institutionalized legal doctrines and practices of argumentation. Not all of the subsequent literature, however, has been as careful as Hart was to emphasize, for example, the importance of the specific role of responsibility within modern legal institutions in distinguishing a criminal-legal conception of responsibility from moral responsibility. For two exceptions, see Peter Cane, *Responsibility in Law and Morality* (Oxford: Hart Publishing 2003) and Lindsay Farmer, *Making the Modern Criminal Law* (2016).

developed—has shown an uneven interest in the broader social, institutional, and cultural conditions under which these legal concepts have developed and by which they have been shaped.[10] The fact, for example, that very little of this work has addressed what is one of the most radical changes in the conception of legal personhood, viewed in modern perspective—the relatively recent acknowledgment of women as legal persons[11]—is one initial clue to the very particular way in which legal philosophers have drawn the boundaries of their intellectual concern.[12]

Indeed, we can push this argument one stage further, echoing and reinforcing this book's insistence that criminal law's practices of responsibility-attribution must be interpreted in the context of the full range of decisions, from legislation *via* prosecution to punishment, which make up the practice of criminalization. For these broader practices are key to the coordinating tasks of criminal law in pursuit of its varying social functions, and are themselves facilitated by the legitimating role which responsibility plays in relation to criminal law. In a world in which the proliferation of overlapping criminal offences has given increasing power to prosecutors through plea-bargaining, William Stuntz has suggested that, in the USA, prosecutors have become not merely the real lawmakers but even the effective adjudicators in the vast majority of cases in which the judge in effect rubber stamps a plea deal and a jury is never empanelled. It is worth quoting his argument, which is almost equally relevant to England and Wales, at length:

> The cumulation of criminal prohibitions that we have seen over the past half-century has made it ever easier for prosecutors to generate guilty

[10] Again, there are honourable exceptions. For example, Antony Duff's work has been pioneering in the degree to which it has incorporated insights into the relevance of legal and criminal justice institutions with a normative analysis, from *Trials and Punishments* (Cambridge: Cambridge University Press 1986) to *Answering for Crime* (Oxford: Hart Publishing 2012).

[11] On the gendering of legal subjectivity from a historical point of view, see, for example, Nicola Lacey, *Women Crime and Character: From Moll Flanders to Tess of the d'Urbervilles* (2008); Lucia Zedner, *Women, Crime and Custody in Victorian England* (1991).

[12] See Nicola Lacey, *Unspeakable Subjects: Feminist Essays in Legal and Social Theory* (Oxford: Hart Publishing 1998); Joanne Conaghan, *Law and Gender* (Oxford: Oxford University Press, 2013); Ngaire Naffine and Rosemary Owens (eds) *Sexing the Subject of Law* (London: Sweet and Maxwell 1997); Ngaire Naffine, *Law and the Sexes: Explorations in Feminist Jurisprudence* (London: Allen and Unwin 1990); see also Naffine, *Law's Meaning of Life: Philosophy, Religion, Darwin and the Legal Person* (Oxford: Hart Publishing 2009).

pleas in street crime cases, making prosecutors the system's prime adjudicators in such cases. When it comes to vice—today, drugs—prosecutors are the system's real lawmakers. When it comes to a range of ordinary street crimes, prosecutors often function as judge and jury; they are the system's real adjudicators. That is how enforcement discretion changed criminal law … Legislative crime definition has a natural tendency to become, in practice, prosecutorial crime definition, as legislatures define broad nominal liability rules, leaving prosecutors to determine what behaviour actually leads to conviction and punishment.[13]

My analogous suggestion is that a change in patterns of prosecution and criminalization amounts, in substance, to a change in the contours of criminal responsibility; that we cannot, in other words, separate the moment of responsibility-attribution from the moments of selection and case-processing which precede (and in most instances supplant) it, or indeed from the moments of penal execution which conclude the criminal process. I therefore conclude, with Stuntz, that:

One unfortunate consequence of the sheer mass of current law and literature on [policing, adjudication and crime definition, punishment …] is that lawyers, judges, and scholars rarely talk about any two of them … in tandem. These are separate subjects, each with its own body of rules and theoretical underpinnings and policy debates. But the subjects interact. Changes in one area tend to produce changes in others … Seeing the system whole, considering change in all its parts together, may be the key to wise reform.[14]

It may be objected in turn that an orientation to reform is not the priority of scholarship concerned with the philosophical foundations of criminal law. But scholars concerned to explore and refine

[13] William J. Stuntz, 'The Pathological Politics of Criminal Law' 100 *Michigan Law Review* (2001) 505–600, at 578. In the English context, the discretionary powers of the police are probably of equal if not greater importance than those of prosecutors. Stuntz further suggests that the judicial development of constitutional devices such as the vagueness doctrine have, perversely, led to a greater incentive for lawmakers, in an attempt to avoid nullification, to enact a welter of very specific crimes whose overlapping nature has further increased the bargaining power of prosecutors and hence further marginalized the criminal trial—an unconscious judicial *auto da fe*.

[14] William J. Stuntz, 'The Political Constitution of Criminal Justice' 119 *Harvard Law Review* (2006) 781–851 at p. 831; see also his *The Collapse of American Criminal Justice* (Cambridge, MA: Harvard University Press 2011).

the normative basis for criminal liability must, surely, be concerned with the conditions under which those principles and values will be most likely to survive. In a world in which the criminal trial is increasingly regarded as an 'expensive luxury'[15]—let alone the American context in which 'criminal law is becoming a sideshow'[16]—we had better try to understand the nature of the environment which confronts the principles to which liberal criminal-law theory is committed.

Normative criminal law theory purports, after all, to have some grounding in the reality of criminal law and to offer an account of the implicit normative structure of an actually existing social practice. But these principles can only be understood in the contexts of both the institutions in which they are mobilized, and the environment in which those institutions exist. To the extent that the refinement of capacity-based principles of responsibility is today juxtaposed with a diminishing practical significance of capacity-responsibility as a principle of attribution, this raises inescapable questions for criminal law theory. Developments in the criminal process, in the penal system, and in the political and economic world, in short, affect the *meaning* as well as the *normative significance* of criminal responsibility; and that meaning, produced within an influential system of social signalling, should be a core concern of criminal law theory. Thus, the story related in this book has several more general implications for method in both legal theory and legal scholarship. Resisting the dichotomy between the imperative to generalization/universalization in legal theory and a slide into particularism and relativism, we can still speak of 'criminal law' and 'criminal responsibility' across the changing practices of responsibility attribution. And we should be interested in both the changes in these phenomena and what causes them. For, without an account of these causal forces, as I have argued in this book, and of the ways in which the patterns of responsibility-attribution which serve to legitimate criminalization and to coordinate its functions are driven by prevailing constellations of ideas, interests, and institutions, our account of criminal law will be impoverished in the sense of being inadequately grounded in its own subject matter.

[15] Andrew Ashworth and Lucia Zedner, 'Defending the Criminal Law: Reflections on the Changing Character of Crime, Procedure and Sanctions' 2 *Criminal Law and Philosophy* (2008) 21–51, at 38.

[16] William J. Stuntz, 'The Pathological Politics of Criminal Law' p. 509.

Someone anxious to defend a primarily philosophical approach to theorizing criminal responsibility will retort that none of this in any way threatens either the normative credentials of her account or its applicability to late twentieth-century English criminal law. The first point may be conceded, though it is obvious that the normative recommendations of particular principles such as responsibility are to some degree founded in social facts—facts about not only human beings but also about the shape of the social world—and vary in their relative strength along with those founding conditions. This is a point to which I shall return below. But even a full concession does not rescue an account such as Hart's from the need to attend to the broader social and institutional context that shapes the significance of doctrines of responsibility in criminal law. For his account purports not merely to be normative but also to have explanatory power. Historical, comparative, or socio-legal understandings of the role of responsibility in criminal law, which affect our interpretation of the shape and relative importance of the concept in criminal law, are therefore factors that neither Hart nor other legal philosophers with similarly descriptive and explanatory commitments cannot ignore.

We should moreover reject the claim that this implies—as Victor Tadros has suggested some of my own work does[17]—that there is nothing of a general nature which can be said about the concept of criminal responsibility, or about the more concrete concepts—intention, recklessness, negligence, knowledge and so forth—out of which doctrines of criminal responsibility are crafted. Here I think we can agree readily with MacCormick and Weinberger when they argue, in their pursuit of a 'socially realistic development of normativism', that the type of ideal entity which we deem really existent is such as always exists only by virtue of its correlation with material objects and processes, and indeed the social existence of norms and institutions depends upon their being in actual operation in the guidance and evaluation of human actions in their social context.[18]

We can accept that there is a 'core' to the idea of responsibility, a core related to the idea of human agency and accountability for

[17] Victor Tadros, *Criminal Responsibility* (Oxford: Oxford University Press 2005) pp. 3–8.

[18] Neil MacCormick and Ota Weinberger, *An Institutional Theory of Law: New Approaches to Legal Positivism* (Dordrecht: Kluwer 1986) p. 6 (a passage in which MacCormick is referring with approval to Weinberger's argument in Chapter 1); see also Neil MacCormick, 'Law as Institutional Fact' 90 *Law Quarterly Review* (1974) 102–29.

conduct which acts as a constant thread amid shifting theories of responsibility over time and space. But this core is a relatively small one, and the inflection which it is given by varying social and institutional conditions and practical imperatives is so decisive that no theorist of criminal responsibility can afford to ignore it. Only if we attend to this socio-institutional basis, and its influence on criminal law's conceptual framework, can we understand, explain, and even predict the ways in which legal decision-makers such as judges interpret and apply the concept. As Hart's enterprise implicitly concedes, one does not have to be a Legal Realist or to deny the distinctively normative, action-guiding quality of law to take the view that legal theory has this sort of explanatory aspect. The argument for a more socially grounded jurisprudential analysis of responsibility can in fact be related back to Hart's general jurisprudence and in particular to his relatively parsimonious conception of law as a system of more or less formally articulated rules.[19]

As has been famously discussed in relation to Hart's theory of adjudication, Hart showed little interest in the operation of the discretion that he saw as characterizing 'hard cases'.[20] Even more clearly, the operation of the range of discretionary powers which shape factors such as which cases come to court and how they are prosecuted stood well beyond his delineated terrain. Yet, as we have seen, there are powerful reasons for thinking that we can understand the full significance of legal concepts such as responsibility only if we take the trouble to inform ourselves about precisely these surrounding forms of power and decision-making, which contribute significantly to the balance which criminal law strikes at any particular time between its competing quasi-moral and regulatory aspects. I shall try to illustrate this point with two examples.

First, within the terrain of criminal law in which a relatively robust responsibility or *mens rea* requirement exists—the law of murder or theft, for example—not only other features of legal doctrine (notably

[19] This is a conception which is also put in doubt by recent analyses of the rhetorical structure of criminal trials and in particular of the influence of cultural frames in the jury's reading of evidential narratives: see, for example, Robert P. Burns, 'The Distinctiveness of Trial Narrative', in Anthony Duff, Lindsay Farmer, Sandra Marshall, and Victor Tadros (eds), *The Trial on Trial* Vol. 1: *Truth and Due Process* (Oxford and Portland: Hart Publishing 2004). As Burns argues, this implies that the normatively and functionally most appealing trial structure is itself socially contingent.

[20] Ronald Dworkin, 'Hard Cases' 88 *Harvard Law Review* (1975) 1057–109; see generally Dworkin, *Taking Rights Seriously* (London: Duckworth 1977).

the scope of defences) but also the (typically rather limited) time frame in which an offence is situated and the shape of the rules of evidence in constraining the kinds of information which may be presented to the court may compromise the investigation of individual responsibility in a full sense. To take a recently much debated example, the tendency to frame prosecutions in relation to single incidents marginalizes the relevance of the experience of background factors, such as long-term domestic abuse, to the volitional dimension of responsibility, hence conducing to a finding of victims of such abuse as fully responsible for an ultimate attack on their abuser.[21] In several jurisdictions, this situation has recently been reversed.[22] I do not want to take a position here on the merits of this change in the law of provocation and self-defence, or on the very limited extent to which criminal defences incorporate factors in a defendant's background which might be thought to compromise their cognitive or volitional capacities or to block inferences of vicious character (let alone features of environment, such as radical social inequality, which might be relevant to the fairness of differently situated individuals' opportunities to conform their behaviour to the law). I merely wish to point out that the legal realization of responsibility depends not merely on the articulation of a liability rule but on a cluster of other assumptions and discretionary powers which we need to understand if we want to have a full view of the meaning and significance of responsibility in criminal law.

The second, converse example has to do with strict liability offences. These, of course, are the most controversial aspects of criminal law from the point of view of Hart's normative theory of capacity-based responsibility. Yet, intriguingly, a welter of empirical evidence suggests that the actual prosecution of these offences is overwhelmingly focused on people whom the prosecuting authority view as responsible in something like the capacity sense.[23] Even if

[21] Donald Nicolson and Rohit Sanghvi, 'Battered Women and Provocation: The Implications of *R v Ahluwalia*' *Criminal Law Review* (October 1993) 728–38; John Gardner and Timothy Macklem, 'Compassion Without Respect? Nine Fallacies in *R v Smith*' *Criminal Law Review* (August 2001) 623–35; V. F. Nourse, 'Passion's Progress: Modern Law Reform and the Provocation Defense' 106 *Yale Law Journal* (1997) 1331–448.

[22] See, for example, in relation to England and Wales *R v Smith* [2000] 4 All ER 289. English law has since been further modified with the replacement of provocation by a new defence of loss of control: Coroners and Justice Act 2009 section 54 (note in particular subsection 3).

[23] W. G. Carson, 'White-collar Crime and the Enforcement of Factory Legislation' 10 *British Journal of Criminology* (1970) 383–98; Keith Hawkins, *Environment and*

the normative notion of outcome-responsibility is rejected, this does not necessarily weaken the case for a capacity-responsibility requirement in the law itself: the prosecutorial discretion which strict liability offences expand may be subject to various forms of abuse. But, as legal theorists, we should be interested in the ways in which broad social attitudes and power relations conduce to or against the realization of idea(l)s of responsibility in the enforcement as much as the formal content of criminal law. This militates in favour of a broader view of law than that adopted in Hart's descriptive jurisprudence, and a generalization of the sort of attention devoted to issues of trial, prosecution, and sentence[24] which is so often absent from philosophical analysis.

These arguments about the relevance to jurisprudence of the social basis for legal ideas, such as responsibility, have, finally, decisive implications for the normative aspect of special jurisprudence. For if conceptual ideas have institutional and other conditions of existence—if, for example, a notion of capacity responsibility can only be realized in criminal law on the basis of certain institutional developments and in the context of a cluster of social and cultural conditions—this has clear implications for the pursuit of normative projects. To the extent that the ambition of special jurisprudence is to affirm, and not merely to characterize or delineate, certain key legal concepts, we must surely be interested in the conditions which facilitate—or hamper—their institutional realization. Yet much special jurisprudence rests at the abstract level of conceptual frameworks and pays little attention to what Lewis Kornhauser has called 'realized institutions' inhabited by particular individuals, and none whatsoever to 'functioning institutions' situated and operating in a specified social and physical environment.[25] To the extent that such 'functioning institutions' are a necessary condition for the realization of our concepts, this is a deficit in the practice of jurisprudence.

Enforcement (Oxford: Clarendon Press 1983); Nicola Lacey, Celia Wells and Oliver Quick, *Reconstructing Criminal Law* (3rd ed., Cambridge: Cambridge University Press 2003) Chapters 1 and 5; Wells and Quick, *Reconstructing Criminal Law* (4th ed., Cambridge: Cambridge University Press 2010) Chapter 19.

[24] There are, of course, exceptions to this rule: see, for example, R. A. Duff, *Trials and Punishments* (Cambridge: Cambridge University Press 1986) and *Punishment, Communication and Community* (Oxford: Oxford University Press 2001).

[25] Lewis Kornhauser, 'Governance Structures, Legal Systems, and The Concept of Law' 79 *Chicago-Kent Law Review* (2004) 355–81, at 362–4.

There is, of course, a judgment to be made about what level of abstraction is appropriate in seeking to theorize complex phenomena such as responsibility. But the bird's eye of analytical jurisprudence has obscured our view of the existence of multiple, overlapping conceptions of responsibility revealed by our historical analysis, by focusing on a particular conceptualization, albeit at a relatively high level of abstraction, and by excluding all phenomena outwith that conceptualization.[26] In doing so, it has missed out on some very important aspects of the social phenomena of law about which—as I have tried to show—things of a reasonable level of generality may be said. The methodological issue here is nicely illustrated by the contrasting positions of Joseph Raz and Tony Honoré on liability for harmful outcomes. While Raz argues that such cases of strict liability in criminal law are not genuine instances of responsibility, since they fall outwith its conceptual contours, Honoré argues in terms of 'outcome responsibility'.[27] It will be evident that my sympathies lie with Honoré's more capacious understanding of responsibility, on the basis that it emerges from a reflexive engagement not only with our intuitions about responsibility but with the variegated practices of responsibility-attribution to be found in the criminal law.

Criminal responsibility, in short, is an idea which is located within a social practice of criminalization, which itself is necessarily located within an institutional framework and structured by the imperatives of legitimation and coordination. Since that framework conditions and shapes the contours of responsibility as an operational idea in criminal law and criminal justice, that framework must itself be an object of interest to a descriptive or classificatory theory of criminal responsibility. It follows that what is needed in order to fully explicate ideas of criminal responsibility is a broad account of the co-evolution of legal doctrine, criminal process, and political economy. These shifts in legal understandings of responsibility are in themselves sufficient to establish the need for legal theory to attune itself to the changing social, intellectual, and institutional environment within

[26] Hence what John Gardner finds puzzling: my claim that jurisprudential conceptualizations tend to suffer from both over-and under-inclusiveness, and do so for similar theoretical reasons: Gardner, *Law as a Leap of Faith* (Oxford: Oxford University Press 2012) 278ff.

[27] Joseph Raz, *From Normativity to Responsibility* (Oxford: Oxford University Press 2011) Part III; Tony Honoré, 'Responsibility and Luck: The Moral Basis of Strict Liability' 104 *Law Quarterly Review* (1988) 530–53.

which legal ideas emerge and legal rules are invoked, interpreted, and enforced. A conceptualization or theorization of responsibility which was inattentive to these broad changes would, quite simply, be irrelevant to our understanding of criminal responsibility, because it would be unmoored from the very phenomena which it purports to illuminate or conceptualize. If my diagnosis of a shift in the alignment of patterns of responsibility attribution, and in particular of the revival of a new, hybrid practice of character responsibility, is persuasive, this is not simply a matter of historical interest: rather, it discloses a shift in the modality of criminal responsibilization which must be of interest to any jurisprudential project which conceives itself to be in some sense descriptive. Moreover my narrative of the shifting contours of criminal responsibility and their articulation with changing institutional structures themselves shaped by changing social needs and creating novel organizational opportunities is, of course, just one example of decisive legal change over time and how it is driven. Equally interesting accounts could be given of the changing gendering of legal subjecthood,[28] of the changing understanding of corporate legal capacity,[29] or, perhaps most spectacularly of all, of the legal subjecthood of animals.[30] In short, history should be seen as central to the very project of special jurisprudence.

I should reiterate, finally, that this methodological claim does not in any sense undermine or question the importance of the normative or evaluative project which has been central to many philosophical accounts. Evidently, the interpretation which I offered of the trajectory of criminal responsibility attribution in late twentieth and early twenty-first century Britain raises a host of evaluative questions, many of them troubling from the point of view of both civil liberties and social justice. So although the focus of this book is on

[28] See Nicola Lacey, *Unspeakable Subjects: Feminist Essays in Legal and Social Theory* (Oxford: Hart Publishing 1998); Joanne Conaghan, *Law and Gender* (Oxford: Clarendon Press 2013); Ngaire Naffine and Rosemary Owens (eds), *Sexing the Subject of Law* (London: Sweet and Maxwell 1997); Ngaire Naffine, *Law and the Sexes: Explorations in Feminist Jurisprudence* (London: Allen and Unwin 1990); see also Naffine, *Law's Meaning of Life* (Oxford: Hart Publishing 2009).

[29] See Celia Wells, *Corporations and Criminal Responsibility* (2nd ed., Oxford: Clarendon Press 2001); Nicola Lacey, 'Philosophical Foundations of the Common Law: Social Not Metaphysical', in Jeremy Horder (ed.), *Oxford Essays in Jurisprudence*, 4th Series (Oxford: Oxford University Press 2000); see also discussion in Chapter 3 above.

[30] E. P. Evans, *The Criminal Prosecution and Capital Punishment of Animals* (1906: London: Faber and Faber 1987); William Ewald, 'Comparative Jurisprudence (I): What Was it Like to Try a Rat?' 143 *University of Pennsylvania Law Review* 1889 (1995).

interpretation and explanation, the reader will doubtless have discerned that I see much reason to be concerned about recent trends in criminal responsibility-attribution in English law, and in particular about the tension between between exclusionary and stigmatizing aspects of the character/risk patterns of attribution and ideals of equality, legality and human rights to which I am strongly committed. I would insist, however, that we can only think about how best to protect and pursue these ideals by trying to understand their conditions of existence, and hence the practical and political context in which we are operating.

Implications for General Jurisprudence: The Evolution of Law and Legality

I now turn to ask, finally, whether the methodological points which I have made in relation to the particular jurisprudence of responsibility apply equally to the central concept with which general jurisprudence has been concerned: that of law itself. Most legal theorists accept that law is a phenomenon whose content is fundamentally shaped by its environment. Most would further concede that its institutional form and *modus operandi* are also historically specific. But does an acknowledgment of this contingency undermine the very project, unsettling the conditions of a 'general jurisprudence' by denying the necessity of any particular institutional feature, modality, or function distinguishing law as a phenomenon?

For many more sociologically and historically minded legal theorists, one particular focus here has been the upshot of Hart's widely accepted view of law as fundamentally a social phenomenon, which they—or, I should say we—see as raising issues which many analytical legal theorists regard as being appropriately bracketed. A good place to start here is therefore with the very robust position taken by Joseph Raz on this question in *The Authority of Law*.[31] While making transparent his Hartian assumption of 'the primacy of the social'—the idea that the existence of law is inextricably bound up with 'its impact on the behaviour of people in the society albeit in a variety of ways',[32] Raz denies that this assumption has any potential to

[31] Joseph Raz, *The Authority of Law* (Oxford: Clarendon Press 1979).

[32] Ibid. p. 103.

disrupt or subvert the quest for a general concept of law. He deals with the issue by carving out a very clear division of labour between legal philosophy and the sociology of law: the former must ally itself with the 'assumption of universality according to which it is a criterion of adequacy of a legal theory that it is true of all the intuitively clear instances of municipal legal systems' and 'must fasten only on those features of legal systems which they must possess regardless of the special circumstances of the societies in which they are in force. This', Raz concludes, 'is the difference between legal philosophy and sociology of law. The latter is concerned with the contingent and with the particular, the former with the necessary and the universal'.[33] One of the universal qualities of law, which in Raz's view commands the attention of legal philosophy and underpins a universal account of law is law's importance: again, intuitions do a significant amount of work here, for this quality is evidenced by the fact that 'we feel that legal systems not only happen to be the most important institutionalized system governing human society, but that that is part of their nature.'[34]

Another robust denial of what I believe to be an interesting methodological issue is to be found in the final chapter of John Gardner's *Law as a Leap of Faith*.[35] Taking as his main targets, Brian Tamanaha, William Twining and my own work,[36] Gardner sets out the case for a 'general jurisprudence' which asserts that there are 'things both interesting and true to say about law in general, law as such, wherever it may be found.[37] One object of Gardner's critique is my argument[38] that Hart's position on the relationship between analytical jurisprudence and descriptive sociology, and on the theorization of law as a social phenomenon, was fractured by a tension between Hart's justified sense of the need to respond to the social quality of

[33] Ibid. p. 104.

[34] Ibid. p. 116.

[35] Oxford: Oxford University Press (2012).

[36] Brian S. Tamanaha, *A General Jurisprudence of Law and Society* (New York: Oxford University Press 2001); William Twining, *General Jurisprudence: Understanding Law from a Global Perspective* (Cambridge: Cambridge University Press 2009); Nicola Lacey, 'Analytical Jurisprudence versus Descriptive Sociology Revisited' 84 *Texas Law Review* (2006) 945–82; see also Roger Cotterrell, 'Why Must Legal Ideas Be Interpreted Sociologically?' 25 *Journal of Law and Society* (1998) 171–92.

[37] Gardner, *Law as a Leap of Faith* p. 301.

[38] In Nicola Lacey, *A Life of H.L.A. Hart: The Nightmare and the Noble Dream* (Oxford: Oxford University Press 2004); and 'Analytical Jurisprudence versus Descriptive Sociology Revisited'.

law and his aspiration to produce a general concept of law which transcended particular social contexts. Gardner is particularly critical of the argument that Hart's concept of law is, in effect, a covert *apologia* for a very particular form of modern, Western law, along the lines suggested by Peter Fitzpatrick in *The Mythology of Modern Law*.[39] While Gardner concedes that Hart may have been guilty of failing to articulate and defend certain normative assumptions, he lines up unambiguously with Hart's aspiration to produce a concept of law which might animate jurisprudence quite generally. In his view, the mistake of those who, like Tamanaha, Twining, and me, insist on the social quality of law as implying a certain degree of institutional and phenomenological contingency, is that in doing so we are fundamentally undermining the very project of jurisprudence.[40]

Gardner asserts that 'some of the true and interesting things to be said about law in general bear on the very nature of law'[41] and that there are 'different senses of "law" and "legal", all of which must be accounted for in a complete explanation of the nature of law'[42] (though, somewhat confusingly, he also denies that he has or aspires to have a 'theory of law' and denies that there is a 'bigger picture' to be revealed or, perhaps, constructed).[43] More important, however, is how we square the circle between Gardner's commitment to understanding jurisprudence as a classificatory enterprise—an interpretation which entails an intimate relationship with, and hence, one would have thought, a sensitivity to, the institutional phenomena which are being classified—and his insistence on the identity of jurisprudence and the project of articulating a general account of 'the very nature of law'.[44]

In framing his own understanding, Gardner lays substantial emphasis on the distinctive modality of law as a social phenomenon. Here again, he is following Joseph Raz, who argued in *The Authority of Law* that legal norm-applying institutions should 'be identified by the way they fulfil their functions rather than by their functions

[39] (London: Routledge 1992). For a more circumspect, but equally telling, formulation of the argument that general theories such as Hart's make implicit assumptions about socio-political structure and culture, see Joanne Conaghan, *Law and Gender* Chapter 5.2.

[40] Gardner, *Law as a Leap of Faith* p. 279.

[41] Ibid. p. 270.

[42] Ibid. p. 176.

[43] Ibid. p. v; on this point, see further Kimberley Brownlee, 'On Gardner on Law in General' *Jurisprudence* 6 (2015) 567–73 http://dx.doi.org/10.1080/20403313.2015.1067487.

[44] Gardner, *Law as a Leap of Faith* p. 270.

themselves'.[45] Law is not distinguished on this view by particular functions or particular institutional qualities. Law will, of course, have these functions and qualities, but they change over time. What is distinctive of law, and in some (not fully specified) way, therefore, more general and, presumably, unchanging, is the modality of law: not what law does, or what it aspires to achieve, but the way in which it does so. Here the well-known modal qualities often associated with the rule of law, with legality, or, as Fuller put it, with law's inner or internal morality,[46] figure large: law subjects human conduct to governance through rule-based regulation which is subject to normative precepts such as publicity, coherence, possibility of compliance, non-retroactivity, generality, consistency, predictability, certainty, and so on.

It is not clear, however, that we should accept without further argument the proposition that law's modality can be taken as an analytic given or an unchanging quality, or that that modality is independent of law's changing social functions or institutional structure. Even less should we accept the idea that law's supremacy or importance is an unchanging given. The relationship between the Polynesian islanders and their legal system, identified in Tamanaha's early work, is a case in point here: the modality of law's normative force was, according to his ethnography, substantially modified by the relationship between state law and other normative orders operating in the same space.[47] Farmer's recent historical analysis shows that the emergence of a modern notion of criminal law, oriented to guaranteeing civil order, produced a new and distinctive modality of legal governance.[48] Many systems, notably those whose state

[45] Raz, *The Authority of Law* p. 106.

[46] For Fuller's classic treatment of the rule of law, a.k.a., the internal morality of law, see Lon Fuller, *The Morality of Law* (New Haven and London: Yale University Press 1964) and 'Positivism and Fidelity to Law—A Reply to Professor Hart' 71 *Harvard Law Review* (1958) 630–72. On Fuller's own grasp of the importance of institutional form to our understanding of law, see Kristen Rundle, *Forms Liberate: Reclaiming the Jurisprudence of Lon Fuller* (Oxford: Hart Publishing 2012).

[47] Brian S. Tamanaha, *A General Jurisprudence of Law and Society*. As Tamanaha also notes, the historical and sociological accounts of law to be found in the work of writings such as Weber and Durkheim posits links between forms of social organization, and not merely the content, but also the form of law (32). For further discussion, see Joanne Conaghan, *Law and Gender*. Chapter 5.4.

[48] Farmer, *Making the Modern Criminal Law*. Chapter Parts I and II; cf, in relation to public law, Martin Loughlin, *Foundations of Public Law* (Oxford: Oxford University Press 2010).

law is inextricably related to theological doctrines and institutions, do not fit the assumption of law's supreme importance or claim to comprehensiveness,[49] and moreover feature forms of legal normativity which at the very least diversify our sense of law's modality. As with the case of responsibility, it is obviously conceptually proper to stipulate that such differences exclude the relevant phenomena from the category, 'law'. But this in my view is to deprive the terrain of jurisprudence of some very significant objects of analysis.

Even within one relatively stable system, such as that of this country, can we really assume that large social developments such as the growth of the regulatory state leave law's modality entirely unchanged? This seems implausible; and a better balance, it seems to me, is indicated by Peter Cane's carefully formulated claim, in a slightly different context, that 'paying careful attention to standard accounts of public law and to differences between those accounts and the image of public law embedded in Hart's theory can tell us something theoretically significant not only (and tautologically) about the nature of *public* law in modern, common law legal systems, but also about the nature of *law*, full stop, *in such systems*'.[50] Conceptions of legality make an interesting case study here,[51] not only because of the persistence of a recognizable discourse of legality over many centuries in the common law, but also because legality is arguably, on Gardner's interpretation of Raz's view, the distinctive modality of law. At a sufficiently high level of abstraction, we can of course produce conceptions of 'law' or 'legality' which are more widely applicable.[52] But we do so at some cost, and there is surely

[49] Raz, *The Authority of Law* pp. 116, 118.

[50] Peter Cane, 'Public Law and the Concept of Law' 33 *Oxford Journal of Legal Studies* (2013) 649–74, final emphasis added so as to underline Cane's careful qualification.

[51] For recent theoretical work on the rule of law, see Jeremy Waldron, 'The Concept and the Rule of Law', 43 *Georgia Law Review* (2008) 1–61, *Law and Disagreement* (Oxford: Clarendon Press 1999) pp. 94–101, and 'Positivism and Legality: Hart's Equivocal Response to Fuller' 83 *New York University Law Review* (2008) 1135–69; Nicola Lacey, 'Philosophy, Political Morality and History: Explaining the Enduring Resonance of the Hart-Fuller Debate' 83 *New York University Law Review* (2008) 1059–87; Tatsuo Inoue, 'The Rule of Law as the Law of Legislation', in Luc J. Wintgens and Philippe Thion (eds), *Legislation in Context: Essays in Legisprudence* (Aldershot: Ashgate 2007). For a fascinating assessment of forms of legalism in vastly differing times and contexts, see Paul Dresch and Hannah Skoda (eds), *Legalism: Anthropology and History* (Oxford: Oxford University Press 2012). For a philosophical approach defending the relevance of empirical knowledge to Hart's conceptual project, Veronica Rodriguez-Blanco, 'A Defense of Hart's Semantics as Nonambitious Conceptual Analysis' 9 *Legal Theory* (2003) 99–124.

[52] Cf. Lindsay Farmer, *Making the Modern Criminal Law* Chapters 3 and 5.

a judgment of balance to be made here, and one which should be addressed openly as an issue of method,[53] rather than swept aside as a matter of perverse misunderstanding of the rules of the game.

At its most basic level, of course, we find the idea of legality reaching back into classical philosophy.[54] A thin concept of the rule of law as signifying regular constraints on political power and authority might plausibly, then, be seen as 'the central case' of the concept. But if we look at thicker, richer conceptions of the concept—and at not only the different purposes for which it has been invoked, but the different ways in which it has been understood and has operated—historical specificity quickly enters the picture. Since Gardner complains that people such as myself 'rarely say enough about what would qualify … as a distinctively social grounding' for a legal theory,[55] let us take a few examples. In a highly centralized and authoritarian system, such as the monarchies of early modern England, it is not clear that the operative concept of the rule of law can intelligibly be read as implying the universal application of law, reaching even to the sovereign. This idea—central to modern notions of legality—was the object of long political contestation, and took centuries to be accomplished. We can, surely, acknowledge that the eighteenth-century conception of the rule of law in England was different to that in the twelfth century without concluding that no such conception existed. Indeed, it existed in part as a critical conception, which informed some of the political conflicts which shaped modern constitutional structures. The conception of universality is itself tied up, in other words, with the emergence of a certain idea of limited government. The interpretation of the requirement that laws should be reasonably susceptible to compliance has similarly changed in tandem with shifting notions

[53] As in Simon Roberts' contribution to the debate: 'After Government? On Representing Law Without the State' 68 *Modern Law Review* (2005) 1–24. Roberts argues that pluralist conceptions of law beyond the state risk diluting the analytic purchase of the concept of law, depriving comparative social science of tools to make important distinctions between centralized, hierarchical, and governing-oriented normative systems and genuinely negotiated normative orders. In his view, for example, Hart's concept of law indeed has an empirical and ethnographic basis, albeit one which Hart himself failed to elaborate. While the first part of his argument is sympathetic from Gardner's point of view, his argument that particular conceptions of law can and must claim empirical support is entirely persuasive and consistent with my argument in this paper.

[54] See Judith N. Shklar, *Legalism: Law, Morals and Political Trials* (Cambridge, MA: Harvard University Press 1964) pp. 1–28; Martin Krygier, *Philip Selznick: Ideals in the World* (Stanford: Stanford University Press 2012) pp. 76–81, Chapters 7 and 8.

[55] Gardner, *Law as a Leap of Faith* p. 282.

of human autonomy and entitlements. Right up to the early nineteenth century, English law, while priding itself on its respect for the rule of law and the 'rights of free-born Englishmen', included a variety of criminal provisions—notably those on vagrancy—which manifestly violated, in relation to certain sub-groups of the population, today's conception of possibility of compliance. This, crucially, was not just a question of a practical inability to match up to acknowledged ideals: it was also a matter of whether this was seen, normatively, as a problem.

In other cases, it is not so much the development of the political values underlying legality as the institutional preconditions for realizing them, which underpin the changing contours of the concept. An example here would be the tenet, widely shared in today's constitutional democracies, that the law should be publicized and intelligible. Even today, this ideal is difficult to realize. But it would have been a far more distant ideal in societies with very low levels of literacy and without developed technologies of communication, such as printing—conditions which fit more easily with customary modes of legality. A further example of this kind relates to the ideal that official action should be congruent with announced law. It seems obvious that this tenet must have a significantly different meaning in today's highly organized, professionalized criminal justice systems than in a system like that of England prior to the criminal justice reforms of the early nineteenth century—a system in which criminal justice enforcement mechanisms were vestigial, with no organized police force or prosecution, and much enforcement practice and indeed adjudication lying in the hands of lay prosecutors, parish constables, and justices of the peace.

These institutional features of eighteenth-century English criminal justice also had significant implications for the law's aspiration to achieve coherence. While the system of precedent is of course conducive to both substantive coherence and even-handedness in enforcement, the relatively disorganized mechanisms for appeal and law reporting gave rise to the possibility of significant regional variations—particularly in relation to criminal adjudication handled by lay justices rather than assize judges. (To get a sense of the relative scales here, recall that it has been estimated that in the mid eighteenth century, there were about 5,000 justices, as opposed to just twelve assize judges).[56] Again, debates about what ought to count as adequate

[56] See Bruce Lenman and Geoffrey Parker, 'The State, the Community, and Criminal Law in Early Modern Europe', in V. A. C. Gatrell, Bruce Lenman, and Geoffrey Parker (eds), *Crime and the Law* (London: Europa 1980) p. 32; see also Peter King, *Crime and Law in England: 1750–1840: Remaking Justice from the Margins* (Cambridge: Cambridge

standards of legality played an important role in underpinning the modernizing reform movement from the late eighteenth century on. But the fact is, that, for many decades, these sorts of discretionary arrangements, inimical to our view of adequate levels of coherence and congruence, were regarded as perfectly consistent with a respect for legality. For the rule of law was, at that time, embedded within a highly personalized model of sovereign authority; one in which the discretionary power of mercy was a core rather than a penumbral feature.[57] Ideals do, of course, underpin arguments for reform; but ideals themselves are constrained by existing institutional capacities. Hence, I agree with E. P. Thompson, among others, in concluding that it would be wrong to infer from the evidence rehearsed here that the rule of law in eighteenth-century England was an empty ideological form, an aspect merely of the rhetoric of those in power.[58]

These historical remarks about changing conceptions of legality raise, in my view, important jurisprudential questions about just how significant, and how unchanging, law's modality truly is; and about how far modality is independent of functionality. If a distinctive modality lends itself to the effective pursuit of certain sorts of functions rather than others, it seems problematic to claim, as Gardner does, that the fact that law's distinctiveness lies in its modality implies 'that the social sciences have no use for the classification of anything as law'.[59] It would be wrong to see the relationship between jurisprudence and the social sciences—or indeed the approach of social sciences—in such impoverished terms. In fact, many of the more innovative forms of social theory, from the classics of Marx, Weber, and Durkheim to more recent thinkers, like Foucault and Luhmann, have been centrally concerned with what we might broadly call the changing modalities of power, legal or otherwise. This lends weight to the contention which underlines the argument of this book: that the modality of legalism as understood by us today was shaped by modern conceptions of good government.

University Press 2006) pp. 47–50; Norma Landau, *The Justice of the Peace, 1679–1760* (Berkeley and Los Angeles: University of California Press 1984).

[57] Douglas Hay, 'Property, Authority, and the Criminal Law', in Douglas Hay, Peter Linebaugh, John G. Rule, E. P. Thompson and Carl Winslow (eds), *Albion's Fatal Tree: Crime and Society in Eighteenth Century England* (Harmondsworth: Penguin 1975).

[58] E. P. Thompson, *Whigs and Hunters: The Origins of the Black Act* (Harmondsworth: Penguin 1975).

[59] Gardner, *Law as a Leap of Faith* p. 293

As Gardner and I agree, jurisprudence is not a purely descriptive exercise, but rather an enterprise of 'classification'.[60] But he also thinks that it is all about 'finding out about law's nature'.[61] Yet classifications are, after all, things we adopt for reasons and purposes: 'getting the classification right'[62]—*pace* Gardner—is not a matter of objective truth,[63] but rather a judgment informed by a theorist's broader interests and concerns. It may be, then, that broader and narrower conceptions of law are useful in different contexts. Where we seem to disagree is in terms of how we should understand the criteria of accountability between the classificatory schema and the institutional arrangements that we both see as founding its subject matter. Hence we have markedly different views of the relationship between 'the institutions and the classifications … law and the idea of it'.[64] For my own part, I find it impossible to abandon the simple, but I think not simple-minded, view that, however many flexibility mechanisms, such as Hart's central case technique,[65] we build into our theoretical method, the rate of institutional change in modern law—indeed its changing modalities—are sufficiently substantial as to necessitate a constant openness to revising the conceptual contours of our idea of law, rather than—as Gardner implies would be necessary—simply preparing ourselves to take the view that law, or legality, or mechanisms of responsibility-attribution, did not exist at a particular time or place, or no longer exist. Law's particular functions can, in other words, inflect its nature and possibly even its modality—as can its distinctive institutional arrangements. To return to our criminal-law example, the way in which eighteenth-century English criminal law constructed, addressed, and regulated its subjects was in an important sense quite different to the way in which early twenty-first-century English criminal law performs its analogous tasks. Both were, however, undoubtedly and in all senses, instances of criminal law. We can intelligibly speak of them as such without committing ourselves to a conceptual framework which denies variation of modality, as of form, function, and substance.

I have taken particular issue with Gardner's formulation of the methodological case for a general jurisprudence, simply because it is

[60] See, for example, Gardner, *Law as a Leap of Faith* p. 277.
[61] Ibid. p. 282.
[62] Ibid. p. 279.
[63] Cf. Scott Shapiro, *Legality* (Cambridge, MA: Harvard University Press 2011) p. 390.
[64] Gardner, *Law as a Leap of Faith* p. 300.
[65] H. L. A. Hart, *The Concept of Law* (Oxford: Clarendon Press 1961) Chapter 1.

a recent, very clear formulation by one of the most influential contemporary analytical legal philosophers. But lest the impression be created that this is a criticism which is directed specifically at a single book, let me conclude by giving a further recent example illustrating the same difficulties which I have identified in relation to Gardner's argument. In his exhaustive recent study of legality,[66] Scott Shapiro argues that we should think of law and legal systems not in terms of the modality of rules, but rather as 'complex and sophisticated tools for creating and applying plans'.[67] This is an intriguing and—at first sight—inclusive conception. But it is not, surely, one which could plausibly have been offered as a conceptualization of the early common law. Rather, as Peter Cane has argued,[68] emerging ideas of legality, particularly in the context of public law, are closely connected to the changing structure of state power. Shapiro's concept of law, in other words, resonates with aspects of law in the modern administrative state. The claim that custom can be accommodated within the concept of law because of its 'plan-like' qualities[69] is surely to sign up to a functionalism which even the sociologists of law so often criticized by analytical legal philosophers generally manage to avoid.

Reflexive Jurisprudence: Beyond Conceptualism/ Empiricism Dichotomy

To give a systematic account of criminal responsibility in modern English law is, therefore, to theorize a concept which is strongly inflected by a particular political, intellectual, and institutional history. The writing of this history, or the placing of this history in comparative context is, of course, a different task from that of conceptualizing criminal responsibility. But to claim that these two projects are not closely intertwined is to leave jurisprudence—and indeed legal scholarship more generally—bereft of any account of how they

[66] Shapiro, *Legality*.

[67] Ibid., front cover flap: 'the task of legal systems is to engage in optimal social planning' (398)—a task which in his view itself entails familiar rule of law type constraints, seen as 'necessary conditions for the existence of social planning' (395).

[68] Cane, 'Public Law and the Concept of Law'.

[69] Shapiro, *Legality* p. 140. For a thoughtful analysis of the way in which Shapiro's vision implicitly rests on assumptions about liberal political order, see Sean Coyle, 'Legality and the Liberal Order' 76 *Modern Law Review* (2013) 401–18.

delineate their own subject matter. While there are, undoubtedly, fine judgments to be made about the boundaries beyond which it is useful to deploy a classification such as 'law' or a conceptual category such as 'responsibility' in our characterization of institutional phenomena, this evolving process must involve a reflexive movement back and forth between institutional arrangements and classificatory regimes. And this reflexive process must be sensitive both to change over time and to the need to craft classificatory regimes which can be applied flexibly so as to capture, not only differing degrees but different modalities of legalism. Moreover this reflexivity is every bit as essential to general as to special jurisprudence. As Cane describes this delicate, but essential, balance, 'There is no compelling reason ... why some sort of non-essentialism,[70] based on rich and careful observation of actual legal systems as opposed to a parsimonious, pre-theoretical, and stipulative set of obvious features, should be an acceptable methodology for particular jurisprudence but not for general jurisprudence'.[71]

To concede that our conception of what counts as, to put it in Hartian terms, the central case of law, or the paradigm of criminal responsibility, may change over time, is not, *pace* Gardner, to 'put paid to all scholarly work on law'[72] or to undermine the enterprise of jurisprudence, but rather to introduce a welcome transparency about how that enterprise is grounded in its subject matter. While, therefore, we can follow Gardner in focusing on classification rather than conceptualization, we must acknowledge that any classification must bear a reflexive and constantly evolving relationship with its own subject matter, as with the attitudes of the agents whose activities constitute the relevant institutional practice. Only by broadening its horizons and its methods in this way will jurisprudence be capable of illuminating not only doctrinal analysis within particular jurisdictions at particular times, but also comparative and historical scholarship which engages with law as one important phenomenon in the social world.

In terms of theoretical method, what does my analysis imply about the most fruitful line of further inquiry into the notion of responsibility, which has been the central concern of this book? If

[70] Cane, 'Public Law and the Concept of Law'.

[71] Ibid.

[72] Gardner, *Law as a Leap of Faith* p. 279.

responsibility works in different ways in different social practices and institutions, and if its meaning shifts over time, is it even a useful analytic construct? Should we speak rather of 'responsibilities', and reject the pursuit of a general interpretive theory of responsibility as theoretically misplaced?

This would, of course, be an over-reaction. Though conceptions of responsibility have indeed shifted over time, core themes can readily be identified—as the main thesis of this book, in relation to character and capacity, risk and outcome, as driven by and realized through not only ideas but also interests and institutions, seeks to demonstrate. As far as variations across practices and institutions is concerned, my suggestion is that, once we let go of the metaphysical fantasy that responsibility just 'is' a certain kind of thing, and think instead of responsibility as a normative device—a matter of construction and ascription—then we can begin to ask common questions about responsibility across social institutions. The result is a method which allows us to trace both the links and the distinctions between the various conceptions being deployed.

Conclusion

Ascriptions of criminal responsibility, I have argued, are best understood in the modern period as a distinctive way of resolving legitimation and coordination problems faced by social institutions: changing conceptions of criminal responsibility track the changing legitimation and coordination problems faced by the criminal process. My analysis suggests that we are seeing not so much a replacement of one paradigm of responsibility by another, but rather an accumulation of conceptions or 'technologies' of responsibility, as new legitimation problems and resources emerge without necessarily obliterating older ones. In the method which I have attempted to describe and to employ, both history and conceptual analysis are used in the service of social theory—in other words, in the pursuit of general insights into the operation and development of modern societies. This is a project which, in my view, simply follows through on the insight of modern linguistic philosophy that the analysis of words must be set in the context of their usage, albeit interpreting that insight in the spirit of the Wittgensteinian precept that such analysis must further be set within the context of a social practice or form of life.

Understood in this way, philosophy, history, law, and the social sciences can be understood as making complementary contributions to the general project of social theory.

For over six hundred years,[73] the English political system has been grappling with how to marshall existing institutional resources in the pursuit of social control and the identification and punishment of crime. Not surprisingly, the problems of disorder, and the mechanisms mobilized to respond to them, have been far from static. In our increasingly heterogeneous and mobile world, both the objects and the mechanisms of social ordering have changed. Yet while the forms of conduct addressed by English criminalization have long been varied and extensive, the impulse to deploy 'outsider' status as a mechanism of labelling and of social control has a very long history.

As we confront the extensive, confusing, and heterogeneous terrain of criminal law and criminal justice today—the regulatory offences and the offences of serious violence, the retributive 'acting out' of vengeful penal populism, and the 'actuarialism' of the 'criminology of everyday life'—it is helpful, I have argued, to reflect on our history. The revival of 'character' and the emergence of 'risk' are not the only show in the sprawling city of contemporary criminal law.[74] Yet there is reason to think that the balance between the quasi-moral and the regulatory aspects of criminal law has shifted over the last thirty years, with an increasing moralization of the regulatory (or police) sphere, and a converse importation of techniques (notably of prevention) developed in the police sphere into the rest of criminal law. Along with the 'acting out' typical of criminal and penal policy in relation to serious crime and terrorism, this underpins the resurgence of short cuts to proof reminiscent of the extreme form of character responsibility, which we might have hoped to have been laid to rest along with the *ancien régime* in English criminal justice.

[73] See Gerald Harriss, *Shaping the Nation: England 1360–1461* (Oxford: Oxford University Press 2005) p. 244.

[74] To take just one example, we might argue that the efflorescence of superficially contractual precursors to criminal liability, such as the non-molestation order or the ASBO, in fact serve a rather different purpose: to pre-empt the criminal trial's evaluative role by specifying the content of the relevant duties or values, leaving the trial merely to determine whether a contractual term has been breached: Lucia Zedner, 'Security, the State, and the Citizen: The Changing Architecture of Crime Control' 13 *New Criminal Law Review* (2010) 379–403, at 393–94. See also Zedner, 'Preventive Justice or Pre-Punishment? The Case of Control Orders' 59 *Current Legal Problems* (2007) 174–203.

Developments in criminal law and criminal procedure are being driven by political pressures, which we see manifested most clearly in the rise in the prison population and the salience of criminal policy to national politics. These political pressures are the product of broader economic and cultural dynamics, themselves shaped by existing institutional arrangements. The days of excluding 'sturdy beggars', or relying on dense networks of 'local knowledge', are gone. But new political pressures, new social preoccupations, and new technologies are changing how our institutions 'think' about criminal responsibility,[75] creating new mechanisms for its attribution, and affecting how such attributions are interpreted in social discourse. Some of these recent developments, I have argued, verge upon forms of character essentialism and character determinism, which sit uncomfortably with the liberal values which twenty-first-century English criminal justice purports to protect.

More radically, I have suggested that, while the resurgence of character and the emergence of risk are made most manifest in these new developments, the seeds of that revival have long lain dormant in doctrinal arrangements ostensibly favourable to the triumph of capacity-responsibility. The balance, in short, between character and capacity in the attribution of criminal responsibility has relatively little to do with doctrinal arrangements in the criminal law, and a great deal to do with the institutional context in which the criminal process operates, and with the interests which bear upon it. While this context of interests and institutions may present itself as a suitable object of social scientific rather than of philosophical investigation, it nonetheless shapes the social practices with which a scholarship committed to an analysis of the philosophical foundations of law must engage. The emergence of short cuts to proof relying on character- and risk-based mechanisms that foster guilt by association or the identification of 'bad apples' may not figure in a normatively polished conception of criminal responsibility—even one based on character. But to the extent that it exists, we must try to assess its implications not only for the implicit structure of criminal responsibility, but also for the feasibility of our normative vision of criminal law.

[75] Mary Douglas, *How Institutions Think* (London: Routledge and Kegan Paul 1987).

Bibliography

Ely Aaronson, *From Slave Abuse to Hate Crime* (New York: Cambridge University Press 2014)

Richard L. Abel, *The Legal Profession in England and Wales* (Oxford: Basil Blackwell 1988)

Larry Alexander and Kimberly Kessler Ferzan, with Stephen J. Morse, *Crime and Culpability: A Theory of Criminal Law* (New York: Cambridge University Press 2009)

C. J. W. Allen, *The Law of Evidence in Victorian England* (Cambridge: Cambridge University Press 1997)

C. K. Allen, *Law in the Making* (Oxford: Clarendon Press 1964)

Harry Annison, *Dangerous Politics: Risk, Political Vulnerability, and Penal Policy* (Oxford: Oxford University Press 2015)

Peter Arenella, 'Character, Choice and Moral Agency: The Relevance of Character to Our Moral Culpability Judgments' 7 *Social Philosophy & Policy* (1990) 59–83

Andrew Ashworth, 'Is the Criminal Law a Lost Cause?' 116 *Law Quarterly Review* (2000) 225

Andrew Ashworth, 'Social Control and "Anti-Social Behaviour": The Subversion of Human Rights?' 120 *Law Quarterly Review* (2004) 263–91

Andrew Ashworth, *Sentencing and Criminal Justice* (4th ed., Cambridge: Cambridge University Press 2005)

Andrew Ashworth and Meredith Blake, 'The Presumption of Innocence in English Criminal Law' *Criminal Law Review* (May 1996) 306–17

Andrew Ashworth and Lucia Zedner, 'Defending the Criminal Law: Reflections on the Changing Character of Crime, Procedure, and Sanctions' 2 *Journal of Criminal Law and Philosophy* (2008) 21–51

Andrew Ashworth and Lucia Zedner, 'Preventive Orders: A Case of Under-Criminalization?', in R. A. Duff, Lindsay Farmer, S. E. Marshall, Massimo Renzo, and Victor Tadros (eds), *The Boundaries of the Criminal Law* (Oxford: Oxford University Press 2010)

Andrew Ashworth and Lucia Zedner, *Preventive Justice* (Oxford: Oxford University Press 2014)

Associated Press, 'Cheney Says No To Closing Prison', *The New York Times*, 13 June 2005 p. A14

John Banville, *The Book of Evidence* (London: Secker & Warburg 1989)

Vanessa Barker, *The Politics of Punishment: How the Democratic Process Shapes the Way America Punishes Offenders* (New York: Oxford University Press 2009)

Michael Bayles, 'Character, Purpose and Criminal Responsibility' 1 *Law and Philosophy* (1982) 5–20

J. M. Beattie, *Crime and the Courts in England, 1660–1800* (Princeton, Princeton University Press 1986)

J. M. Beattie, 'London Juries in the 1690s', in J. S. Cockburn and T. A. Green (eds), *Twelve Good Men and True: The Criminal Trial Jury in England, 1200–1800* (Princeton: Princeton University Press 1988)

J. M. Beattie, 'Scales of Justice: Defence Counsel and the English Criminal Trial in the Eighteenth and Nineteenth Centuries' 9 *Law and History Review* (1991) 221–67

John M. Beattie, *Policing and Punishment in London, 1660–1750: Urban Crime and the Limits of Terror* (Oxford and New York: Oxford University Press 2001)

Ulrich Beck, *Risk Society: Toward a New Modernity* (transl. Mark Ritter, London: Sage 1992)

Katherine Beckett, *Making Crime Pay: Law and Order in Contemporary American Politics* (New York: Oxford University Press 1997)

John Bender, *Imagining the Penitentiary: Fiction and the Architecture of Mind in Eighteenth-Century England* (Chicago and London: University of Chicago Press 1987)

David Bentley, *English Criminal Justice in the 19th Century* (London: Hambledon Press 1998)

Guyora Binder, 'The Meaning of Killing', in Markus D. Dubber and Lindsay Farmer (eds), *Modern Histories of Crime and Punishment* (Stanford: Stanford University Press 2007)

Guyora Binder, *Felony Murder* (Stanford: Stanford University Press 2012)

Tom Bingham, *The Rule of Law* (London: Allen Lane, Penguin Books 2010)

William Blackstone, *Commentaries on the Laws of England* Vol. IV (1769: Chicago: University of Chicago Press 1979)

Susanna Blumenthal, *Law and the Modern Mind: Consciousness and Responsibility in American Legal Culture* (Cambridge, MA: Harvard University Press, 2016)

Mark Bovens, *The Quest for Responsibility* (Cambridge and New York: Cambridge University Press 1998)

John Braithwaite, 'Shame and Modernity' 33 *British Journal of Criminology* (1993) 1–18

John Braithwaite, *Restorative Justice and Responsive Regulation* (Oxford: Oxford University Press 2001)

Paul A. Brand, *The Origins of the English Legal Profession* (Oxford: Blackwell 1992)

Charlotte Brontë, *Jane Eyre* (1847: London: Penguin Classics 2006)

Darryl Brown, 'History's Challenge to Criminal Law Theory' 3 *Criminal Law and Philosophy* (2009) 271–87

Kimberley Brownlee, 'On Gardner on Law in General' 6 *Jurisprudence* (2015) 567–73 http://dx.doi.org/10.1080/20403313.2015.1067487

Alan Brudner, *Punishment and Freedom: A Liberal Theory of Penal Justice* (Oxford: Oxford University Press 2009)

Robert P. Burns, 'The Distinctiveness of Trial Narrative', in Anthony Duff, Lindsay Farmer, Sandra Marshall, and Victor Tadros (eds), *The Trial on Trial* Vol. 1: *Truth and Due Process* (Oxford and Portland: Hart Publishing 2004)

David J. A. Cairns, *Advocacy and the Making of the Adversarial Criminal Trial, 1800–1865* (Oxford: Clarendon Press 1998)

Peter Cane, 'Public Law and the Concept of Law' 33 *Oxford Journal of Legal Studies* (2013) 649–74

Peter Cane, *Responsibility in Law and Morality* (Oxford: Hart Publishing 2002)

W. G. Carson, 'White-Collar Crime and the Enforcement of Factory Legislation' 10 *British Journal of Criminology* (1970) 383–98

James Chalmers, '"Frenzied Law-Making": Over-Criminalisation by Numbers' 67 *Current Legal Problems* (2014) 483

James Chalmers and Fiona Leverick, 'Tracking the Creation of Criminal Offences' *Crim LR* (2013) 543–60

James Chalmers and Fiona Leverick, 'Quantifying Criminalization', in R. A. Duff et al. (eds), *Criminalization: The Political Morality of the Criminal Law* (Oxford University Press 2015), Chapter 2

C. M. V. Clarkson, 'Kicking Corporate Bodies and Damning their Souls' 59(4) *Modern Law Review* (1996) 557

Raymond Cocks, *Foundations of the Modern Bar* (London: Sweet & Maxwell 1983)

Raymond Cocks, 'Statutes, Social Reform, and Control', in William Cornish, J. Stuart Anderson, Raymond Cocks, Michael Lobban, Patrick Polden, and Keith Smith (eds.), *The Oxford History of the Laws of England* Vol. XIII (Oxford: Oxford University Press 2010) Part 2

Stanley Cohen, *Folk Devils and Moral Panics* (1972: London and New York: Routledge Classics 2011)

Hugh Collins, *Marxism and Law* (Oxford: Clarendon 1982)

Wilkie Collins, *The Moonstone* (1868: London: Penguin Classics 1998)

Wilkie Collins, *The Woman in White* (1860: London: Penguin Classics 1999)

Joanne Conaghan, *Law and Gender* (Oxford: Clarendon Press 2013)

Carolyn A. Conley, *The Unwritten Law: Criminal Justice in Victorian Kent* (Oxford: Oxford University Press 1991)

Penelope J. Corfield, *Power and the Professions in Britain, 1700–1850* (London and New York: Routledge 1995)

Roger Cotterrell, 'Why Must Legal Ideas Be Interpreted Sociologically?' 25 *Journal of Law and Society* (1998) 171–92

Sean Coyle, 'Legality and the Liberal Order' 76 *Modern Law Review* (2013) 401–18

Crown Prosecution Service, *Table of Offences* http://www.cps.gov.uk/publications/docs/annex_1b_table_of_offences_scheme_c_class_order.pdf (accessed 18 September 2015)

Mirjan R. Damaška, *The Faces of Justice and State Authority: A Comparative Approach to the Legal Process* (New Haven: Yale University Press 1991)

Mirjan R. Damaška, *Evidence Law Adrift* (New Haven: Yale University Press 1997)

Chris Danta, 'The Metaphysical Cut: Darwin and Stevenson on Vivisection' 36 *Victorian Review* (2010) 51–65

Maksymilian Del Mar, 'Legality as Relative Institutionalization: MacCormick's Diffusionism and Transnational Legal Theory' 5(2) *Transnational Legal Theory* (2014) 177–217

Alessandro de Giorgi, *Re-Thinking the Political Economy of Punishment: Perspectives on Post-Fordism and Penal Politics* (Aldershot: Ashgate 2006)

Thomas De Quincey, *Confessions of an Opium Eater* (1821: London: Signet Classics 1966)

Mary Douglas, *How Institutions Think* (London: Routledge and Kegan Paul 1987)

David Downes and Rod Morgan, 'No Turning Back: The Politics of Law and Order into the Millennium', in Mike Maguire, Rod Morgan, and Robert Reiner (eds), *The Oxford Handbook of Criminology* (4th ed., Oxford: Oxford University Press 2007)

Paul Dresch and Hannah Skoda (eds), *Legalism: Anthropology and History* (Oxford: Oxford University Press 2012)

John S. Dryzek, 'The Informal Logic of Institutional Design', in Robert E. Goodin (ed.), *The Theory of Institutional Design* (Cambridge: Cambridge University Press 1996)

Markus D. Dubber, 'The Right to be Punished: Autonomy and its Demise in Modern Penal Thought', 16 *Law and History Review* (1998) 113–46

Markus D. Dubber, *The Police Power: Patriarchy and the Foundations of American Government* (New York: Columbia University Press 2005)

Markus D. Dubber and Mariana Valverde (eds), *The New Police Science: The Police Power in Domestic and International Governance* (Palo Alto, CA: Stanford University Press 2006)

Markus D. Dubber (ed.) *Foundational Texts in Modern Criminal Law* (Oxford and New York: Oxford University Press 2014)

Antony Duff, *Trials and Punishments* (Cambridge: Cambridge University Press 1986)

Antony Duff, *Punishment, Communication and Community* (Oxford: Oxford University Press 2001)

Antony Duff, Lindsay Farmer, Sandra Marshall, and Victor Tadros (eds), *The Trial on Trial I: Truth and Due Process* (Oxford: Hart Publishing 2004)

Antony Duff, Lindsay Farmer, Sandra Marshall, and Victor Tadros (eds), *The Trial on Trial II: Judgment and Calling to Account* (Oxford: Hart Publishing 2005)

Antony Duff, Lindsay Farmer, Sandra Marshall, and Victor Tadros (eds), *The Trial on Trial III: Towards a Normative Theory of the Criminal Trial* (Oxford: Hart Publishing 2007)

Antony Duff, Lindsay Farmer, Sandra Marshall, Massimo Renzo, and Victor Tadros (eds), *The Boundaries of the Criminal Law* (Oxford: Oxford University Press 2010)

Antony Duff, Lindsay Farmer, Sandra Marshall, Massimo Renzo, and Victor Tadros (eds), *The Structures of the Criminal Law* (Oxford: Oxford University Press 2011)

Antony Duff, Lindsay Farmer, Sandra Marshall, Massimo Renzo, and Victor Tadros (eds), *The Constitution of the Criminal Law* (Oxford: Oxford University Press 2013)

Antony Duff, Lindsay Farmer, Sandra Marshall, Massimo Renzo, and Victor Tadros (eds), *Criminalization: the Political Morality of the Criminal Law* (Oxford: Oxford University Press 2015)

Antony Duff and Stuart Green (eds) *Philosophical Foundations of Criminal Law* (Oxford: Oxford University Press 2011)

R. A. Duff, 'Codifying Criminal Fault', in I. H. Dennis (ed.), *Criminal Law and Criminal Justice* (London: Sweet and Maxwell, 1987)

R. A. Duff, *Intention, Agency and Criminal Liability* (Oxford: Basil Blackwell 1990)

R. A. Duff, 'Choice, Character and Criminal Liability' 12 *Law and Philosophy* (1993) 345–83

R. A. Duff, 'Virtue, Vice and Criminal Liability: Do We Want an Aristotelian Criminal Law?' 6 *Buffalo Criminal Law Review* (2002) 147–84

R. A. Duff, *Answering for Crime: Responsibility and Liability in the Criminal Law* (Oxford: Hart Publishing 2007)

Daniel Duman, 'The Creation and Diffusion of a Professional Ideology in Nineteenth Century England' 27 *Sociological Review* (1979) 113–38

Daniel Duman, 'Pathway to Professionalism: The Legal Profession in the Nineteenth Century' 13 *Journal of Social History* (1980) 615–28

Troy Duster, *The Legislation of Morality: Law, Drugs, and Moral Judgment* (New York: Free Press 1970)

Ronald Dworkin, *Law's Empire* (London: Fontana 1986)

Ronald Dworkin, 'Hard Cases' 88 *Harvard Law Review* (1975) 1057–109

Ronald Dworkin, *Taking Rights Seriously* (London: Duckworth 1977)

Joel Peter Eigen, *Witnessing Insanity* (New Haven: Yale University Press 1995)

Joel Peter Eigen, 'Lesion of the Will: Medical Resolve and Criminal Responsibility in Victorian Insanity Trials' 33 *Law and Society Review* (1999) 425–59

Joel Peter Eigen, *Unconscious Crime: Mental Absence and Criminal Responsibility in Victorian London* (Baltimore and London: Johns Hopkins University Press 2003)

Joel Peter Eigen, '"An Inducement to Morbid Minds": Politics and Madness in the Victorian Courtroom', in Markus D. Dubber and Lindsay Farmer (eds), *Modern Histories of Crime and Punishment* (Stanford: Stanford University Press 2007)

George Eliot, *Daniel Deronda* (1876: London: Penguin Classics 1995)

George Eliot, *Felix Holt: The Radical* (1866: London: Penguin Classics 1995)

Clive Emsley, *Crime and Society in England, 1750–1900* (2nd ed., London and New York: Longman 1996)

Clive Emsley, 'The History of Crime and Crime Control Institutions', in Mike Maguire, Rod Morgan, and Robert Reiner (eds), *The Oxford Handbook of Criminology* (3rd ed., Oxford: Oxford University Press 2002)

Richard V. Ericson, Patricia M. Baranek, and Janet B. L. Chan, *Visualizing Deviance: A Study of News Organizations* (Toronto: University of Toronto Press 1987)

E. P. Evans, *The Criminal Prosecution and Capital Punishment of Animals* (1906: London: Faber and Faber 1987)

William Ewald, 'Comparative Jurisprudence (I): What Was it Like to Try a Rat?' 143 *University of Pennsylvania Law Review* 1889 (1995)

Lindsay Farmer, *Criminal Law, Tradition and Legal Order: Crime and the Genius of Scots Law, 1747 to the Present* (Cambridge: Cambridge University Press 1997)

Lindsay Farmer, 'Of Treatises and Textbooks: The Literature of Criminal Law in Nineteenth Century Britain', in Angela Fernandez and Markus D. Dubber (eds), *Law Books in Action: Essays on the Anglo-American Legal Treatises* (Oxford: Hart 2012)

Lindsay Farmer, 'Criminal Law as an Institution: Rethinking Theoretical Approaches to Criminalization', in R. A. Duff, Lindsay Farmer, S. E. Marshall, Massimo Renzo, and Victor Tadros (eds), *Criminalization: The Political Morality of the Criminal Law* (Oxford: Oxford University Press 2014)

Lindsay Farmer, *Making the Modern Criminal Law: Criminalization and Civil Order* (Oxford: Oxford University Press 2016)

Malcom M. Feeley and Deborah H. Little, 'The Vanishing Female: The Decline of Women in the Criminal Process, 1687–1912' 25 *Law and Society Review* (1991) 719–57

Malcolm Feeley and Jonathan Simon, 'The New Penology: Notes on the Emerging Strategy of Corrections and its Implications' 39 *Criminology* (1992) 449–74

Joel Feinberg, *The Moral Limits of Criminal Law,* Vol. 1: *Harm to Others* (New York: Oxford University Press 1987)

Joel Feinberg, *The Moral Limits of Criminal Law,* Vol. 2: *Offense to Others* (New York: Oxford University Press 1987)

Joel Feinberg, *The Moral Limits of Criminal Law,* Vol. 3: *Harm to Self* (New York: Oxford University Press 1989)

Joel Feinberg, *The Moral Limits of Criminal Law,* Vol. 4: *Harmless Wrongdoing* (New York: Oxford University Press 1990)

S. A. Field, 'State, Citizen and Character in French Criminal Process' 33 *Journal of Legal Studies* (2006) 522–46

Henry Fielding, 'Essay on the Knowledge of the Characters of Men', in his *Miscellanies* Vol. 1, edited by Henry Knight Miller (1743: Oxford: Clarendon Press, 1972)

Henry Fielding, *The History of Tom Jones, A Foundling* (1749: Oxford: Oxford World's Classics 1996)

S. E. Finer, *The History of Government from the Earliest Times III: Empires, Monarchies, and the Modern State* (Oxford: Oxford University Press 1997)

Herbert Fingarette, *Self-Deception* (2nd ed., Berkeley and Los Angeles: University of California Press 2000)

Herbert Fingarette and Ann Fingarette Hasse, *Mental Disability and Criminal Responsibility* (Berkeley: University of California Press 1979)

Margot C. Finn, *The Character of Credit: Personal Debt in English Culture, 1740–1914* (Cambridge: Cambridge University Press 2003)

John Finnis, 'The Priority of Persons', in Jeremy Horder (ed.), *Oxford Essays in Jurisprudence* (Fourth Series) (Oxford: Clarendon Press 2000)

John Martin Fischer and Mark Ravizza, *Responsibility and Control: A Theory of Moral Responsibility* (New York: Cambridge University Press 1998)

Peter Fitzpatrick, *The Mythology of Modern Law* (London: Routledge 1992)

George P. Fletcher, *Rethinking Criminal Law* (Boston and Toronto: Little, Brown 1978)

George P. Fletcher, *Basic Concepts of Criminal Law* (New York: Oxford University Press 1998)

Richard R. Follett, *Evangelicalism, Penal Theory and the Politics of Criminal Law: Reform in England, 1808–30* (Basingstoke: Palgrave 2001)

Michel Foucault, *The History of Sexuality* (London: Peregrine 1976)

Michel Foucault, *Discipline and Punish* (transl. Alan Sheridan, Harmondsworth: Penguin 1977)

Cathrine O. Franks, *Law, Literature and the Transmission of Culture in England, 1837–1925* (Farnham: Ashgate 2010)

Peter French (ed.), *The Spectrum of Responsibility* (London: St Martin's Press 1991)

Sigmund Freud and Josef Breuer, *Studies in Hysteria* (1895: London: Penguin Books 2004)

Lon Fuller, 'Positivism and Fidelity to Law—A Reply to Professor Hart' 71 *Harvard Law Review* (1958) 630–72

Lon Fuller, *The Morality of Law* (New Haven and London: Yale University Press 1964)

Thomas P. Gallanis, 'The Rise of Modern Evidence Law' 84 *Iowa Law Review* (1999) 499–560

Thomas P. Gallanis, 'Making Sense of Blackstone's Puzzle: Why Forbid Defense Counsel?' 53 *Studies in Law, Politics, and Society* (2010) 35–57

John Gardner, 'The Gist of Excuses' 1 *Buffalo Criminal Law Review* (1998) 575–98

John Gardner, *Law as a Leap of Faith* (Oxford: Oxford University Press 2012)

John Gardner and Timothy Macklem, 'Compassion Without Respect? Nine Fallacies in *R v Smith*' *Criminal Law Review* (August 2001) 623–35

David Garland, *Punishment and Welfare: A History of Penal Strategies* (Aldershot: Gower Publishing 1985)

David Garland, *Punishment and Modern Society* (Oxford: Oxford University Press 1990)

David Garland, 'The Limits of the Sovereign State: Strategies of Crime Control in Contemporary Society' 36 *British Journal of Criminology* (1996) 445–71

David Garland (ed.), *Mass Imprisonment: Social Causes and Consequences* (London: Sage 2001)

David Garland, *The Culture of Control: Crime and Social Order in Contemporary Society* (Oxford: Oxford University Press 2001)

Elizabeth Gaskell, *Mary Barton: A Tale of Manchester Life* (1848: New York: Penguin 1996)

Moira Gatens and Genevieve Lloyd, *Collective Imaginings* (London: Routledge 1999)

V. A. C. Gatrell, 'The Decline of Theft and Violence in Victorian and Edwardian England', in V. A. C. Gatrell, Bruce Lenman, and Geoffrey Parker (eds), *Crime and the Law: The Social History of Crime in Western Europe Since 1500* (London: Europa Publications 1980)

Lorraine Gelsthorpe, 'Feminism and Criminology', in Mike Maguire, Rod Morgan, and Robert Reiner (eds), *The Oxford Handbook of Criminology* (2nd ed., Oxford: Oxford University Press 1997)

Anthony Giddens, *Modernity and Self-Identity: Self and Society in the Late Modern Age* (Palo Alto, CA: Stanford University Press 1991)

Paul Gilroy, *There Ain't No Black in the Union Jack* (2nd ed., London: Routledge 2002)

Carlos Gómez-Jara Díez, 'Enemy Combatants versus Enemy Criminal Law' 11 *New Criminal Law Review* (2008) 529–62

Thomas A. Green, *Verdict According to Conscience: Perspectives on the English Criminal Trial Jury, 1200–1800* (Chicago and London: University of Chicago Press 1985)

Thomas A. Green, 'A Retrospective on the Criminal Trial Jury, 12001800', in J. S. Cockburn and T. A. Green (eds), *Twelve Good Men and True: The Criminal Trial Jury in England, 1200–1800* (Princeton: Princeton University Press 1988)

Thomas A. Green, *Freedom and Criminal Responsibility in American Legal Thought* (New York: Cambridge University Press 2014)

Chris Greer and Robert Reiner, 'Mediated Mayhem: Media, Crime and Criminal Justice' in Mike Maguire, Rod Morgan, and Robert Reiner (eds), *The Oxford Handbook of Criminology* (5th ed., Oxford: Oxford University Press 2012) 245–78

Jonathan H. Grossman, *The Art of Alibi: English Law Courts and the Novel* (Baltimore: Johns Hopkins University Press 2002)

Ian Hacking, *Rewriting the Soul: Multiple Personality and the Sciences of Memory* (Princeton, NJ: Princeton University Press 1995)

Matthew Hale, *The History of the Common Law of England*, edited by Charles M. Gray (1713: Chicago: University of Chicago Press 1971)

Jerome A. Hall, *Theft, Law and Society* (2nd ed., Indianapolis: Bobbs-Merrill 1952)

Leigh Hancher and Michael Moran, 'Organising Regulatory Space', in Leigh Hancher and Michael Moran (eds) *Capitalism, Culture and Economic Regulation* (Oxford: Clarendon Press 1989)

Bernard Harcourt, 'From the Ne'er-Do-Well to the Criminal History Category: The Refinement of the Actuarial Model in Criminal Law' 66 *Law and Contemporary Problems* (2003) 99–152

Thomas Hardy, *Tess of the d'Urbervilles* (1891: New York: Bantam Classics 2004)

Ruth Harris, *Murders and Madness: Medicine, Law and Society in the Fin de Siècle* (Oxford: Clarendon Press 1989)

Gerald Harriss, *Shaping the Nation: England 1360–1461* (Oxford: Oxford University Press 2005)

H. L. A. Hart, 'Definition and Theory in Jurisprudence' *70 Law Quarterly Review* 37 (1954)

H. L. A. Hart, *The Concept of Law* (Oxford: Clarendon Press 1961)

H. L. A. Hart, *Punishment and Responsibility* (Oxford: Clarendon Press 1968)

H. L. A. Hart, 'Discretion' (1956) 127 *Harvard Law Review* (2013) 652.

H. L. A. Hart and A. M. Honoré, *Causation in the Law* (1959: 2nd ed. Oxford University Press 1985)

Keith Hawkins, *Environment and Enforcement* (Oxford: Clarendon Press 1983)

Douglas Hay, 'Property, Authority and the Criminal Law', in Douglas Hay, Peter Linebaugh, John G. Rule, E. P. Thompson, and Carl Winslow (eds), *Albion's Fatal Tree: Crime and Society in Eighteenth Century England* (Harmondsworth: Penguin 1975)

Douglas Hay, 'The Class Composition of the Palladium of Liberty: Trial Jurors in the Eighteenth Century', in J. S. Cockburn and T. A. Green (eds), *Twelve Good Men and True: The Criminal Trial Jury in England, 1200–1800* (Princeton: Princeton University Press 1988)

Douglas Hay (ed.), *Criminal Cases on the Crown Side of King's Bench: Staffordshire, 1800 (1740–1800)* (Staffordshire Record Society 2010)

Douglas Hay and Paul Craven (eds), *Masters, Servants and Magistrates in Britain and the Empire, 1562–1955* (Chapel Hill: University of North Carolina Press 2004)

Frances Heidensohn, *Women and Crime* (London: Macmillan 1985)

Frances Heidensohn and Marisa Silvestri, 'Gender and Crime', in Mike Maguire, Rod Morgan, and Robert Reiner (eds), *The Oxford Handbook of Criminology* (5th ed., Oxford: Oxford University Press 2012) Chapter 12 pp. 336–69

Paddy Hillyard, 'The Normalization of Special Powers', in P. Scraton (ed.), *Law, Order and the Authoritarian State* (Philadelphia: Open University Press 1987)

Tony Honoré, 'Responsibility and Luck: The Moral Basis of Strict Liability' 104 *Law Quarterly Review* (1988) 530–53, reprinted in his *Responsibility and Fault* (Oxford: Hart Publishing 1999)

Jeremy Horder, *Provocation and Responsibility* (Oxford: Clarendon Press 1982)

Jeremy Horder, 'Criminal Culpability: The Possibility of a General Theory' 12 *Law and Philosophy* (1993) 193–215

Jeremy Horder, 'Criminal Law: Between Determinism, Liberalism and Criminal Justice' 49 *Current Legal Problems* (1996) 159–86

Jeremy Horder, 'Two Histories and Four Hidden Principles of *Mens Rea*' 113 *Law Quarterly Review* (1997) 95–119

Jeremy Horder, 'Bureaucratic "Criminal" Law: Too Much of a Bad Thing?', in R. A. Duff et al. (eds), *Criminalisation: The Political Morality of the Criminal Law* (Oxford: Oxford University Press, 2014), ch 4

Jeremy Horder, *Ashworth's Principles of Criminal Law* (Oxford: Oxford University Press, 2016)

Carolyn Hoyle, 'Victims, the Criminal Process and Restorative Justice', in Mike Maguire, Rod Morgan, and Robert Reiner (eds), *The Oxford Handbook of Criminology* (5th ed., Oxford: Oxford University Press 2012)

Kyron Huigens, 'Virtue and Inculpation' 108 *Harvard Law Review* (1995) 1423–80

Kyron Huigens, 'Homicide in Aretaic Terms', *The New Culpability: Motive, Character and Emotion in Criminal Law* (ed. Guyora Binder), 6 *Buffalo Criminal Law Review* (2002) 97–146

Lynn Hunt, *Inventing Human Rights* (New York: W. W. Norton 2007)

Douglas Husak, *Overcriminalization* (New York: Oxford University Press 2007)

Tatsuo Inoue, 'The Rule of Law as the Law of Legislation', in Luc J. Wintgens and Philippe Thion (eds), *Legislation in Context: Essays in Legisprudence* (Aldershot: Ashgate 2007)

Lee Jackson, *Dirty Old London: The Victorian Fight with Filth* (New Haven and London: Yale University Press 2014)

Elizabeth P. Judge, *Character Witnesses: Credibility and Testimony in the Eighteenth Century Novel* (D.Phil. thesis, Dalhousie University 2004) http://dalspace.library.dal.ca/handle/10222/54642

JUSTICE, *Breaking the Rules* (London: JUSTICE 1980)

Dan M. Kahan and Martha C. Nussbaum, 'Two Conceptions of Emotion in Criminal Law' 96 *Columbia Law Review* (1996) 269–374

Leo Katz, 'Villainy and Felony: A Problem Concerning Criminalization', 6 *Buffalo Criminal Law Review* (2002) 451–82

Mark Kelman, 'Interpretive Construction in the Substantive Criminal Law' 33 *Stanford Law Review* (1981) 591–673

C. S. Kenny, *Outlines of Criminal Law* (1st ed., Cambridge: Cambridge University Press 1902)

Peter King, 'Decisions and Decision-Makers in English Criminal Law, 1750–1800' 27 *Historical Journal* (1984) 25–58

Peter King, 'Illiterate Plebeians, Easily Misled: Jury Composition, Experience and Behaviour in Essex, 1735–1815', in J. S. Cockburn and T. A. Green (eds), *Twelve Good Men and True: The Criminal Trial Jury in England, 1200–1800* (Princeton: Princeton University Press 1988)

Peter King, 'Punishing Assault: The Transformation of Attitudes in the English Courts' 27 *Journal of Interdisciplinary History* (1996) 43–74

Peter King, *Crime, Justice and Discretion, 1740–1820* (Oxford: Oxford University Press 2000)

Peter King, *Crime and Law in England, 1750–1840: Remaking Justice from the Margins* (Cambridge: Cambridge University Press 2006)

Richard Kinsey, John Lea, and Jock Young, *Losing the Fight against Crime* (Oxford: Blackwell 1986)

Elizabeth Kolsky, 'Crime and Punishment on the Tea Plantations of Colonial India', in Markus D. Dubber and Lindsay Farmer (eds), *Modern Histories of Crime and Punishment* (Stanford: Stanford University Press 2007)

Lewis Kornhauser, 'Governance Structures, Legal Systems, and The Concept of Law' 79 *Chicago-Kent Law Review* (2004) 355–81

Martin Krygier, *Philip Selznick: Ideals in the World* (Stanford University Press 2012)

Nicola Lacey, *State Punishment: Political Principles and Community Values* (London: Routledge 1988)

Nicola Lacey, 'Contingency and Conceptualism: Reflections on an Encounter between Critique and Philosophical Analysis of Criminal Law', in R. A. Duff (ed.), *Philosophy and the Criminal Law* (Cambridge: Cambridge University Press 1998) pp. 9–59

Nicola Lacey, 'Philosophy, History and Criminal Law Theory' 1 *Buffalo Criminal Law Review* (1998) 295–328

Nicola Lacey, *Unspeakable Subjects: Feminist Essays in Legal and Social Theory* (Oxford: Hart Publishing 1998)

Nicola Lacey, 'Partial Excuses to Homicide', in Andrew Ashworth and Barry Mitchell (eds), *Rethinking English Homicide Law* (Oxford: Clarendon Press 2000)

Nicola Lacey, 'Philosophical Foundations of the Common Law: Social Not Metaphysical', in Jeremy Horder (ed.), *Oxford Essays in Jurisprudence* (Fourth Series) (Oxford: Clarendon Press 2000) pp. 17–39

Nicola Lacey, 'In Search of the Responsible Subject: History, Philosophy and Criminal Law Theory' 64 *Modern Law Review* (2001) 350–71

Nicola Lacey, 'Responsibility and Modernity in Criminal Law' 9 *Journal of Political Philosophy* (2001) 249–77

Nicola Lacey, *A Life of H.L.A. Hart: The Nightmare and the Noble Dream* (Oxford: Oxford University Press 2004)

Nicola Lacey, 'Criminalization as Regulation: The Role of Criminal Law', in Christine Parker, Colin Scott, Nicola Lacey, and John Braithwaite (eds) *Regulating Law* (Oxford: Oxford University Press 2004) pp. 144–67

Nicola Lacey, 'Analytical Jurisprudence versus Descriptive Sociology Revisited' 84 *Texas Law Review* (2006) 945–82

Nicola Lacey, 'Historicizing Contrasts in Tolerance', in Tim Newburn and Paul Rock (eds), *The Politics of Crime Control* (Oxford: Oxford University Press 2006) pp. 197–226

Nicola Lacey, 'Character, Capacity, Outcome: Towards a Framework for Assessing the Shifting Pattern of Criminal Responsibility in Modern English Law', in Markus D. Dubber and Lindsay Farmer (eds), *Modern Histories of Crime and Punishment* (Stanford: Stanford University Press 2007) pp. 14–41

Nicola Lacey, 'Space, time and function: intersecting principles of responsibility across the terrain of criminal justice' *Criminal Law and Philosophy* Vol. 1 (2007) 233–50

Nicola Lacey, 'Philosophy, Political Morality and History: Explaining the Enduring Resonance of the Hart-Fuller Debate' 83 *New York University Law Review* (2008) 1059–87

Nicola Lacey, *The Prisoners' Dilemma: Political Economy and Punishment in Contemporary Democracies* (Cambridge: Cambridge University Press 2008)

Nicola Lacey, *Women, Crime and Character: From Moll Flanders to Tess of the d'Urbervilles* (Oxford: Oxford University Press 2008)

Nicola Lacey, 'Historicising Criminalisation: Conceptual and Empirical Issues' 72 *Modern Law Review* (2009) 936–61

Nicola Lacey, 'Psychologising Jekyll, Demonising Hyde: The Strange Case of Criminal Responsibility' 4 *Criminal Law and Philosophy* (2010) 109–33

Nicola Lacey, 'The Way We Lived Then: The Legal Profession and the Nineteenth Century Novel' 33 *Sydney Law Review* (2011) 599–621

Nicola Lacey, 'The Resurgence of Character: Responsibility in the Context of Criminalization', in Anthony Duff and Stuart Green (eds), *Philosophical Foundations of Criminal Law* (Oxford: Oxford University Press 2011) pp. 151–78

Nicola Lacey, 'Political Systems and Criminal Justice: The Prisoners' Dilemma after the Coalition' 65 *Current Legal Problems* (2012) 203–39

Nicola Lacey, 'Principles, Policies and Politics of Criminal Law', in Julian Roberts and Lucia Zedner (eds) *Principled Approaches to Criminal Law and Criminal Justice: Essays in Honour of Andrew Ashworth* (Oxford: Oxford University Press 2012) pp. 19–35

Nicola Lacey, 'What Constitutes Criminal Law?', in R. A Duff, Lindsay Farmer, S. E. Marshall, Massimo Renzo, and Victor Tadros (eds), *The Constitution of the Criminal Law* (Oxford: Oxford University Press 2012) pp. 12–29

Nicola Lacey 'The Path Not Taken: H. L. A. Hart's Harvard Essay on Discretion', 127 *Harvard Law Review* (2013) 636–51

Nicola Lacey, 'Comparative Criminal Justice: An Institutional Approach' 24 *Duke Journal of Comparative and International Law* (2014) 501–27

Nicola Lacey, 'Jurisprudence, History, and the Institutional Quality of Law' 101 *Virginia Law Review* (2015) 919–45

Nicola Lacey, 'Responsibility without Consciousness' 36 *Oxford Journal of Legal Studies* (2016) doi: 10.1093/ojls/gqv032

Nicola Lacey and David Soskice, 'Why are the Truly Disadvantaged American, when the UK is Bad Enough? A Political Economy Analysis of Local Autonomy in Criminal Justice, Education, Residential Zoning' (2013) *Law Society Economy Working Papers* no. 11, http://ssrn.com/abstract=2264749

Nicola Lacey and David Soskice, 'Crime, Punishment and Segregation in the United States: The Paradox of Local Democracy', 17 (4) *Punishment and Society* (2015) 454–81

Nicola Lacey, Celia Wells, and Dirk Meure, *Reconstructing Criminal Law: Critical Perspectives on Crime and the Criminal Process* (1st ed., London, Weidenfeld and Nicolson 1990)

Nicola Lacey and Celia Wells, *Reconstructing Criminal Law: Critical Perspectives on Crime and the Criminal Process* (2nd ed., London: Butterworths 1998)

Nicola Lacey, Celia Wells, and Oliver Quick, *Reconstructing Criminal Law* (3rd ed., Cambridge: Cambridge University Press 2003)

Nicola Lacey and Hanna Pickard, The Chimera of Proportionality: Institutionalising Limits on Punishment in Contemporary Social and Political Systems', 78(2) *Modern Law Review* (2015) 216–40

Nicola Lacey and Hanna Pickard, 'To Blame or to Forgive? Reconciling Punishment and Forgiveness in Criminal Justice', 35 *Oxford Journal of Legal Studies* (2015) 665–96 doi: 10.1093/ojls/gqv012

Norma Landau, *The Justice of the Peace, 1679–1760* (Berkeley and Los Angeles: University of California Press 1984)

John Langbein, 'The Criminal Trial before the Lawyers' 45 *University of Chicago Law Review* (1978) 263–316

John H. Langbein, 'Shaping the Eighteenth Century Criminal Trial: A View from the Ryder Sources' 50 *University of Chicago Law Review* (1983) 1–136

John. H. Langbein, 'Historical Foundations of the Law of Evidence' 96 *Columbia Law Review* (1996) 1168–90

John H. Langbein, *The Origins of Adversary Criminal Trial* (Oxford: Oxford University Press 2003)

Tapio Lappi-Seppälä, 'Penal Policy in Scandinavia', in Michael Tonry (ed.), *Crime and Justice* Vol. 36: *Crime, Punishment, and Politics in Comparative Perspective* (Chicago: University of Chicago Press 2007)

Tapio Lappi-Seppälä, 'Trust, Welfare, and Political Culture: Explaining Difference in National Penal Policies', in Michael Tonry (ed.), *Crime and Justice* Vol. 37: *A Review of Research* (Chicago: Chicago University Press 2008)

Magali Sarfatti Larson, *The Rise of Professionalism: A Sociological Analysis* (Berkeley: University of California Press 1977)

Law Commission of England and Wales, *Criminal Liability in Regulatory Contexts: A Consultation Paper,* No. 195 (London: The Stationary Office 2010)

Bruce Lenman and Geoffrey Parker, 'The State, the Community and Criminal Law in Early Modern Europe', in V. A. C. Gatrell, Bruce Lenman and Geoffrey Parker (eds), *Crime and the Law: The Social History of Crime in Western Europe since 1500* (London: Europa 1980)

David P. Leonard, 'Character and Motive in Evidence Law' 34 *Loyola of Los Angeles Law Review* (2001) 439–537

David Leonard, *The New Wigmore: A Treatise on Evidence: Evidence of Other Misconduct and Similar Events* (Austin: Wolters Kluwer, Aspen Publishers 2009)

Amy E. Lerman and Vesla M. Weaver, *Arresting Citizenship: the Democratic Consequences of American Crime Control* (Chicago: University of Chicago Press 2014)

Lawrence Lessig, *Code and Other Laws of Cyberspace* (New York: Basic Books 1999)

Michael Lobban, 'The English Legal Treatise and English Law in the Eighteenth-Century' 13 *Iuris Scripta Historica* (1997) 69–88

Martin Loughlin, *Foundations of Public Law* (Oxford: Oxford University Press 2010)

Arlie Loughnan, 'Manifest Madness: Towards a New Understanding of the Insanity Defence' 70 *Modern Law Review* (2007) 379–401

Arlie Loughnan, *Manifest Madness: Mental Incapacity in Criminal Law* (Oxford: Oxford University Press 2012)

Arlie Loughnan, 'Historicizing Criminal Responsibility', in Z. Hoskins and C. Flanders (eds) *The New Philosophy of Criminal Law* (Rowman Littlefield International, 2016), pp. 137–55

Deidre Shauna Lynch, *The Economy of Character: Novels, Market Culture, and the Business of Inner Meaning* (Chicago: University of Chicago Press 1998)

Neil MacCormick, 'Law as Institutional Fact' 90 *Law Quarterly Review* (1974) 102–29

Neil MacCormick and Ota Weinberger, *An Institutional Theory of Law: New Approaches to Legal Positivism* (Dordrecht: Kluwer 1986)

Oliver MacDonagh, 'The Nineteenth Century Revolution in Government: A Reappraisal' 1 *Historical Journal* (1958) 52–67

Donal MacIntyre, 'Major on crime: "Condemn more, understand less"', *The Independent*, 21 February 1993

Randall McGowen, 'The Image of Justice and Reform of the Criminal Law in Early Nineteenth-Century England' 32 *Buffalo Law Review* (1983) 89–125

Henry Sumner Maine, *Ancient Law: Its Connection with the Early History of Society and its Relation to Modern Ideas* (1861: London: Oxford University Press 1959)

Henry Mares, 'Criminal Informations of the Attorneys-General in the King's Bench from Egerton to North', in Matthew Dyson and David Ibbetson (eds), *Law and Legal Process: Substantive Law and Procedure in English Legal History* (Cambridge: Cambridge University Press 2013)

Allyson N. May, 'Advocates and Truth-Seeking in the Old Bailey Courtroom' 26 *The Journal of Legal History* (2005) 83–90

Allyson N. May, *The Bar and the Old Bailey, 1750–1850* (Chapel Hill: University of North Carolina Press 2006)

Alan C. Michaels, 'Acceptance: The Missing Mental State' 71 *Southern California Law Review* (1998) 953–1036

Robert Mighall, 'Diagnosing Jekyll: The Scientific Context to Dr Jekyll's Experiment and Mr Hyde's Embodiment', in Robert Louis Stevenson (ed.), *The Strange Case of Dr Jekyll and Mr Hyde and Other Tales of Terror*, edited by Robert Mighall (London: Penguin 2002)

John Stuart Mill, *On Liberty* (1859: London: Penguin 1974)

Lisa L. Miller, *The Perils of Federalism: Race, Poverty, and the Politics of Crime Control* (New York: Oxford University Press 2008)

Michael S. Moore, *Law and Psychiatry: Rethinking the Relationship* (Cambridge: Cambridge University Press 1984)

Michael Moore, *Placing Blame* (Oxford: Oxford University Press 1998)

Morgan Harris Burrows LLP, Ministry of Justice Research Series 5/09 (Office for Criminal Justice Reform, March 2009)

Linda Mulcahy, *Legal Architecture: Justice, Due Process and the Place of Law* (London: Routledge 2011)

Tim Murphy, *The Oldest Social Science?* (Oxford: Clarendon Press 1998)

Andrew Murray and Colin Scott, 'Controlling the New Media: Hybrid Responses to New Forms of Power' 65 *Modern Law Review* (2002) 491–516

Ngaire Naffine, *Law and the Sexes: Explorations in Feminist Jurisprudence* (London: Allen and Unwin 1990)

Ngaire Naffine, *Feminism and Criminology* (Oxford: Polity Press 1997)

Ngaire Naffine, *Law's Meaning of Life: Philosophy, Religion, Darwin and the Legal Person* (Oxford: Hart 2009)

Ngaire Naffine and Rosemary Owens (eds), *Sexing the Subject of Law* (London: Sweet and Maxwell 1997)

Tim Newburn, '"Tough on Crime": Penal Policy in England and Wales', in Michael Tonry (ed.), *Crime and Justice* Vol. 36: *Crime, Punishment, and Politics in Comparative Perspective* (Chicago: University of Chicago Press 2007)

Tim Newburn and Robert Reiner, 'Crime and Penal Policy', in Anthony Seldon (ed.), *Blair's Britain, 1997–2007* (Cambridge: Cambridge University Press 2007)

Donald Nicolson and Rohit Sanghvi, 'Battered Women and Provocation: The Implications of *R v Ahluwalia*' *Criminal Law Review* (October 1993) 728–38

Richard Nobles and David Schiff, *Understanding Miscarriages of Justice* (Oxford: Oxford University Press 2000)

Alan Norrie, *Law, Ideology and Punishment: Retrieval and Critique of the Liberal Idea of Criminal Justice* (Dordrecht: Kluwer 1991)

Alan Norrie, *Crime, Reason and History: A Critical Introduction to Criminal Law* (1993: 2nd ed., Cambridge: Cambridge University Press 2001)

Alan Norrie, *Crime, Reason and History: A Critical Introduction to Criminal Law* (3rd ed., Cambridge: Cambridge University Press 2014)

V. F. Nourse, 'Passion's Progress: Modern Law Reform and the Provocation Defense' 106 *Yale Law Journal* (1997) 1331–448

V. F. Nourse, 'Hearts and Minds: Understanding the New Culpability', *The New Culpability: Motive, Character and Emotion in Criminal Law* (ed. Guyora Binder), 6 *Buffalo Criminal Law Review* (2002) 361 88

Daniel Ohana, 'Trust, Distrust and Reassurance: Diversion and Preventive Orders Through the Prism of *Feindstrafrecht*' 73 *Modern Law Review* (2010) 721–51

Daniel Ohana, 'Günther Jakobs's *Feindstrafrecht*: A Dispassionate Account', in Markus Dubber (ed.) *Foundational Texts in Modern Criminal Law* (Oxford: Oxford University Press 2014)

Pat O'Malley (ed.), *Crime and the Risk Society* (Aldershot and Brookfield: Ashgate 1998)

David Ormerod, *Smith and Hogan's Criminal Law* (13th ed., Oxford: Oxford University Press 2011)

Fania Oz-Salzberger, 'New Approaches towards a History of the Enlightenment: Can Disparate Perspectives Make a General Picture?' 29 *Tel Aviver Jahrbuch für deutsche Geschichte* (2000) 171–82

Evgeny Pashukanis, *Law and Marxism: A General Theory* (1924: transl. Barbara Einhorn, London: Pluto 1978)

Ellen Frankel Paul, Fred D. Miller Jr., and Jeffrey Paul (eds), *Responsibility* (Cambridge: Cambridge University Press 1999)

Harold Perkin, *The Rise of Professional Society: England Since 1880* (London: Routledge 2002)

Phillip Pettit, 'Institutional Design and Rational Choice', in Robert E. Goodin (ed.), *The Theory of Institutional Design* (Cambridge: Cambridge University Press 1996)

Phillip Pettit, *Republicanism: A Theory of Freedom and Government* (Oxford: Clarendon Press 1999)

David Philips, *Crime and Authority in Victorian England: The Black Country, 1835--1860* (London: Rowman and Littlefield 1977)

David Philips, 'A New Engine of Power and Authority: The Institutionalisation of Law Enforcement in England, 1780–1830', in V. A. C. Gatrell, Bruce Lenman, and Geoffrey Parker (eds), *Crime and the Law: The Social History of Crime in Western Europe since 1500* (London: Europa 1980)

Coretta Phillips and Ben Bowling, 'Racism, Ethnicity, Crime and Criminal Justice', in Mike Maguire, Rod Morgan, and Robert Reiner (eds), *The Oxford Handbook of Criminology* (3rd ed., Oxford: Oxford University Press 2002)

Coretta Phillips and Ben Bowling, 'Ethnicities, Racism, Crime and Criminal Justice' in Mike Maguire, Rod Morgan, and Robert Reiner (eds), *The Oxford Handbook of Criminology* (5th ed, Oxford: Oxford University Press 2012)

Coleman Phillipson, *Three Criminal Law Reformers: Beccaria, Bentham, Romilly* (London and Toronto: J. K. Dent and Sons 1923)

Thomas Piketty, *Capital in the 21st Century* (transl. Arthur Goldhammer, Cambridge, MA and London: Harvard University Press 2014)

Samuel H. Pillsbury, 'A Problem in Emotive Due Process: California's Three Strikes Law' 6 *Buffalo Criminal Law Review* (2002) 483–524

Patrick Polden, *A History of the County Court,* 1846–1971 (Cambridge: Cambridge University Press 1999)

Patrick Polden, 'The Legal Professions', in William Cornish, J. Stuart Anderson, Raymond Cocks, Michael Lobban, Patrick Polden, and Keith Smith (eds), *The Oxford History of the Laws of England* Vol. XI (Oxford: Oxford University Press 2010) Part IV

Roy Porter (ed.), *Rewriting the Self: Histories from the Renaissance to the Present* (London: Routledge 1997)

John Pratt, *Penal Populism* (London: Routledge 2006)

John Pratt, 'Scandinavian Exceptionalism in an Era of Penal Excess', Parts I ('The Nature and Roots of Scandinavian Exceptionalism') and II ('Does Scandinavian Exceptionalism Have a Future?') 48 *British Journal of Criminology* (2008) 119–37 and 275–92

W. Prest (ed.), *The Professions in Early Modern England* (London: Croom Helm 1987)

Wesley Pue, 'Exorcising Professional Demons: Charles Rann Kennedy and the Transition to the Modern Bar' 5 *Law and History Review* (1987) 135–74

Dana Y. Rabin, *Identity, Crime, and Legal Responsibility in Eighteenth-Century England* (Basingstoke: Palgrave Macmillan 2004)

Leon Radzinowicz, *A History Of English Criminal Law Since 1750* (Oxford: Oxford University Press 1948–1986)

Leon Radzinowicz and Roger Hood, *The Emergence of Penal Policy in Victorian and Edwardian England* (Oxford: Clarendon Press 1990)

Paul Raffield, 'The Elizabethan Rhetoric of Signs: Representations of *Res Publica* at the Early Modern Inns of Court' 7 *Law, Culture and the Humanities* (2010) 244–63

Peter Ramsay, 'What is Anti-Social Behaviour?' *Criminal Law Review* (November 2004) 908–25

Peter Ramsay, 'The Theory of Vulnerable Autonomy and the Legitimacy of the Civil Preventative Order', in Bernadette McSherry, Alan Norrie, and Simon Bronitt (eds), *Regulating Deviance: The Redirection of Criminalisation and the Futures of Criminal Law* (Oxford: Hart Publishing 2009)

Peter Ramsay, *The Insecurity State: Vulnerable Autonomy and the Right to Security in the Criminal Law* (Oxford: Oxford University Press 2012)

Peter Ramsay, 'Pashukanis and Public Protection', in Markus D. Dubber (ed.), *Foundational Texts in Modern Criminal Law* (Oxford: Oxford University Press 2015)

Joseph Raz, *The Authority of Law* (Oxford: Clarendon Press 1979)

Joseph Raz, *From Normativity to Responsibility* (Oxford: Oxford University Press 2011)

W. J. Reader, *Professional Men: The Rise of the Professional Classes in Nineteenth-Century England* (London: Weidenfeld 1966)

Mike Redmayne, 'The Relevance of Bad Character' 61 *Cambridge Law Journal* (2002) 684–714

Mike Redmayne, 'The Ethics of Character Evidence' 61 *Current Legal Problems* (2008) 371–99

Mike Redmayne, *Character in the Criminal Trial* (Oxford: Oxford University Press 2015)

Robert Reiner, *Law and Order: An Honest Citizen's Guide to Crime and Control* (London: Polity Press 2007)

Robert Reiner, 'Media-Made Criminality: The Representation of Crime in the Mass Media', in Mike Maguire, Rod Morgan, and Robert Reiner (eds), *The Oxford Handbook of Criminology* (4th ed, Oxford: Oxford University Press 2007) 302–37

Robert Reiner, Sonia Livingstone, and Jessica Allen, 'Casino Culture: Crime and Media in a Winner-Loser Society', in K. Stenson and R. Sullivan (eds), *Crime, Risk and Justice: The Politics of Crime Control in Liberal Democracies* (Cullompton: Willan 2001)

Paul Roberts, 'Strict Liability and the Presumption of Innocence: An Exposé of Functionalist Assumptions', in A. P. Simester (ed.), *Appraising Strict Liability* (Oxford: Oxford University Press 2005)

Simon Roberts, 'After Government? On Representing Law Without the State' 68 *Modern Law Review* (2005) 1–24

Paul Roberts and Adrian Zuckerman, *Criminal Evidence* (2nd ed., New York: Oxford University Press, 2010)

Veronica Rodriguez-Blanco, 'A Defense of Hart's Semantics as Nonambitious Conceptual Analysis' 9 *Legal Theory* (2003) 99–124

Richard Rorty, 'The Historiography of Philosophy: Four Genres', in Richard Rorty, J. B. Schneewind, and Quentin Skinner (eds), *Philosophy in History* (Cambridge: Cambridge University Press 1984)

Nikolas Rose, *The Psychological Complex: Psychology, Politics and Society in England, 1869–1939* (London: Routledge and Kegan Paul 1985)

Nikolas Rose, *Governing the Soul: The Shaping of the Private Self* (London and New York: Routledge 1990)

Nikolas Rose, *Powers of Freedom* (Cambridge: Cambridge University Press 1999)

Hamish Ross, *Law as a Social Institution* (Oxford: Hart Publishing 2001)

Dick W. P. Ruiter, *Institutional Legal Facts* (Dordrecht: Kluwer 1993)

Kristen Rundle, *Forms Liberate: Reclaiming the Jurisprudence of Lon Fuller* (Oxford: Hart Publishing 2012)

Georg Rusche and Otto Kirchheimer, *Punishment and Social Structure* (first published, in German, 1939; New York: Russell Sage 1969)

Mick Ryan, *Penal Policy and Political Culture in England and Wales* (Winchester: Waterside Press 2003)

Elyn R. Saks with Stephen H. Behnke, *Jekyll on Trial: Multiple Personality Disorder and Criminal Law* (New York and London: New York University Press 1997)

Frederick Schauer, 'Hart's Anti-Essentialism', in Luís Duarte d'Almeida, James Edwards, and Andrea Dolcetti (eds) *Reading Hart's Concept of Law* (Oxford: Hart Publishing 2013) pp. 237–46

J. B. Schneewind, *The Invention of Autonomy: A History of Modern Moral Philosophy* (Cambridge: Cambridge University Press 1998)

Wendie Ellen Schneider, '"Enfeebling the Arm of Justice": Perjury and Prevarication in British India', in Markus D. Dubber and Lindsay Farmer (eds), *Modern Histories of Crime and Punishment* (Stanford: Stanford University Press 2007)

Ferdinand Schoeman (ed.), *Responsibility, Character and the Emotions* (Cambridge: Cambridge University Press 1987)

Jonathan Schonsheck, *On Criminalization* (New York: Springer Verlag 1994)

Jan-Melissa Schramm, 'Is Literature More Ethical than Law? Fitzjames Stephen and Literary Responses to the Advent of Full Legal Representation of Felons', in Michael Freeman and Andrew Lewis (eds), *Current Legal Issues Volume 2: Law and Literature* (Oxford: Oxford University Press 1999)

Jan-Melissa Schramm, *Testimony and Advocacy in Victorian Law, Literature and Theology* (Cambridge and New York: Cambridge University Press 2000)

Jan-Melissa Schramm, '"The Anatomy of a Barrister's Tongue": Rhetoric, Satire and the Victorian Bar in England' 32 *Victorian Literature and Culture* (2004) 285–303

Colin Scott, 'Analysing Regulatory Space: Fragmented Resources and Institutional Design' *Public Law* (Summer 2001) 329–53

Richard Sennett, *The Fall of Public Man* (Cambridge: Cambridge University Press 1977)

Stephen Shapin, *A Social History of Truth: Civility and Science in Seventeenth-Century England* (Chicago: University of Chicago Press 1983)

Geoffrey C. Shaw, 'Hart's Lost Essay: *Discretion* and the Legal Process School', 127 *Harvard Law Review* (2013) 636–51

George Sher, *Who Knew? Responsibility without Awareness* (Oxford and New York: Oxford University Press 2009).

Judith N. Shklar, *Legalism: Law, Morals and Political Trials* (Cambridge, MA: Harvard University Press 1964)

Andrew Simester (ed.), *Appraising Strict Liability* (Oxford: Oxford University Press 2005)

A. P. Simester and Andrew von Hirsch, 'Regulating Offensive Conduct through Two-Step Prohibitions', in A. P. Simester and Andrew von Hirsch (eds), *Incivilities: Regulating Offensive Behaviour* (Oxford: Hart Publishing 2006)

Jonathan Simon, *Governing Through Crime: How the War on Crime Transformed American Democracy and Created a Culture of Fear* (New York: Oxford University Press 2007)

Kenneth W. Simons, 'Does Punishment for "Culpable Indifference" Simply Punish for Bad Character?', *The New Culpability: Motive, Character and Emotion in Criminal Law* (ed. Guyora Binder), 6 *Buffalo Criminal Law Review* (2002) 219–315

A. W. B. Simpson, 'The Circulation of Yearbooks in the Fifteenth Century' 73 *Law Quarterly Review* (1957) 492–505

A. W. B. Simpson, 'The Rise and Fall of the Legal Treatise: Legal Principles and the Forms of Legal Literature' 48 *University of Chicago Law Review* (1981) 632–79

A. W. Brian Simpson, *Cannibalism and the Common Law* (Chicago: Chicago University Press 1984)

Carol Smart, *Women, Crime and Criminology* (London: Routledge 1976)

Bruce P. Smith, 'The Presumption of Guilt and the English Law of Theft, 1750–1850' 23 *Law and History Review* (2005) 133–71

Bruce P. Smith, 'The Myth of Private Prosecution in England, 1750–1850', in Markus D. Dubber and Lindsay Farmer (eds), *Modern Histories of Crime and Punishment* (Stanford: Stanford University Press 2007)

Keith Smith, 'Criminal Law', in William Cornish, J. Stuart Anderson, Raymond Cocks, Michael Lobban, Patrick Polden, and Keith Smith (eds), *The Oxford History of the Laws of England* Vol. XIII (Oxford: Oxford University Press 2010) Part 1

K. J. M. Smith, *Lawyers, Legislators and Theorists: Developments in English Criminal Jurisprudence* (Oxford: Clarendon 1998)

Roger Smith, *Trial by Medicine: Insanity and Responsibility in Victorian Trials* (Edinburgh: Edinburgh University Press 1981)

Roger Smith, *Inhibition: History and Meaning in the Sciences of Mind and Brain* (London: Free Association Books 1992)

David Soskice, '*Capital in the 21st Century:* A Critique' 65 *The British Journal of Sociology* (2014) 650–66

Patricia Meyer Spacks, *Imagining a Self: Autobiography and Novel in Eighteenth-Century England* (Cambridge, MA: Harvard University Press 1976)

Richard Sparks, *Television and the Drama of Crime* (London: Sage 1992)

James Fitzjames Stephen, 'The Morality of Advocacy' 3 *Cornhill Magazine* (1861) 447–59

James Fitzjames Stephen, *A General View of the Criminal Law of England* (London: Macmillan 1863)

Robert Louis Stevenson, *The Strange Case of Dr Jekyll and Mr Hyde and Other Tales of Terror*, edited by Robert Mighall (London: Penguin 2002)

Bram Stoker, *Dracula* (1897: Oxford: Oxford World's Classics 1998)

Julius Stone, 'The Rule of Exclusion of Similar Fact Evidence: England' 46 *Harvard Law Review* (1933) 954–85

P. F. Strawson, 'Freedom and Resentment', in Gary Watson (ed.), *Free Will* (Oxford: Oxford University Press 1982)

John W. Strong et al. (eds), *McCormick on Evidence* (5th ed., St. Paul: West Group 1999)

William J. Stuntz, 'The Pathological Politics of Criminal Law' 100 *Michigan Law Review* (2001) 505–600

William J. Stuntz, 'The Political Constitution of Criminal Justice' 119 *Harvard Law Review* (2006) 781–851

William J. Stuntz, *The Collapse of American Criminal Justice* (Cambridge, MA: Harvard University Press 2011)

Victor Tadros, *Criminal Responsibility* (Oxford: Oxford University Press 2005)

Victor Tadros, 'Justice and Terrorism' 10 *New Criminal Law Review* (2007) 658–89

Victor Tadros, 'Crimes and Security' 71 *Modern Law Review* (2008) 940–70

Brian S. Tamanaha, *A General Jurisprudence of Law and Society* (New York: Oxford University Press 2001)

Charles Taylor, *Sources of the Self: The Making of Modern Identity* (Cambridge, MA: Harvard University Press 1989)

Charles Taylor, *Modern Social Imaginaries* (Durham, NC: Duke University Press 2004)

Gunther Teubner, *Law as an Autopoietic System* (Oxford: Blackwell 1993)

E. P. Thompson, *Whigs and Hunters: The Origins of the Black Act* (Harmondsworth: Penguin 1975)

J. J. Tobias, *Crime and Industrial Society in the Nineteenth Century* (London: Ratsford 1967)

William Twining, *General Jurisprudence: Understanding Law from a Global Perspective* (Cambridge: Cambridge University Press 2009)

Tom R. Tyler, *Why People Obey the Law* (London: Yale University Press 1990)

Martha Merrill Umphrey, 'The Dialogics of Legal Meaning' 33 *Law and Society Review* (1999) 393–423

Mariana Valverde, *Diseases of the Will: Alcohol and the Dilemmas of Freedom* (Cambridge: Cambridge University Press 1998)

Loïc Wacquant, '"Suitable Enemies": Foreigners and Immigrants in the Prisons of Europe' 1 *Punishment and Society* (1999) 215–22

Peter Wagner, *Liberty and Discipline: A Sociology of Modernity* (London: Routledge 1993)

Dror Wahrman, *The Making of the Modern Self: Identity and Culture in Eighteenth-Century England* (New Haven: Yale University Press 2004)

Jeremy Waldron, *Law and Disagreement* (Oxford: Clarendon Press 1999)

Jeremy Waldron, 'Positivism and Legality: Hart's Equivocal Response to Fuller' 83 *New York University Law Review* (2008) 1135–69

Jeremy Waldron, 'The Concept and the Rule of Law', 43 *Georgia Law Review* (2008) 1–61

Nigel Walker, *Crime and Insanity in England:* Volume One, *The Historical Perspective* (Edinburgh: Edinburgh University Press 1968)

Judith Walkowitz, *Prostitution in Victorian Society: Women, Class, and the State* (Cambridge: Cambridge University Press 1980)

Gary Watson (ed.), *Free Will* (Oxford: Oxford University Press 1982)

Dorothy Wedderburn et al., *Justice for Women: The Need for Reform: The Report of the Committee on Women's Imprisonment* (London: Prison Reform Trust 2000)

Ota Weinberger, *Law, Institution and Legal Politics* (Dordrecht: Kluwer 1991)

Celia Wells, *Corporations and Criminal Responsibility* (2nd ed., Oxford: Clarendon Press 2001)

Celia Wells and Oliver Quick, *Reconstructing Criminal Law* (4th ed., Cambridge: Cambridge University Press 2010)

Alexander Welsh, *Strong Representations: Narrative and Circumstantial Evidence in England* (Baltimore: The John Hopkins University Press 1992)

James Q. Whitman, *Harsh Justice: Criminal Punishment and the Widening Divide Between America and Europe* (Oxford: Oxford University Press 2003)

James Q. Whitman, *The Origins of Reasonable Doubt: Theological Origins of the Criminal Trial* (New Haven: Yale University Press 2008)

Martin Wiener, *Reconstructing the Criminal: Culture, Law and Policy in England, 1830-1914* (Cambridge: Cambridge University Press 1991)

Martin J. Wiener, 'Judges and Jurors: Courtroom Tensions in Murder Trials and the Law of Criminal Responsibility in Nineteenth Century England' 17 *Law and History Review* (1999) 467–506

Martin J. Wiener, *Men of Blood: Violence, Manliness and Criminal Justice in Victorian England* (Cambridge University Press 2006)

Martin Wiener, 'Criminal Law at a Fault Line of Imperial Authority: Interracial Homicide Trials in British India', in Markus D. Dubber and Lindsay Farmer (eds), *Modern Histories of Crime and Punishment* (Stanford: Stanford University Press 2007)

Oscar Wilde, *The Picture of Dorian Gray* (1891: London: Penguin Classics 2000)

Bernard Williams, 'Persons, Character and Morality', in his *Moral Luck* (Cambridge: Cambridge University Press 1981)

Glanville Williams, *Criminal Law: The General Part* (2nd ed., London: Stevens and Sons 1961)

Arlene Fish Wilner, 'Henry Fielding and the Knowledge of Character' 18 *Modern Language Studies* (1988) 181–94

Richard Wollheim (1985) 'Crime, Punishment and Pale Criminality' 8(1) *Oxford Journal of Legal Studies* (1988) 1–16

Sir Llewellyn Woodward, *The Age of Reform, 1815-1870* (2nd ed., Oxford: Oxford University Press 1962)

Jock Young, *The Exclusive Society* (London: Sage 1999)

Lucia Zedner, *Women, Crime, and Custody in Victorian England* (Oxford and New York: Oxford University Press 1991)

Lucia Zedner, 'Victims', in Mike Maguire, Rod Morgan, and Robert Reiner (eds), *The Oxford Handbook of Criminology* (2nd ed., Oxford: Oxford University Press 1997)

Lucia Zedner, 'Policing Before and After the Police: The Historical Antecedents of Contemporary Crime Control' 46 *British Journal of Criminology* (2006) 78–96

Lucia Zedner, 'Preventive Justice or Pre-Punishment? The Case of Control Orders' 59 *Current Legal Problems* (2007) 174–203

Lucia Zedner, *Security* (London: Routledge 2009)

Lucia Zedner, 'Fixing the Future? The Pre-emptive Turn in Criminal Justice', in Bernadette McSherry, Alan Norrie, and Simon Bronitt (eds), *Regulating Deviance: The Redirection of Criminalisation and the Futures of Criminal Law* (Oxford: Hart Publishing 2009)

Lucia Zedner, 'Security, the State, and the Citizen: The Changing Architecture of Crime Control' 13 *New Criminal Law Review* (2010) 379–403

Lucia Zedner and Ian Loader, 'Police Beyond Law' 10 *New Criminal Law Review* (2007) 142–52

Index

n = footnote. *t* = table/diagram.